ISLAM
REVEALED

OTHER WORKS BY AUTHOR

The Glory of Christ: A Commentary on Ephesians (in Arabic). Jerusalem, Jordan: Published by Author, 1965.

An Ambassador for Jesus. Mobile, Ala: Havard Printing, 1968.

The Ultimate Reality. Mobile, Ala: Havard Printing, 1971. Also printed in Bangalore, India: Revival Literature Agency, 1971.

The Fig Tree. Mobile, Ala: Havard Printing, 1973.

The Liberated Palestinian. Wheaton, Ill: Victor Books, 1976. Printed also in Finnish by Tammer-Paino Oy: Helsinki, Finland, 1977.

Where Jesus Walked. Mobile, Ala: Havard Printing, 1978.

Jesus, Prophecy and the Middle East. Orlando, Fla: Christ for the World Publishers, 1979, 1st edition. The following 4 editions by Thomas Nelson Publishers, Nashville, Tenn. (40,000 in print). Also published in English by Maranatha Revival Crusade: Secunderabad, India, 1984.

The Exciting Discovery of the Ark of the Covenant. Winona, Minn: Justin Books, 1984. Also published by Asia for Christ: Secunderabad, India, 1986.

For more information, write:

ANIS SHORROSH EVANGELISTIC ASSOCIATION
P.O. Box 7577
Spanish Fort, Al 36577

ISLAM
REVEALED

A Christian Arab's View of Islam

Dr. ANIS A. SHORROSH

Foreword by Dr. Adrian Rogers

THOMAS NELSON PUBLISHERS
Nashville

Published in Nashville, Tennessee, by Thomas Nelson, Inc.

Printed in the United States of America.

Scripture quotations are from THE NEW KING JAMES VERSION of the Bible. Copyright © 1979, 1980, 1982, Thomas Nelson, Inc., Publishers.
All verses from the Quran are quoted from Muhammad Marmaduke Pickthall's *The Glorious Qur'an*. Muslim World League, Grand Central Station, New York City, N.Y., 1977.

This volume is dedicated to the memory of my father, Aghustien Shorrosh, who did not hesitate to witness for Christ, even to fanatic Muslim friends. One outcome of his efforts was eleven long years of hospital confinement, followed by his tragic death in 1948. Fellow Israelis planted a land mine near the Jordanian border that accidentally blew him up while he was trying to cross to join his family. During his lifetime, he set a profound Christian example, which can be articulated in this way: "Christ does not only deserve our living for Him, but also our dying for Him."

I have suffered much throughout my life as a result of the missing earthly father-figure in my home. In spite of that, the heavenly Father has taught me how much better He is as my Father when I trust him. Does not the Bible proclaim, "God is the Father of widows and orphans"?

Furthermore, this book is dedicated to Muslims in general and Arab Muslims in particular who sincerely pray daily "lead us to the straight path." Christ Jesus is the Straight path, as well as the Truth and the Life. He is also the Word who became flesh to save every human being who calls on Him, the world's Savior, through faith in His finished work on the cross and in His victory over death through His resurrection.

CONTENTS

�֍ �֍ ✖

ACKNOWLEDGMENTS

❊ ❊ ❊

I am grateful for God's wisdom and strength in allowing me to write this book.

My dear wife, Nell, typed the entire manuscript at least seven different times. This book couldn't have been done without her patient, loving help.

The counsel and advice of Dr. James Hefley, my friend and excellent editor, provided a readable and accurate manuscript. Dr. Samuel Shahid, Sparky Sparks, Professor Ebrahim J. Suleman, Bob and Gretchen Passantino, and many others also assisted in the evaluation and editing of this book.

The prayerful support of our own association members continued to be the backbone of our ministry.

Dr. Adrian Rogers, a close friend for many years and a well-known and powerful gospel preacher, graciously penned the foreword.

My sincere thanks also go to a dedicated Indian couple, Mobin and Gladys Khan. They searched for several valuable, out-of-print publications on Islam, then sent them to me from California for my research. I met Mobin in Varanasi, India, shortly after his conversion to Christ from Islam in 1970. Our organization sponsored his college and doctoral studies. Today he directs International Outreach, Inc., a worldwide ministry to Muslims.

FOREWORD

✳ ✳ ✳

There is only one Anis Shorrosh. He is unique. He understands all sides of the questions which keep the Bible lands in such turmoil.

My friend is a Palestinian Arab. He understands the feelings and aspirations of the Palestinian refugees, for he was once a refugee himself in Jordan. He has walked in their shoes. He knows what it is like to be a man without a country.

He also understands Muslims better than any Christian I know. He grew up among Muslims. There are far more Muslims in his hometown of Nazareth than Christians. After becoming a Christian minister, he served as pastor of the East Jerusalem Baptist Church for three years. Muslims comprise a majority of the population of the area known as East Jerusalem.

He has probably spoken to more Muslims outside of the Holy Land than any other Arab-Christian minister in the world. He understands the Quran and Muslim theology. He knows where Christians and Muslims agree and where they disagree. This book is evidence of that.

He has debated Ahmed Deedat, one of the foremost Islamic spokesmen in the world, in England's prestigious Royal Albert Hall. Interest in this debate was so great that thousands flocked to attend and couldn't even get in the door. In fact, police had to be called to forestall a riot.

Anis also understands Jews. He grew up in a town which is now part of the modern state of Israel, and he later lived in Jerusalem. When he goes to the Holy Land, he is "home." He knows the holy sites and has taken numerous pilgrims to see them.

I might add that the Jews respect him. How many other Palestinian Arabs do they know who can say truthfully, "I love the Jews because of Jesus"?

And he understands Christianity, both the real and the cultural or political kind. Anis comes from a Palestinian Arab family group who are Christians in a cultural and ancestral sense. Some have been born again through repentance and faith in the Lord Jesus Christ; some have not.

Arabs are not alone in this, of course. I have pastored churches in the American Bible Belt for 30 years. In every community where I have served, I have found some people who were cultural Christians and some who were Christians by a personal experience with Jesus Christ. Anis knows how to distinguish between those who merely wear Christian clothes and those who carry Jesus in their hearts.

In 1948, when Anis was only fourteen years old, the Jewish army swept into his hometown of Nazareth. Anis's father was killed while trying to return home. His body was never found. Anis's uncle was killed in the battle of Nazareth. Anis's mother gathered up her children at night and fled with them on camelback across the Jordan River to Jordan. Anis's biography, *The Liberated Palestinian*, tells the story of his dramatic conversion while an embittered refugee, and how Southern Baptist missionaries influenced him to come to America where he earned college and seminary degrees.

I first met Anis in a seminary classroom. Everybody knew him for his infectious smile and amazing ability to learn. Years later I came to know him better when I invited him to speak to the church which I then pastored in Merritt Island, Florida, near Cape Canaveral. How the people enjoyed him! They laughed and cried every night. Many made decisions for Christ.

Anis went on to earn his doctorate in seminary, and became a world-wide evangelist of the Gospel of Christ, and author of several books. This is his latest and most prodigious effort. It is "meaty" reading. After you have completed it, you will probably find yourself returning often for help in understanding the great debate between Islam and Christianity. I know it will be on my reference shelf.

I compliment my friend, Dr. Anis Shorrosh, on this work of love, and I pray that it will be enlightening and a blessing to many thousands.

DR. ADRIAN ROGERS
President of the Southern Baptist Convention
Pastor of Bellevue Baptist Church, Memphis, Tennessee

INTRODUCTION

✣ ✣ ✣

THE DEBATE STORY

Our twenty-fourth pilgrimage to the Holy Land ended joyfully on June 29, 1985 in the city of Vienna, Austria. While my group of twenty-four boarded their flight back to the U.S., I hurried to catch my plane to London, England, for several preaching engagements in London, Oxford, and Birmingham.

At one of the Arabic-speaking churches in London, the minister's wife informed me that a Muslim, Mr. Ahmed Deedat of Durban, South Africa, was advertising a debate on the crucifixion of Christ for Sunday, the 7th of July, in the world-famous Royal Albert Hall. I had just been to the hall on July fourth to attend a program celebrating America's independence.

My wife, Nell, and our daughter, Victoria, had just arrived from the United States to join me for the next ten days, and I had an important engagement Sunday, but I still felt compelled to go that afternoon to the debate. My first great surprise was seeing the long line of people waiting to get the free tickets. Finally I penetrated the barriers and found a seat.

The non-Muslim speaker, a former dean of the-

ology from an American school in Tennessee, was
unable to present a strong case for Christ's crucifixion and failed miserably during his rebuttal time.
It was a disastrous experience for the Christians
present. During the debate I interrupted the Muslim
speaker, Mr. Deedat, once, then at the question and
answer period I asked him if the Quran contradicts
itself. I strongly believe that it was then God planted
the desire in my heart to challenge Mr. Deedat to a
public debate.

My desire was realized the following Sunday.
Without either of us knowing about the other's
plans, we were both speaking that Sunday in Birmingham, England. When I discovered Deedat's
presence, as soon as I concluded the service at the
church where I was speaking, I hurried my family to
lunch, then walked across the street from our hotel
to the Birmingham Hall where Deedat was speaking. The place was filled to capacity, but no one was
debating Deedat. He quoted numerous Bible verses
which referred to the Holy Spirit and shocked me as
he announced to the audience (90% of whom were
Muslims) that these were promises of Jesus about
Muhammad's coming!

Eventually the question and answer period came.
I was up on my feet before anyone else, sensing the
moving of God's Spirit, and challenged Deedat to
meet me anywhere in the world to reveal the truth in
a formal debate. After some commotion and consultation with his platform colleagues, he agreed.
Royal Albert Hall would be the place. *Is Jesus God?*
would be the topic.

When I urged him to split the expenses of renting
the famed hall, he refused, answering, "You challenged me, you pay." I had no funds to pay for such
an undertaking, but God's Spirit led me to agree.

I began extensive research, ordering books from various countries in Arabic and English, studying the Quran in the original Arabic, my native language. Fred Massabni, a veteran of twenty-five years of ministering among Muslims, assisted me in my preparation for the debate. He is a Syrian by birth, is over 70 years old, sprite, joyful, Spirit-filled, and experienced.

My wife, Mr. Sparky Sparks, Mr. and Mrs. R. G. Wilson, and Mr. Massabni flew with me to London four days ahead of the debate. Our middle son, Paul, who was serving as an associate pastor in Germany, came with two of his friends. Other prayer supporters flew in from other countries.

On Sunday, December 15, 1985, people lined up at all fourteen gates two hours before the appointed hour of 7:30 P.M. The pushing and shoving was uncharacteristic of Londoners. There were Asian Muslims, Arab Christians, and English folks, with Muslims accounting for 75% of the crowd. The Lord had led me to bring beautiful Christmas music and pipe it into the massive hall. It became a soothing factor to these who were shaken by the struggle to enter the hall. Still, the riot police had to be called during the debate to quiet the 2,000 people milling outside and trying to push through the gates to join the capacity crowd of 5,000 already inside. Mr. Clive Culver was our chairman for the occasion and General Secretary of the Evangelical Alliance of England. It turned out that I would speak first. I greeted the crowd in Arabic and English, then proceeded to present Mr. Ahmed Deedat with a giant print New King James version of the Bible, and to give each of his twenty colleagues a bookmarker from the Holy Land. Turning to my opponent, I hugged him in a characteristic Mid-eastern bear hug. The audience exploded in applause because of this demonstration of love.

The debate lasted two hours and twenty minutes. Except for Deedat's misquoting of two stories from my biography, *The Liberated Palestinian* by James and Marti Hefley, and for which he later apologized, the entire event was tremendous. Although many felt neither side won, I was not displeased. My aim was to keep a low profile and win another opportunity to challenge this forty-year veteran orator and scholar of Islam, when I could then take the offensive.

Deedat has been defying and ridiculing Christians for many years. He agreed to a second debate with me to be held on July 20, 1986, in Birmingham, England. We agreed that the topic would be *The Quran or the Bible: Which One is the Word of God?*

This book is the fruit of my study and research for both debates. As I prepared for the second debate and worked on the first draft of this book, no word came from the Deedat camp. Before the first debate, he had communicated often, calling me early in the morning and late at night, sending a cable, writing long letters. After the first debate, I wondered why I had not heard from him about the agreed-upon second debate. Finally a short cable arrived with these words:

Exhibition Centre Birmingham booked Sunday twentieth July STOP We will incur all expenses approximately twenty thousand pounds STOP My young secretary will debate STOP Subject—Is the Bible God's Word? Format same as with Floyd Clark STOP Admission to meeting two pounds per person STOP Please wire if hundred percent agreeable STOP Ahmed Deedat

I cabled back after prayer and consultation with my associates:

Mr. Deedat thanks for telex. Date is OK in Birmingham England but why is topic changed? Why aren't you debating? Letter follows. Thanks. Shorrosh

I received no response to either my telex or my follow-up letter. Since then, the second debate date has come and gone, and Deedat has lectured eighteen times in England with no opponents or debaters.

I was determined to present the best Christian defense possible against Islam—if not in debate, then in this book. My work and research, and the prayers of Christians around the world, were not going to be wasted!

But God's plans are always better than our own! Deedat finally contacted me again in September 1987, and our second debate is now set for August 7, 1988, in Birmingham, England, at the National Exhibition Center, which has a seat capacity of twenty thousand.

It is my earnest prayer that this debate, and this book, *Islam Revealed,* will become the most successful defenses against Islam ever produced to the glory of God! Christians, as well as Muslims who earnestly seek the truth, will be guided through the debate and the book to Him who is the Truth, Jesus Christ (see John 14:6).

ANIS SHORROSH
June 1988

Post Script March 1990, the debate did take place with capacity crowd of 11,000 people—97% Muslims. The great success God granted us is recognized by the loud shouting and jeering, the closing of a major Islamic office of Mr. Deedat in England, his going into silence from August until December including the suspension of his monthly news magazine, the salvation of several Muslims who attended the debate, and finally several threats on my life.

PART ONE

ISLAM: THE EVIDENCE EXAMINED

CHAPTER ONE

THE RELIGION OF ISLAM

❋ ❋ ❋

Nearly one out of five human beings claims the Muslim religion. Islam is an Arabic word which means submission or surrender. As Muslims use it, Islam becomes a description of the religion of surrendering one's life to Allah, the one true God.

THE FOUNDATION

The Quran

The Quran is held in the greatest esteem and reverence among Muslims as their holy scripture. They dare not touch it without first being washed and purified. They read it with the greatest care and respect, never holding it below their waist. They swear by it and consult it on all occasions. They carry it with them to war, write sentences of it on their banners, suspend it from their necks as a charm, and always place it on the highest shelf or in some place of honor in their houses. It is said that the devil runs away from the house in which a portion of the Quran, Surat al-Baqarah (The Cow) 2, is read.[1]

A person able to memorize and repeat the whole Quran by heart is called a Hafiz, or protector. A

Hafiz is not required to understand its meaning but only to pronounce each word correctly. Blind people sometimes memorize it to obtain the title.

Sunna

Next to the Quran in Islamic life is Tradition (Hadith). While the former is regarded as supreme, the whole system of Islamic government is largely founded on the latter. A command given by Muhammad or an example set by him is called *Sunna*, a rule. The belief of Muslims is that their prophet, in all that he did and said, was guided by God, and that his words and acts became forever divine rules of faith and practice.[2] A Muslim places the Sunna on the same level as the Bible, but he regards the Quran as far superior to both—"the very words of God." Muhammad said:

> **He who loves not my Sunna is not my follower. He who in distress holds fast to the Sunna will receive the reward of a hundred martyrs.[3]**

The Sunna is taken from a much larger tradition. For example, one Muslim, Bukhari, collected twenty thousand of them, of which he rejected ten thousand, accounting them untrue. Of the remaining ten thousand, he accepted only 7,275, declaring the rest to be untrustworthy. Abu Da'ud accepted as authentic only 4,800 rules out of 50,000.

Ijma

Muslims are also guided by what is called *Ijma*, the consent of the leading companions of Muhammad and their followers. The highest rank a Muslim divine can reach is that of a Mujtahid (One who strives). Such a person can make what is called an Ijtihad, a deduction from a legal or theological question. The Ijtihad of the four successors of Muhammad are considered the most authoritative of the class.

Four systems of Muslim law, founded by the four great Imams, are recognized by all except the Shi'ite sect of Islam. Today, the Qadi (judge) must make no conviction, and the Mufti (religious leader who is qualified to give legal decisions) would not give fatwa (legal decisions) contrary to the opinion of the four Imams. To follow any other course is not lawful. Change and progress are therefore impossible in Islam.

Qiyas

Qiyas is the fourth foundation of Islam. Also called Analogy, the Qiyas denotes the reasoning of the learned with regard to the teaching of the Quran, Hadith, and Ijma.

The Quran is considered so sacred that only the companions of the prophet, who were in constant communication with him, are deemed worthy of explaining it. The work of learned divines since then has been to memorize the Quran by heart and to master the Traditions, along with the writings of the earliest commentators. A Muslim theology student must complete a course of instruction in grammer, rhetoric, logic, law, and dogmatics before beginning the study of *Ilm-il-usul* (science of principles), the aggregate of the Quran, Tradition, Ijma, and Qiyas. A good memory, not judgment or analytical thinking, is the great virtue of a Muslim theologian.

COMPILATION OF THE QURAN

From the Reciters by Zeyd

The word *Quran* means the Reading or the Recitation. A second and popular name is Al'Kitab, The Book. A third and a very respected name is Al-Mashaf, A Handwritten Book. Altogether fifty-five different names are applied to the Quran.[4]

The delivery and writings of the Quran extended over a twenty-three year period. Passages were taken down from Muhammad's lips from time to time by some writers, or they were first committed to memory, then at some subsequent period recorded. For this purpose, the crude writing material then in use among the Arabs was employed. There was no fixed repository for these materials, but they were probably kept in the room of one of Muhammad's wives or left in charge of the persons who first wrote them down. Many passages were preserved only in the memories of his followers and were never committed to writing during his lifetime.

After Muhammad's death, many reciters of the Quran were slain in the Battle of Yamama. 'Umar therefore suggested to Abu Bakr that all the chapters of the Quran should be collected. The task was committed to Zeyd, the chief scribe or secretary of Muhammad. He sought out the fragments of the Quran from every quarter, gathering them together from palm leaves and tablets of white stone and from the memories of faithful men. The first complete manuscript was compiled twenty years after Muhammad's death and was entrusted to the care of Hafasa, one of Muhammad's widows.

Years later, the Khalifa 'Uthman appointed Zeyd to make a fresh revision of the work, and all previous copies were called in and burned. This second revision, it is supposed, has been handed down unaltered.[5]

The Language of the Quran

The Quran is written in a kind of rhyming Arabic prose, the jingling sound of which greatly delights the Arabs. Pickthall's translation of Surat al'Fatihah (The Opening) 1 expresses this sound:

> In the name of Allah, the Beneficent, the Merciful. Praise be to Allah, Lord of the Worlds: The Beneficent, the Merciful: Owner of the Day of Judgment. Thee (alone) we worship; Thee (alone) we ask for help. Show us the straight path: The path of those whom Thou hast favoured; Not (the path) of those who earn Thine anger nor of those who go astray.

◆ ◆

بِسْمِ اللهِ الرَّحْمٰنِ الرَّحِيمِ ﴿١﴾
اَلْحَمْدُ لِلّٰهِ رَبِّ الْعٰلَمِينَ ﴿٢﴾
الرَّحْمٰنِ الرَّحِيمِ ﴿٣﴾

مٰلِكِ يَوْمِ الدِّيْنِ ۞

اِيَّاكَ نَعْبُدُ وَاِيَّاكَ نَسْتَعِيْنُ ۞

اِهْدِنَا الصِّرَاطَ الْمُسْتَقِيْمَ ۞

صِرَاطَ الَّذِيْنَ اَنْعَمْتَ عَلَيْهِمْ ۙ غَيْرِ الْمَغْضُوْبِ

عَلَيْهِمْ وَلَا الضَّآلِّيْنَ ۞

Muslims regard this chapter as the essence of the
Quran and repeat it as Christians do the Lord's
Prayer.

Arrangement of the Quran

The Quran is regarded as holy by Muslims and is
divided into 114 Surats (rows or chapters), containing about 6,200 verses, 80,000 words, and
330,000 letters. It is further arranged into 30 sections, called Juz, or Sipara, enabling a Muslim to
recite the whole book in the thirty days of the fast
month of Ramadan.[6] The Ruku' are recited sections
of about ten verses before which the Muslim makes a
bow of reverence.

The Quran was first printed in Arabic at Rome in
1530. The first translation in French was done in
1647, and from it the first English translation was
made soon after 1657.

The Surats are not placed chronologically according to content or composition. The opening prayer
stands first, then the longest chapters. Some of the
Surats contain verses delivered at different times
and put together without regard to subject. Sir
William Muir considers that the shorter chapters belong, as a general rule, to Muhammad's early ministry; so to begin at the end of the Quran and read

backwards would give the best conception of the stages of Muhammad's teaching. Muir identifies eighteen Surats consisting of short rhapsodies, which may have been composed by Muhammad before he conceived the idea of a divine mission, none of which are in the form of a message from Allah.

Contents

According to tradition, four Surats are supposed to belong to the beginning of Muhammad's ministry. Nineteen Surats probably date from the commencement of Muhammad's public ministry to the Abyssinian (Ethiopian) emigration. Twenty-two Surats are thought to have been given from the sixth to the tenth year of Muhammad's ministry. Thirty-one Surats are assigned to the period from the tenth year of Muhammad's ministry to the flight from Mecca to Medina. They contain some narratives from the Gospels. Twenty Surats are supposed to have been given at Medina. The second Surat is the longest in the book. Its name is "The Cow," named after the heifer described within the Surat (although misidentified as yellow instead of red, as recorded in the Old Testament) as having been sacrificed by the Israelites under the direction of Moses. Muslims assert from this Surat that Abraham and his firstborn, Ishmael, built the Ka'bah, Islam's holiest shrine.

THE CREED OF ISLAM

To become a Muslim, one needs only to repeat with sincerity this simple creed:
La ilaha
il' Allah,
Muhammadan

Rasoulu Allah

Translated, this means, "There is no god but Allah, and Muhammad is the messenger of Allah." This is the *Shahada* (witness) and expresses the very heart of the Islamic creed.

Following this, the true Muslim must accept five main articles of *Iman* (faith):

1. Belief in Allah as the one true God.
2. Belief in angels as the instruments of God's will.
3. Belief in the four inspired books: Torah, Zabur, Injil, and Quran, of which the Quran is the final and most complete.
4. Belief in the twenty-eight prophets of Allah, of whom Muhammad is the last.
5. Belief in a final day of judgment.

Allah (God)

The first and most important doctrine in the creed of Islam is the doctrine of Allah. Muhammad knew from childhood the native pre-Islamic belief in Al-ilah, meaning "the god," a vague high God who created the world and became Allah or God.[7] He also knew of the Najran tribe, which was almost totally Christian and had considerable influence in northern Arabia. We should never forget that Muhammad's father's name, Abd–Allah, means "the slave of God." In other words, Muhammad was definitely aware of a belief in the one God among his people.

The essence or being of Allah includes his existence, eternity, unsubstantiality, unembodiedness, essentiality, omnipresence, formlessness, and uniqueness. His attributes include life, power, knowledge, will, sensibility, and speech. Creation, preservation, revelation, and predestination constitute the works of Allah.

By Islamic tradition, there are ninety-nine most beautiful names of Allah. The titles and the frequency of usage include: The Omniscient (158), The One (21), The Mighty (44), The Unique (89), The Forgiving (96), and The Wise (95). Infrequently used titles include The Slayer, The Provider, and The Avenger.[8] Every devout Muslim begins his conversation with "In the name of God, the Merciful, the Compassionate."

The Quran focuses on the absolute unity and uniqueness of God. Islam maintains an uncompromising monotheism. The only unpardonable sin is *shirk*, or the associating or joining of other gods to the one God. While the Bible and Christianity are also both uncompromisingly monotheistic, Islamic monotheism denies the biblical doctrine of the trinity, misassociating it with tritheism.

Angels

A belief in angels is essential to the acceptance of the manner in which Allah revealed himself both to Muhammad and to various other prophets before him. This belief includes all kinds of creatures inhabiting the invisible world.

Muslims believe in four archangels: Gabriel (the angel of revelation), Michael (the angel of providence), Israfil (the angel of doom), and Izra'il (the angel of death). Ministering angels include recording angels, throne-bearers, and questioners of the dead. A third category is the fallen angels, the chief of which is Iblis, or Shaytan. A fourth group includes Jinn, a group of spirits midway between men and angels, some good and some bad.

The Holy Books

Islam recognizes that four sets of scriptures contain revelations of Allah's will. These are the Torah of Moses, the Psalms of David, the Injil (Gospel) of Jesus, and the Quran, which represents the final and complete revelation, superceding all previous revelations and conflicting claims to truth. (Although Muslims talk about the Torah, Psalms, and Gospel, they do not mean by those terms the same Old and New Testaments that Christians have in their Bibles. They believe that the original Torah, Psalms, and Gospel have been corrupted and lost. What Christians have in the Old and New Testaments are not God's Word or revelation.)

Prophets

Islam claims to be open to revelation from Allah whenever and wherever it occurs. This is true at least in theory. Muslims believe their religion is simply "the religion of God." God speaks and acts in history to reveal Himself through prophets.

Twenty-eight prophets are particularly recognized in the Quran. These include Adam, Noah, Abraham, Moses, Isaac, Jacob, Ishmael, Joseph, David, Solomon, Elijah, Elisha, and Jonah from Old Testament times. There are others from New Testament times: Zachariah, John the Baptist, and Jesus. The five prophetic predecessors to Muhammad specially mentioned are Adam, Noah, Abraham, Moses, and Jesus. The Quran affirms the Virgin Birth of Jesus (although not His *eternal* pre-existence), but teaches that the Crucifixion and Resurrection did not happen as the Bible says. The Quran includes some of the miracles and moral teachings of Jesus but does not mention His lordship or His divinity.[9]

Muhammad is considered the last and the greatest of the prophets. He is the Seal of the Prophets, after whom no more will come. Muslims believe that he was "prepared for and attested to by all the preceding prophets." The Muslims consider Islam as, not the youngest, but the oldest monotheistic religion in the world.

Resurrection and the Hour of Judgment

Readers of the Quran soon find that Allah is portrayed as stern and harsh rather than compassionate. Allah's harshness is intensified in the Quranic description of Judgment Day and its consequences.[10] Muhammad's original message warned people of the terrible divine judgment that was to come. About 852 verses of the Quran emphasize this fearful theme.

Judgment Day will be preceded by signs, then announced by a trumpet blast (see 1 Thessalonians 4:16–17). The dead will arise bodily from their graves and join the living, then all will be examined one by one and assigned to Paradise or hell. No one can escape this judgment. Vivid pictures are given of the balance scales which will be used to weigh the good and evil deeds of each soul, even to the weight of a mustard seed. Pious believers in Allah can expect abundant sensual pleasures in Paradise. There will be perpetual luxury, physical comfort, food, clear water, mansions, servants, lovely maidens, and virgins. The wicked will suffer and swelter in the hot blasts, foul smoke, and molten metal of hell.

Predestination

The sixth belief, predestination, is not mandatory, but it is still accepted by many Muslims. "If Allah wills it"

إِنْ شَاءَ اللّٰهِ

is the comment of the devout Muslim. Predestination is the belief that all events are determined by Allah. The function of humans is to submit to that divine determination with obedient thankfulness. However, the predestined must still face Allah's justice.

DUTIES OR PILLARS OF ISLAM

To Muslims, belief in Islam and observance of ritual are not enough to reach heaven. A man must walk the straight path—accepting the doctrines (Iman) of the faith, performing the required duties (Din) and living in the moral precepts stated in the Quran and Hadiths. There is a definite relationship between doctrine and duty in Islam. Islam is, therefore, more a way of life than just a set of beliefs. The greatest virtue is complete submission to the will and authority of Allah. Five specific duties, known traditionally as the Five Pillars, are demanded of every Muslim.

The Creed (Kalima or Shahada)

"There is no God but Allah, and Muhammad is the messenger of Allah" is the bedrock belief of Muslims. One must declare this doctrine publicly to become a Muslim. It is repeated constantly by Muslim believers.

Daily Prayers (Salat) and Friday
Public Service

Prayer as a ritual is central to a devout Muslim. It is performed upon rising, at noon, in mid-afternoon, after sunset, and before retiring. The worshiper must recite the prescribed prayers, the first surat and other selections from the Quran in Arabic while facing the Ka'bah in Mecca. The Hadith (Book of Tradition) has turned these prayers into a mechanical procedure of standing, kneeling, hands and face on the ground, and so forth. The call to prayer is sounded by the "muezzin" (a Muslim crier) from a tower called a "minaret" which is part of the "mosque" (the place of public worship).

One can easily recognize the similarities between the minaret and the belfry of a church, between the call to prayer and the ringing of bells to announce a church function. In fact, tradition has it that Muhammad himself did not like bells, and therefore initiated the vocal call to prayer.

The Muslims have a Friday public service similar to the Christian's Sunday worship service. However, few women attend these services and, much like in the Orthodox Jewish services, men worship in the central hall while women are either in the back of the hall or in a separate room. Furthermore, the ceremonial washing of feet, hands, and face prior to prayer finds its origin in Exodus 30:18–21, where God instructed the Jewish priests to do that two thousand years before Muhammad!

The Fast of Ramadan

Faithful Muslims fast from sunup to sundown each day during this holy month. The fast develops self-control, devotion to Allah, and identification with the destitute. No food or drink may be consumed, and no smoking or sexual pleasures may be enjoyed during daylight hours. Many Muslims eat only two meals a day during Ramadan, one before sunrise and one shortly after sunset.

Almsgiving (Zakat)

Muhammad, himself an orphan, is said to have had a strong desire to help the needy. Almsgiving in Islam originally was voluntary, but all Muslims are now required to give one-fortieth of their income for the destitute. There are other rules and regulations for giving produce, cattle, and other wealth, along with freewill offerings.[11]

Since those to whom alms are given are helping the giver to attain salvation, they need feel no sense of debt to the giver. On the contrary, it is the giver's responsibility and duty to give, and he should consider himself lucky he has someone to whom he can give.

The Pilgrimage to Mecca (Hajj)

Every Muslim is expected to make a pilgrimage at least once in his lifetime. This can be extremely arduous on the old or infirm, so they may send someone in their place. Hajj is an essential part in gaining salvation. It involves a set of ceremonies and rituals, many of which center around the Ka'bah shrine in Mecca, to which the pilgrimage is directed. This Muslim pilgrimage serves to heighten and solidify Islamic faith.[12]

The Jihad

Some Muslim scholars may take issue with me on this matter, but a sixth religious duty almost invariably associated with the five pillars is Jihad, or Holy War. The Kharjites raised Jihad to a sixth pillar of Islam in the early days of Islam.[13] When the situation warrants, men are required to go to war in order to spread Islam or defend it against infidels.

One who dies in a Jihad is guaranteed eternal life in Paradise.

The severest atrocities in contemporary Lebanon, the largest number of bombings, and the most frequent kidnappings, for example, are perpetrated by Al Jihad groups. In Iran they call themselves Al Mujahideen and provide the largest number of fanatic terrorist fighters as well as soldiers in the war with Iraq. In a brochure, *Islam at a Glance*, distributed in July 1985, in Birmingham, England, it is admitted, "to struggle in the path of Allah with the pen, speech, and the sword is Jihad." The news media has lately announced that a new group, called Hizb Allah, the party of God, has claimed responsibility for bombings and kidnappings in Lebanon. Khomeini, the current ruler over Iran, has even preached that "the purest joy in Islam is to kill and be killed for Allah."[14]

SECTS OF ISLAM

According to the Traditions, Muhammad predicted that his followers would become divided into seventy-three sects, every one of whom would go to hell, except one sect, the religion professed by himself and his companions. However the number of Islamic sects, now over 150, has far exceeded Muhammad's prediction.

Sunnis

The Sunnis, by far the largest sect in the Muslim world, take the title of the Najiyah, meaning those who are "being saved." They acknowledge the first four Khalifs as the rightful successors of Muhammad. They received the "six correct books" and be-

long to one of the schools of jurisprudence founded
by the four Imams.

Shi'ites

Shi'ite means "follower." Shi'ites are the followers
of 'Ali, maintaining that he was the first true Khalifa
and Imam, the successor to the Prophet. Another
name for Shi'ites is "followers of the twelve," which
the Sunnis derisively call the "Rafidi," or "forsakers
of the truth." The Shi'ites strenuously maintain that
they alone are right in their understanding of Islam, and like the Sunnis, they call themselves "al-
Muminun," or the "true believers." They believe in
the divine right of the successors of 'Ali. His rightful
successor is now concealed, they say, but will appear
at the end of the world as the "Mahdi," the one
rightly guided by Allah, thus able to guide others.
They have split into many smaller sects. Furthermore, Shi'ites reject the "six correct books" of the
Sunnis, and have five collections of their own.

Shi'ites are numerous in Iran, where they have
deposed the Shah and in his place, installed the
Ayatollah Khomeini and enforced Islamic law as the
rule of the government. Khomeini has gone beyond
that by declaring that his command is as good as
that of the prophet Muhammad![15]

Wahhabis

The founder of the Wahhabi sect was 'Abd al-
Wahhab, born in Nejd in A.D. 1691. He maintained
that the Muslims had departed from the precepts of
Muhammad. He accepted only the Quran and the
Traditions, rejecting the two other foundations, Ijma
and Qiyas. He condemned the worship of dead holy
men at tombs. He said,

They (worshippers) run there to pay the tribute of their fervent prayers. By this means they think that they can satisfy their spiritual and temporal needs. From what do they seek this benefit? From walls made of mud and stone, from corpses deposited in tombs. The true way of salvation is to prostrate one's self before Him who is everpresent and to venerate Him—the one without associate or equal.[16]

The war cry of the Wahhabis was "Kill and strangle all infidels which give companions to Allah." On the day of battle, the Wahhabi founder gave each soldier a letter addressed to the Treasurer of Paradise. It was enclosed in a bag which the warrior suspended from his neck. The soldier believed that by dying in battle he would go straight to Paradise, without being examined by the angels Munkar and Nakir. Many Iranian prisoners today have confided to their Iraqi captors that they were duped into hanging a small Quran around their necks so they would become invisible in battle and not be seen by their enemies!

The Wahhabis condemn astrology, trusting in omens, and believing in lucky or unlucky days, as well as praying at tombs. They disallow the use of a rosary but attach great merit to counting the ninety-nine names of God on their fingers.

Suffis

The meaning of the name Suffi is disputed. Suffis are a Muslim sect that have set aside the literal meaning of the words of Muhammad for a supposed spiritual interpretation. Their system is a Muslim adaptation of the Indian Vedantic philosophy. They believe that only Allah exists. All visible things are not really distinct from Him. There is no real difference between good and evil. Allah fixes the will of man. In fact, transmigration is accepted. The principal occupation of the Suffi is meditation on the unity of God and the remembrance of God's name so as to obtain absolution.[17]

Suffis are most numerous in Iran, once called Persia. The three chief Persian poets, Jami, Sa'di, and Hafiz were Suffis who dwelt on love to God. Many of the writings of the Persian Suffis contain indecent passages. The Suffis are divided into innumerable sects which find expression in the numerous orders of Faqirs, or Darweshes.

Faqir is an Arabic word meaning "poor." Darwesh is its Persian counterpart, derived from "dar," a "door," one who begs from door to door. Faqirs are divided into two great classes, those who govern their conduct according to the principles of Islam and those who do not, although they all call themselves Muslims.

Bahaiism

The Bahai sect began with a man who was born in 1817 in Tehran, Persia, and whose real name was Mirza Hussayn Ali. In 1847 he declared that he was the glory of Allah, "Bahau Allah" from two Arabic words. His acquaintance with a religious movement led by a man called the Bab (Gate) convinced him that he himself was the prophet that the Bab had predicted would appear.

In 1850, the Persian government executed the Bab for his teachings, and Mirza took over the leadership of the movement. In 1863, ten years after he was banished to Baghdad, Bahau Allah declared he was the expected prophet. From 1868 till his death in 1892, he lived in a prison colony in what is now

Akka, Israel.[18] He tried to unite the three mono-theistic religions of Judaism, Christianity, and Islam through his writings, which comprise 100 volumes.

Bahais believe in good works, nondiscrimination, and a federated world government. Their headquarters are in Haifa, Israel, and they have over 17,000 local counsels, called local spiritual assemblies, with 1,500,000 adherents.[19] Ten percent of them live in India.

Ahmadiya

Ahmadiya is Islam's newest sect. Its members are not recognized as Muslims in Pakistan because they accept Mizra Qadyani as their prophet in addition to Muhammad. They also believe that Jesus was crucified, but did not actually die. He only swooned on the cross and was resuscitated three days later in the tomb. Their number is growing, largely because they believe in sending missionaries to proclaim their faith. (I became acquainted with them while in Pakistan in 1986.)

FEASTS AND FASTS OF ISLAM

Ramadan

Ramadan, referred to before, is the most holy fast of Islam. During the holy month of Ramadan, faithful Muslims fast from both food and sex every day during daylight hours. The fast is meant to develop self-control, devotion to God, and identification with the destitute. However, some Muslims gorge themselves so much after dark each evening that the "fast" often seems more like a feast. Ramadan marks the anniversary of the first month of the first year on the Muslim calendar, which was adopted in A.D. 622.

'Idu'l-Fitr (Breaking the Fast)

The "Feast of the Breaking of the Fast" is the first day after Ramadan when food is eaten during daylight hours. On that day Muslims give alms before saying their prayers in the mosque. After hearing the sermon, the people mingle, visit, and enjoy a festive meal.

El-Dahiya (Feast of Sacrifice)

The Feast of Sacrifice is the most important feast of the whole year. The pre-Islamic Arabs, interestingly enough, offered similar animal sacrifices as part of the concluding ceremonies to their own pilgrimages to the Ka'bah in Mecca. Muhammad simply adapted their practice to his religion and called it El-Dahiya.

The feast is said to be in memory of Abraham attempting to sacrifice Ishmael (not Isaac) when Gabriel substituted a ram for the lad. It is considered highly meritorious to sacrifice one animal for each member of the family. But since this would involve an expenditure which few could bear, it is allowable to sacrifice one animal for the entire household.

IMPORTANT FACTS AND FIGURES

Islam is one of the driving forces among world religions today. Its growth is closely tied to nationalism. But growth does not mean truth.[20]

A Muslim's Openness to the Gospel

Great tensions now grip the Muslim world. Riots
involving eighty-five million Muslims threaten to rip
apart the fabric of Indian society. Overpopulated
Bangladesh struggles for survival. Iran is convulsed
with revolution within and the Iraqi war without.
Pakistan had a new neighbor on its western
border—the Russian army. But now the Russians
are withdrawing. Turkey is torn by religious unrest
and social instability. Egypt, desperately in need of
peace, is threatened by fanatical Muslim broth-
erhoods. Chad has been engulfed in a gruesome civil
war with Libya. Nigeria, almost 50 percent Muslim,
is leading the boycott against South Africa's ap-
artheid policy. Morocco and Algeria are quarreling
over Western Sahara. Somalia is a nation plagued
with famine and refugee problems. The forty-six
million Muslims in Central Russia are becoming in-
creasingly restive. The Iraq/Iran war has opened old
animosities between Arabs and Persians. Libya fer-
ments Muslim insurrection in the Philippines. The
Democratic Republic of Yemen hosts Russian
troops.[21] And the thorniest problem of all is the ex-
iled Palestinian agitation for a return to their homeland.

The myth of an impregnable Islam is no longer
valid. Muslims can, will, and are coming to Christ!
Indonesian Muslims have been turning to Christ at
an amazing rate. It is estimated that over half of all
Christian converts from Islam are Indonesian. Re-
sponses to Bible correspondence courses have been
remarkable. Muslim-convert churches have been
planted in Afghanistan, Pakistan, Kashmir-India,
Bangladesh, and Nigeria. Churches made up of former Muslims have come into being in western India

through radio broadcasts. Turks are being reached in Germany, and Iranians are turning to Christ.

Muslims In North America

In the United States, Muslims claim to number around three million. Nearly 612 mosques have been built and extensive plans have been drawn for a number of others around the country. Over 150 chapters of Muslim Student Associations are on our university campuses. The Muslim Student Association wants to get on every college campus in the country. In Atlanta, Muslims have purchased a large farm, which they are using for agricultural training and rural development. Just outside Indianapolis, there has been widespread Muslim land purchasing and building. In New Mexico, an entire Islamic community is being developed. Islamic financial investment in real estate, agriculture, small businesses, and banking are rapidly increasing. Sixty percent of the conversions to Islam in North America are occurring in the black community.[22]

Former U.S. president Jimmy Carter emphatically states the following evaluation of the Muslim world in his recent book, *The Blood of Abraham:*

Despite the common language, customs, and religion, and regardless of the desire of influential and prosperous leaders for harmony and unity of purpose, the Islamic world is still torn by strife that is not limited to combat with Israel. Iran and Iraq's conflict demonstrates Islam's love for bloodshed and warfare.[23]

MUSLIMS IN THE WORLD
893,230,200 MUSLIMS WORLDWIDE

COUNTRY	MUSLIM POPULATION	%
Afghanistan	14,256,000	99.0
Albania	1,812,500	62.5
Algeria	21,186,000	99.0
Australia	310,000	2.0
Austria	76,000	1.0
Bahrain	400,000	100.0
Bangladesh	83,664,000	84.0
Belgium	99,000	1.0
Benin	546,000	14.0
Bhutan	56,000	4.0
Brazil	537,600	.4
Brunei	128,000	64.0
Bulgaria	720,000	8.0
Burma	1,556,000	4.0
Burundi	94,000	2.0
Cameroon	1,598,000	17.0
Canada	125,500	.5
Cent. African Rep.	208,000	8.0
Chad	2,500,000	50.0
China	20,690,000	2.0
Comoros	495,000	99.0
Congo	17,000	1.0
Cyprus	126,000	18.0
Dem. Kampuchea	91,500	1.5
Denmark	25,000	.5
Djibouti	282,000	94.0
Egypt	44,180,000	94.0
Ethiopia	13,760,000	43.0
Fiji	14,000	2.0
Finland	1,500	—
France	2,192,000	4.0
Gabon	10,000	1.0

Population figures are from the 1984 World Population Data Sheet of the Population Reference Bureau, Inc., 2213 M. Street, N.W., Washington, D.C. 20037, and the Samuel Zwemer Institute, P. O. Box 365, Altadena, CA 91001.)

COUNTRY	MUSLIM POPULATION	%
Germany, East	15,000	—
Germany, West	1,842,000	3.0
Ghana	2,216,500	15.5
Greece	150,000	1.5
Guinea	4,200,000	75.0
Guinea-Bissau	260,000	32.5
Guyana	120,000	15.0
Hong Kong	27,000	.5
Hungary	32,100	.3
India	82,104,000	11.0
Indonesia	140,592,000	87.0
Iran	43,362,000	98.0
Iraq	14,100,000	94.0
Israel	462,000	11.0
Italy	171,000	.3
Ivory Coast	2,162,000	23.5
Jordan	3,255,000	93.0
Kenya	1,746,000	9.0
Kuwait	1,552,000	97.0
Lebanon	1,560,000	60.0
Liberia	374,000	17.0
Libya	3,589,000	97.0
Madagascar	686,000	7.0
Malawi	1,380,000	20.0
Malaysia	7,650,000	50.0
Maldives	200,000	100.0
Mali	6,840,000	90.0
Mauritania	1,800,000	100.0
Mauritius	180,000	18.0
Mongolia	133,000	7.0
Morocco	23,293,200	98.7
Mozambique	2,814,000	21.0
Nepal	332,000	2.0
Netherlands	288,000	2.0
Niger	5,197,500	82.5
Nigeria	38,323,500	43.5
Norway	16,400	.4
Oman	990,000	99.0
Pakistan	94,381,000	97.0
Philippines	2,725,000	5.0
Poland	2,500	—

COUNTRY	MUSLIM POPULATION	%
Portugal	30,300	—
Qatar	295,500	98.5
Reunion	30,000	6.0
Romania	35,000	—
Rwanda	174,000	3.0
Saudi Arabia	10,692,000	99.0
Senegambia	6,095,000	85.0
Sierra Leone	1,072,500	27.5
Singapore	400,000	16.0
Somalia	5,529,000	97.0
South Africa	317,000	1.0
South Korea	33,000	—
Spain	15,000	—
Sri Lanka	1,127,000	7.0
Sudan	15,403,000	73.0
Surinam	80,000	20.0
Sweden	24,900	.3
Switzerland	58,500	.9
Syria	9,090,000	90.0
Taiwan	192,000	1.0
Tanzania	6,360,000	30.0
Thailand	2,068,000	4.0
Togo	174,000	6.0
Trinidad & Tobago	72,000	6.0
Tunisia	6,860,000	98.0
Turkey	49,698,000	99.0
Uganda	1,072,500	7.5
U.S.S.R.	46,580,000	17.0
United Arab Emirates	1,425,000	95.0
United Kingdom	1,412,500	2.5
United States	2,363,000	1.0
Upper Volta	1,340,000	20.0
Vietnam	58,300	.1
Western Sahara Reg.	125,000	90.0
Yemen (Aden-South)	2,079,000	99.0
Yemen (Sana-North)	5,841,000	99.0
Yugoslavia	3,910,000	17.0
Zaire	644,000	2.0
Zambia	66,000	1.0
Zimbabwe	6,300	.9

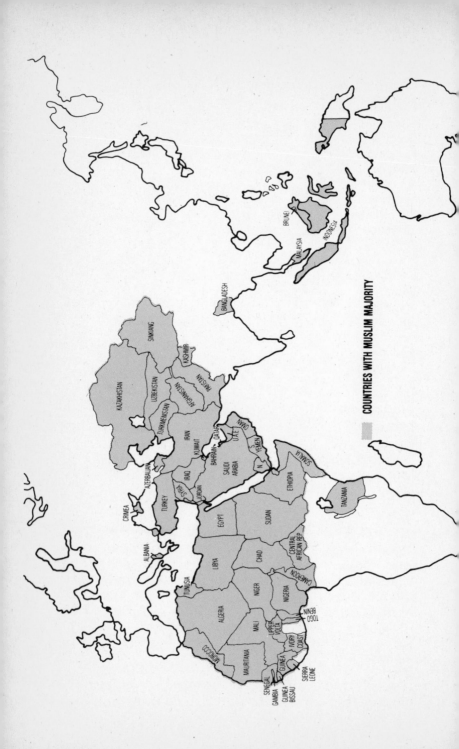

COUNTRIES WITH MUSLIM MAJORITY

CHAPTER TWO

THE LIFE OF MUHAMMAD

❋ ❋ ❋

MUHAMMAD'S EARLY YEARS

There are two main sources for the life of Muhammad, both of which are Islamic. As far as is known, no ancient non-Muslim source on the life of Muhammad exists. To construct a reliable biography of Muhammad apart from these Islamic sources is impossible.

The Quran does not purport to be a biography of Muhammad. However, the many biographical references in the Quran are invaluable because they are contemporary with Muhammad. Their authenticity appears to be indisputable. It is incumbent upon anyone, Muslim or non-Muslim, attempting to write about Muhammad to utilize the Quranic evidence as honestly and judiciously as possible, without distorting its witness.

The ancient biographies of Muhammad based on the traditions which have been preserved are *The Life History of Muhammad*, by Ibn-Ishaq (A.D. 768), edited by Ibn-Hisham (A.D. 833); and *The Expeditions of Muhammad*, by Al-Waqidi (A.D. 822). Both have been combined in an English translation by

A. Guillaume, titled *The Life of Muhammad*. It was
published by Oxford University Press in London in
1955. A similar book titled *Muhammad: His Life
Based on the Earliest Sources*, by Martin Lings, was
published first by the Islamic Texts Society in
London in 1983.

His Birth at Mecca A.D. 570.

Muhammad, the prophet of Arabia, was born at
Mecca in 570. He sprang from the Quraish, a tribe
that ruled over the city and the surrounding area.
His father was 'Abdu'llah, the son of 'Abdu'l-Muttalib, a leading citizen; his mother's name was
'Amina. 'Abdu'llah died on a trading trip at Yathrib,
and soon after 'Amina gave birth to their son. When
this news was brought to 'Abdu'l-Muttalib, the
grandfather, he went to 'Amina's house, and, taking
the child in his arms, gave thanks to God and called
the baby Muhammad, "The Praised One."[1]

Quraish mothers customarily gave their infants
out to a nurse in some Bedouin tribe to gain them
the healthy air of the desert. Muhammad was entrusted to Halima, who nursed the infant until he
was two years old before taking him back to 'Amina.
Delighted with his healthy look, Muhammad's
mother said, "Take the child with thee back again,
for much do I fear for him the unwholesome air of
Mecca." So Halima took him back. Two years later
she appeared again, but this time she was troubled.
The child had had numerous fits, which made
Halima think he was demon possessed. She was per-
suaded to carry him back once more, but after subsequent epileptic fits, she returned him to his
mother when he was five. Muhammad gratefully re-
membered Halima's care.

The Death of 'Amina

'Amina took the child on a trip to Yathrib. She died on the way home, leaving Muhammad in the care of his grandfather, who died two years later at age eighty.[2]

Uncle Abu Talib Raises Muhammad

The child was then committed to the care of his paternal uncle, Abu Talib. When Muhammad was twelve years old he was taken by his uncle on mercantile journeys to Damascus and other cities.

Muhammad's youth passed without any other incidents of interest. He was employed, like other lads, in tending the sheep and goats of Mecca on the neighboring hills and valleys. Many years later, when passing near some shrubs with purple berries, he cried, "Pick me out the blackest ones, for they are sweet. Even such I used to gather, feeding the flocks in the valley of Mecca: and truly no prophet hath been raised up but first he hath done the work of a shepherd."[3]

MUHAMMAD'S FIRST MARRIAGE

Khadija, A Rich Widow of Mecca

When Muhammad reached his twenty-fifth year, his uncle, Abu Talib, recommended that he enter the service of Khadija, a rich widow merchant of Mecca. He accompanied her trading caravan as far as Syria. Khadija was so pleased with him that on his return, she offered to marry him. Muhammad agreed, although she was forty years of age and had been twice married before. She bore him two sons and four daughters. Both sons died in infancy. Muhammad loved her faithfully until her death.

His Personal Appearance

As an adult, Muhammad was somewhat above middle height, with a lean but commanding figure. His head was massive, with a broad and noble forehead. He had thick black hair, slightly curling, which hung over his ears; his eyes were large, black, and piercing; his eyebrows arched and joined; his nose high and acquiline; and he had a long, bushy beard. When he was excited, the veins would swell across his forehead. His eyes were often bloodshot and always restless. Decision marked his every movement. He used to walk so rapidly that his followers half-ran behind him and could hardly keep up with him.

'Ayisha's Evaluation of Muhammad

'Ayisha, the youngest of his eleven wives, said,

He was a man just such as yourselves; he laughed often and smiled much. At home he would mend his clothes and cobble his shoes. He used to help me in my household duties; but what he did oftenest was to sew. He used to eat with his thumb and two fore-fingers; and when he had done, he would lick them, beginning with the middle finger. He had a special liking for sweetmeats and honey. He was also fond of cucumbers and undried dates. When a lamb or a kid was being cooked, Muhammad would go to the pot, take out the shoulder, and eat it. He never travelled without a toothpick.[4]

'Ayisha used to say that the prophet loved three things—women, scents, and food.

Muhammad at one time was very poor, but prospered later in life. He had twenty milch camels, yielding two large skinsful of milk every evening. He also had seven goats. He would say, "There is no house possessing a goat but a blessing abideth thereon; and there is no house possessing three goats but the angels pass the night there praying for its inmates until the morning."[5]

PROPHETIC CLAIMS—FLIGHT TO MEDINA

Rebuilding of the Ka'bah

The Ka'bah, having been damaged by a flood, had to be rebuilt. The Ka'bah was the cubed stone building which housed the 360 idols of the local Arab tribes. The Ka'bah, from *kaab*, meaning square, contained a black stone alleged to have been given to the first man, Adam, and subsequently found by the patriarch Abraham to identify the place of Allah's worship.

A quarrel arose among the leading families as to which of them should deposit the black stone in its rightful place. They agreed that the first citizen approaching the pagan temple should decide between them. Muhammad then came in sight. He had been called "the Faithful One," and all cried, "We are content." Spreading his mantle on the ground, he bade them to place the stone upon it. "Now," said he, "let a chief man from each of you seize a corner of this mantle and raise the stone." When the sacred stone was lifted to the proper height, Muhammad guided the beams to the proper place. The building was then completed. A black curtain was later thrown over the edifice and hung like a veil all around.[6]

Literacy, Dreams, and Early Followers

Around Muhammad's fortieth year, the idolatry and moral debasement of his people pressed heavily upon him, and his soul was troubled about what might be the true religion. He often meditated in a cave on the side of Mount Hira', two or three miles from Mecca. The view from this place was dreary: only barren black and grey hills and white sandy valleys met the eye. He would stroll with his faithful wife, Khadija, to Mt. Hira'. During this period, he probably composed some of the chapters of the Quran which express the yearning of an inquirer.[7] No scribe accompanied Muhammad at that time.

Many experts on the life of Muhammad believe he was illiterate. However, such a claim is not true. The myth may be an attempt to magnify the work of Muhammad in producing the Quran, thus substantiating the so-called miraculous nature of the book. Here are my reasons for rejecting this notion.

First, we are told that when the treaty with the Meccans was to be signed by Muhammad, they refused to acknowledge him as the Apostle of Allah. Relenting to their demands, he struck out that title and wrote instead Muhammad, son of 'Abdu'llah, then signed the peace treaty.[8]

A second incident supporting Muhammad's literacy occurred on his deathbed. Realizing that he was dying, he motioned to 'Ayisha, his favorite wife, to bring him something on which he could write the name of his successor, but he was too weak to perform the task.[9]

Third, he served for many years as a trading camel-caravan merchant, who would naturally know reading, writing, and arithmetic as he travelled to Damascus and other cities.

Fourth, while visiting the St. Catherine's Monastery at Mt. Sinai in 1979, I was shown a personal letter said to be signed by Muhammad himself, guaranteeing the freedom of the monks and their monastery and dated in 632. The document was issued because the monks honored Islam by building a small mosque within their walled fortress. If this document is verified as coming from Muhammad's hand, it presents strong proof for his literacy.

Fifth, the most eloquent and articulate in the Arabic language are the Bedouins. Muhammad lived with them until he was five years old. He then travelled with them as an adult and learned their classical language, which to this day is not any different from the Quranic Arabic. In other words, just as Shakespeare and the King James Bible present us with beautiful seventeenth-century English, so does the Quran with seventh-century Arabic.

Finally, in Surat al-'Alaq (The Clot) 96:1-5, Gabriel, the angel of inspiration, commands Muhammad to read and Muhammad reads! If Muhammad could read, could he not also write? Why would Allah also refer to Muhammad as the one "who taught by the pen" if the prophet could not write?

Now Muhammad's writing ability may be disputed, but his dreams and visions are not. At times we are told that Muhammad's mind was so troubled that escape by suicide was suggested. Once when seeking a precipice from which to jump, it is said that he was suddenly arrested by the angel Gabriel seated on a throne in the sky, who called, "O Muhammad, thou who art the Prophet of the Lord, I am Gabriel."

At times Muhammad's excitement took the shape of a trance or vision. At the moment of inspiration, the tradition says, sweat dropped from his forehead,

and he fell to the ground. Once, as he lay wrapped in
his garment and stretched upon his carpet, Gabriel
again addressed him, bidding him, "Arise and
preach!" Muhammad then believed himself to be a
commissioned apostle, the Prophet of Allah sent to
reclaim a fallen people.[10]

The first convert to Islam was Muhammad's wife,
Khadija; the next two were Ali, his cousin, and Zeyd,
his adopted son; and afterwards his friend, Abi Bakr,
a prosperous merchant. Others followed till Muhammad had about forty adherents. When he began to
preach publicly, he called the new way Islam, or
"surrender" to the will of God.

Problems with the Meccans

The Meccans at first gave little heed to the teaching of Muhammad; but no sooner did he condemn
their idols than they became angry and persecuted
his new converts. Zeyd was attacked while leading a
party in prayer. He defended himself and struck one
of his opponents with a camel's goad.[11] This was the
first blood spilled for the cause of Islam.

As the believers increased in number, so did the
enmity of the persecutors. Muhammad recommended those of his followers who were without
protection to seek asylum in a foreign land. Some
went for a time to Abyssinia (Ethiopia). Muhammad
tried to protect his followers by arranging a compro-
mise with the Meccans, which admitted their gods
into his system as intercessors. He recited the following lines as inspired:

**Have ye thought upon Al-Lāt and Al-'Uzza and
Manāt, the third, the other?**

أَفَرَءَيْتُمُ اللَّاتَ وَالْعُزَّى ۝

وَمَنَوٰةَ الثَّالِثَةَ الْأُخْرَى ۝ [12]

Al-Lat, Al'Uzza, and Manat were the three protecting
Arabic deities of Mecca. "These are exalted god-
desses," Muhammad instructed his followers, "and
verily their intercession is to be sought." The com-
promise brought reconciliation and led the Meccans
to bow before the God of Muhammad. But Muhammad soon repented of what he had done.[13] He gave
the message as now found in the Quran, confessing
that the previous verses were inspired by Satan.

**Are yours the males and His the females? That in-
deed was an unfair division! They are but names
which ye have named, ye and your fathers, for which
Allah hath revealed no warrant.**

Salman Rushdie's *Satanic Verses* caused a world-
wide furor among the Muslims in February 1989.

◆ ◆

أَلَكُمُ الذَّكَرُ وَلَهُ الْأُنثَى ۝

تِلْكَ إِذًا قِسْمَةٌ ضِيزَى ۝

إِنْ هِيَ إِلَّا أَسْمَاءٌ سَمَّيْتُمُوهَا أَنتُمْ وَآبَاؤُكُم

مَّا أَنزَلَ اللَّهُ بِهَا مِن سُلْطَٰنٍ [14]

Death of Khadija and Marriage to Sauda

In the tenth year of his mission and the fiftieth of
his life, Muhammad lost his faithful wife, Khadija,
who died at sixty-five. Abu Talib, his uncle and
guardian, died a few weeks afterward. Khadija was

the only wife of Muhammad during her lifetime. His grief over her death at first was inconsolable; but within two months he married Sauda, a widow. He also betrothed himself to 'Ayisha, the daughter of his best friend Abu Bakr, then only seven years of age.[15] Muhammad eventually married fifteen women, eleven of whom are mentioned in this chapter because of their importance. From several historical accounts, it is clear that he married someone new every year after Khadija's death.

In the sixtieth year of his life, Muhammad was joined by two leading citizens of Mecca, his uncle Hamza and 'Umar. Noted for bravery, Hamza was called the "Lion of God." Umar was a former persecutor, who confessed to Muhammad, "Verily, I testify that thou art the prophet of God." Filled with delight, Muhammad cried aloud, "Allahu Akbar" (Allah is greater).

The Quraish elders of Mecca became alarmed at the progress of Muhammad's religion and tried for a time to suspend all dealings with him and his followers; but the interdict had to be cancelled due to popular pressure.

The Flight to Medina

Soon after the death of Abu Talib, Muhammad and Zeyd went to Ta'if, a city to the east of Mecca. The people refused to listen to their message because they had a god of their own. Hooting and yelling, the citizens drove the two visitors through the streets and pelted them with stones. Blood flowed from Muhammad, and his companion was wounded in the head. On their way back to Mecca, Muhammad said that a company of Jinn, or spirits, pressed around them to hear the preaching of Islam.

Two hundred and seventy miles north of Mecca is Yathrib. Twelve idolaters from that city accepted Islam during the annual pilgrimage and pledged their faith to Muhammad. This was called "the first pledge of Aqaba," named after the location where they met at night. The twelve (on their return to Medina) became zealous missionaries of Islam and spread the faith from house to house. They wrote to Muhammad for a teacher able to instruct inquirers.[16] The Prophet Muhammad's hopes were now fixed on Yathrib, which was renamed Medina after he took up residence there.

Another year passed for Muhammad without any progress at Mecca, then tidings came to him of the growth of Islam at Yathrib. Arriving at Mecca for the pilgrimage, the enthusiastic band of disciples from Yathrib surrounded him and placed their life and property at his service.

After two months nearly all of the Islamic believers had left for Yathrib with their households except for Muhammad and Abu Bakr. The Quraish became determined to slay Muhammad, but being warned of their design, he fled with Abu Bakr to a cave near Mecca, where they hid for three days. Miracles were reported to have happened there. Allegedly, a spider wove her web across the mouth of the cave and branches sprouted over it on which wild pigeons settled as camouflage. On the evening of the fourth day, Muhammad and Abu Bakr set out for Yathrib. The date was June 25, 622. Muhammad was fifty-three years of age. Muslims observe this as "The Hijra," or Flight, which marks the beginning of the Muslim calendar.[17]

MUHAMMAD THE CONQUEROR

Medina's Chief and Muhammad's Marriage to 'Ayisha

The first year of Muhammad's residence at Yathrib, now renamed Medina, was chiefly occupied in building the great Mosque and in providing houses for himself and his followers. Shortly afterward he celebrated his marriage with 'Ayisha, then a ten-year-old girl.

The Battle of Badr

Muhammad heard that a rich caravan of the Quraish was on its way from Syria to Mecca, so he took 305 men out to plunder it. The Quraish of the caravan, with others who joined them from Mecca, numbered about a thousand. In the battle which took place at Badr, about fifty of the Quraish were slain and about as many taken prisoners, while Muhammad lost only fourteen. Among those killed was the leader of the caravan, Abu Jahl, who had greatly opposed Muhammad at Mecca. When his head was cast at Muhammad's feet, it is said that the prophet exclaimed, "It is more acceptable to me than the choicest camel of Arabia." After the battle was over, two of the prisoners were executed. Those who declared themselves believers in the one God Allah were set free. The rest were kept for ransom.

There was a sharp contention about the division of the spoil. Muhammad, in the name of Allah, took one-fifth of the plunder and divided the remainder among his warriors. It was Allah who had given the victory and to Allah the spoil belonged, Muhammad said. Afterward he proclaimed an ordinance which is recognized to this day by the Muslims: "Know that whatsoever thing ye plunder, verily one-fifth thereof is for God and for the Prophet."

The battle of Badr is memorable as the occasion on which Muhammad first drew the sword in assertion of his claim as the commissioned apostle of the Most High Allah. The ensuing victory was alleged to be a sign of this truth. Hence Muhammad was received in triumph on his return to Medina.[18]

The first blood shed at Medina under devotion to Muhammad was a woman's. Asma, daughter of Merwan, belonged to a family which still clung to the ancestral faith. She made no secret that she disliked Islam, and she composed verses on the folly of putting faith in a stranger who had slain so many of his own people in battle.

These verses quickly spread from mouth to mouth. The Muslims were offended, and 'Umair, a blind man of Asma's tribe, vowed that he would kill her. In the dead of night, he crept to the apartment where Asma lay asleep with her children. Stealthily, he removed her suckling baby and plunged his sword into her breast, pinning her to the couch. The next morning, in the mosque at prayer, 'Umair acquainted Muhammad (who was aware of the scheme) with what he had done. Muhammad turned to the bystanders and said, "Behold a man that hath assisted the Lord and His prophet. Call him not blind, call him rather ' 'Umair,' the seeing."[19] On his way home 'Umair encountered members of Asma's family who criticized him for the murder. He defended it openly and threatened the whole clan with the same fate. They were so alarmed that they pledged loyalty to the Muslim party to avoid a blood-feud.

The Battle Against the Jewish Tribes

Medina was founded by refugee Jews from Syria,
and many still remained in the city. At first Muhammad tried to win them over by representing himself
as only a teacher of the creed of Abraham, but they
refused to acknowledge him as a prophet. Muhammad now felt himself strong enough to use force.

The members of one of the Jewish tribes were
goldsmiths and lived in a fort outside the city.
Muhammad summoned them to acknowledge him
as the apostle of God, lest they should suffer the fate
of the Quraish. The Jews refused, and an insult
hurled at a Muslim maiden gave Muhammad the
pretext to attack them. Placing his great white banner, fresh from the field of Badr, in the hands of
Hamza, he marched against the Jewish tribes and
besieged their fort.

After some time they surrendered. One by one, as
they came out of their fortress, they were pinioned
for execution. 'Abdu'llah ibn 'Ubai could not bear
the sight, and begged for mercy; but Muhammad
turned away from him. Then seizing Muhammad by
the arm, 'Abdu'llah repeated his request.

"Let me alone," retorted Muhammad. But 'Abdu'llah did not relax his grasp. "Wretch, let me go,"
cried the prophet.

"Nay," answered 'Abdu'llah, "I will not let thee go
until thou showest mercy on my friends who stood
by me on the day of battle."

"Then let them go," said Muhammad sullenly.
"The Lord curse them and him too!"

They were freed but banished, and all their houses
and goods were distributed among Muhammad and
his followers.[20]

The Battle of Uhud

At Mecca there was a burning desire to avenge the defeat at Badr. Twelve months later, three thousand Quraish marched north and camped at Uhud, a mountain three miles northeast of Medina. Muhammad, clad in armor, led out his army of one thousand men, halted for the night, and at early dawn advanced on Uhud. He was soon abandoned by 'Abdu'llah and three hundred men. In the battle that ensued, the Muslims were defeated. Khalid, commanding the right wing of the Quraish, raised the cry, "Muhammad is slain!" The confusion of the Faithful was great and defied all Muhammad's attempts to rally them. During this turmoil, Muhammad was wounded in the face. The retreat, however, was still ably conducted, and the Quraish did not attempt a pursuit thinking that he was dead. Seventy Muslims were slain, and Muhammad comforted their friends by declaring the dead as martyrs in Allah's cause and now alive with Allah in Paradise.[21]

MORE WIVES FOR MUHAMMAD

The Fourth Wife—Hafsa, Daughter of 'Umar

About this time Muhammad took a fourth wife, Hafsa, the daughter of 'Umar. There was much rivalry between Hafsa and 'Ayisha, but the latter succeeded in maintaining her supremacy.

None of Muhammad's marriages at Medina produced a male heir. It was only later, through his youngest daughter Fatima, that his line was perpetuated. When she was seventeen, she was given in marriage to 'Ali, Muhammad's childhood friend and cousin, then twenty-five. Within twelve months she gave birth to Hasan, and the year after to Husain.[22]

The Fifth Wife—Zainab, His Adopted Son's Ex-wife

One day Muhammad went to visit the house of his adopted son Zeyd, but Zeyd was not there. Muhammad accidentally saw Zeyd's wife, Zainab, unveiled. Smitten by her beauty, Muhammad exclaimed, "Praise belongeth unto God who turneth the hearts of men even as He will." These words were overheard by Zainab, who, proud of her conquest, told her husband of it. Zeyd went at once to Muhammad and offered to divorce his wife for him. At first Muhammad refused, for it was a thing unheard of to marry the divorced wife of an adopted son; but Zeyd carried out his proposal. Muhammad at last resolved to have Zainab. Sitting by 'Ayisha, he professed to have a revelation from Allah, and said, "Who will run and tell Zainab that the Lord hath joined her to me in marriage?" Zainab was overjoyed and gave the messenger all the jewels she had on her person. This event demonstrates that the traditional view that Muhammad's numerous marriages were for political reasons or to care for some widows is not true.[23]

The marriage caused great scandal. To save his reputation, Muhammad sought to justify his conduct by affirming that it was done by Allah's command:

> So when Zeyd had performed the necessary formality (of divorce) from her, We gave her unto thee in marriage, so that (henceforth) there may be no sin for believers in respect of wives of their adopted sons, when the latter have performed the necessary

formality (of release) from them. The commandment of Allah must be fulfilled.

◆ ◆

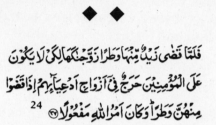

فَلَمَّا قَضَى زَيْدٌ مِّنْهَا وَطَرًا زَوَّجْنَكَهَا لِكَيْ لَا يَكُونَ
عَلَى الْمُؤْمِنِينَ حَرَجٌ فِى أَزْوَاجِ أَدْعِيَآئِهِمْ إِذَا قَضَوْا
مِنْهُنَّ وَطَرًا وَكَانَ أَمْرُ اللهِ مَفْعُولًا ٢٤ ۝

Afterward, Zainab vaunted herself as the only wife of Muhammad who had been given in marriage by Allah Himself.

The same Surat, at 33:50, allows Muhammad more than four wives:

> **O Prophet! Lo! We have made lawful unto thee thy wives unto whom thou hast paid their dowries, and those whom thy right hand possesseth of those whom Allah hath given thee as spoils of war, and a believing woman if she give herself unto the Prophet and the Prophet desire to ask her in marriage—a privilege for thee only, not for the (rest of) believers.**

◆ ◆

يَٰٓأَيُّهَا النَّبِىُّ إِنَّآ أَحْلَلْنَا لَكَ أَزْوَاجَكَ الَّٰتِىٓ ءَاتَيْتَ
أُجُورَهُنَّ وَمَا مَلَكَتْ يَمِينُكَ مِمَّآ أَفَآءَ اللهُ عَلَيْكَ
وَامْرَأَةً مُّؤْمِنَةً إِن
وَهَبَتْ نَفْسَهَا لِلنَّبِىِّ إِنْ أَرَادَ النَّبِىُّ أَن يَسْتَنكِحَهَا
خَالِصَةً لَّكَ مِن دُونِ الْمُؤْمِنِينَ

In verse 59 of the same Surat, rules are laid down
for the seclusion of women, especially in the case of
Muhammad's wives. The latter were not to be spoken to unless they were behind a curtain. It was also
said that Allah had forbidden them from ever marry-
ing after Muhammad's death. They were virtually
"captives" in the prophet's houses.

The Sixth Wife—Juwariyah

During his residence at Medina, Muhammad gratified the ruling passion of the Arabs and gained
many adherents by his numerous expeditions for
plunder. In one case, 1,000 camels, 5,000 sheep, and a
great many women and children became the spoil of
the Muslims. Among the captives was Juwariyah,
the wife of one of the chiefs, distinguished for her
beauty. Muhammad ransomed her, took her to be his
wife, and built a special room for her reception.[25]

The Seventh Wife—Raihana, A Jewess

At the conclusion of the battle against the Quraiza
Jews, Raihana was kept by Muhammad as his seventh wife. Her husband and male relatives had all
perished in the massacre. Muhammad offered her
marriage, but she preferred to remain his bond-
slave. She declined Islam, but she had no escape
from the embrace of her conqueror.[26]

The Eighth Wife—Maryam
An Egyptian Christian Slave Girl

A year after the battle with the Quraiza Jews,
Muhammad sent letters to various foreign sov-
ereigns inviting them to embrace Islam. The mes-

sage was unheeded except by Al-Moqawqas, the governor of Egypt. He sent Muhammad two Christian slave girls, Maryam and her sister Sirin, and a white mule. Muhammad chose Mary, or Maryam, the fairer slave, for himself. The fondness of Muhammad for Mary was resented by his numerous wives. To show his displeasure for their attitude, he lived for a month with Mary alone, even though he had instructed Muslims to marry as many as four wives provided they were treated equally. Furthermore, he warned the other wives by revelation,

> It may happen that his Lord, if he divorce you, will give him in your stead wives better than you, submissive (to Allah), believing, pious, penitent, inclined to fasting, widows and maids.[27]

The Ninth Wife—Safiyya from the Khaibar Jews

In the seventh year of the Hijra, Muhammad attacked Khaibar, a Jewish settlement on the way to Syria. The Jews surrendered the citadel on condition that the people be free to leave the country, giving up all their wealth to the conquerors. The chief, Kinana, was accused of keeping back part of his treasure, upon which he was tortured to death.

Among the female captives was Safiyya, the widow of Kinana and just fifteen years of age. One of Muhammad's followers begged to have her for himself, but the prophet, struck with her beauty, threw his mantle over her, and took her to his harem. The wedding was celebrated by a feast. This is further evidence that Muhammad's marriages were neither for political nor humanitarian purposes but purely for passion.[28]

The Tenth Wife—Um Habeeba

On his return to Medina in 628, Muhammad married his tenth wife—Um Habeeba, the widowed daughter of Abu Sufyan. She had emigrated with her husband and other Muslims in 615 to Abyssinia to escape persecution. But her husband had renounced Islam, become a Christian, and died. Muhammad sent for her with a marriage proposal. The marriage was consumated in 628.[29]

The Eleventh Wife—Maimuna of Mecca

During a short stay at Mecca in 629, for the Lesser Pilgrimage, Muhammad also arranged to marry Maimuna, his eleventh wife. This marriage gained for him two of his most important converts: Khalid, Ibn al Waleed, called the "Sword of God," and 'Amr, a leading chief of Mecca.[30]

ISLAMIC BATTLES

The Siege of Medina

The Quraish and Bedouins made another attempt to capture Medina with an army of ten thousand men. Following the advice of a Persian, Muhammad had a trench dug around Medina, a technique unknown until then in Arabia. Muhammad encouraged the citizens in their work by bearing baskets of the excavated earth and by joining them in their songs. The Quraish were unable to cross the trench, supplies ran short, camels died, and drenching rain fell. The camp eventually disbanded, and the attackers returned home. Muhammad attributed their "retreat" to the intervention of Allah.

During the sixth year of the Hijra, there were as

many as seventeen expeditions, which generally ended in the capture of flocks and herds or other booty. These served to spread the terror of Muhammad's name.

The Battle with the Quraiza Jews

Not long after the siege was lifted from Medina, Muhammad marched with three thousand men against the Quraiza Jews. The besieged Jews, numbering over two thousand souls, surrendered at last. The Jewish men, with hands tied behind their backs, were kept in one place. The women and children were placed under the charge of a renegade Jew. The spoil was put aside for division. A wounded chief named Sa'd was asked to decide the fate of the captives. His judgment was that the men should be put to death, the women and children sold into slavery, and the spoil divided among the Islamic army. A shrill of horror ran through the assembly, but Muhammad stopped all questioning. "Truly," said he, "the judgment of Sa'd is the judgment of the Lord, pronounced on high from above the seventh heaven."

During the night trenches were dug across the marketplace. In the morning Muhammad commanded the male captives to be brought out in companies of five or six at a time. As each party came up, they were made to sit down in a row on the brink of the trench. There they were beheaded, and their bodies cast into the trench. The butchery lasted all day and continued by torchlight into the night.[31]

Zainab, a Jewess, lost her husband, father, and brother in this bloody battle, and she planned a revenge. She cooked a goat, steeped it in poison, and placed the dish before Muhammad for his evening

supper. Accepting the gift, he took for himself his
favorite piece, the shoulder, and distributed portions to Abu Bakr and other friends. "Hold," cried
Muhammad, as he spat out the first mouthful, "this
shoulder has been poisoned." One who had
swallowed part of the meat soon died. Muhammad
was seized with excruciating pains. Zainab defended
herself, saying,

> **Thou hast inflicted grievous injuries on my people,
> and slain, as thou seest, my husband and my father.
> Therefore, said I within myself, If he be a prophet he
> will reject the gift, knowing that it is poisoned; but if
> only a pretender we shall be rid of our troubles.**[32]

The Conquest of Mecca

A truce, scheduled to last ten years, had been established with the Quraish; but within two years
Muhammad decided he was strong enough to conquer Mecca, breaking the truce. A dispute among the
tribes afforded him his pretext. In January 630, he
set out for Mecca at the head of ten thousand men.
On the eighth day, he halted on the heights next to
the city. Abu Sufyan, the great opponent of Muhammad, sought a personal interview. When they met,
Muhammad said to him, "Has the time not yet come
for thee to acknowledge that there is but one God
and that I am his Apostle?" He replied that he was
still in some doubt. At this 'Abbas, threatening him
with his sword, said, "Believe and testify thy faith at
the peril of thy neck." Abu Sufyan then repeated the
formula of belief, and he was sent to prepare the city
for the approach of Muhammad.

The Quraish knew resistance would be hopeless.
Muhammad made his triumphant entry into Mecca,
unchallenged, on his favorite camel. On his way he

recited Surat al-Fath (Victory) 48. He then rode around the Ka'bah seven times, touching the black stone with his stick. He ordered daily prayers to be said in the direction of the Ka'bah from that time on. He also ordered the destruction of the 360 idols within the temple, and he personally destroyed a wooden pigeon suspended from the roof which was regarded as one of the deities of the Quraish. His uncle 'Abbas was appointed to give drink to pilgrims out of the well, Zamzam. Alms were accepted by Muhammad's uncle for this drinking water.

During his stay at Mecca, Muhammad sent out troops into the district to destroy the temples of 'Uzza, Suwa, and Manat, and the idols of the neighboring tribes. His high-strung deputy Khalid, ordered a whole tribe to be slain because they would not acknowledge Muhammad as Allah's prophet. Muhammad distanced himself, declaring that he was innocent of what Khalid had done.[33]

MUHAMMAD'S LAST DAYS

Farewell Pilgrimage

In the tenth year of the Hijra, at age sixty-three, Muhammad set out with thousands of followers and all his wives for Mecca. He led a hundred camels, marked by his own hand for sacrifice, in solemn order. At the Ka'bah he carefully performed all the ceremonies of the Lesser Pilgrimage, then proceeded to do those of the Greater. On the eighth day of the holy month, he set out for Mina, a short distance from Mecca, where he spent the night. The next day he went to 'Arafat, a small conical hill. Ascending the summit, he declared the valley sacred, saying,

**This day have I perfected your religion for you and
completed My favour unto you, and have chosen for
you as religion AL-ISLĀM. Whoso is forced by hunger, not by will, to sin: (for him) lo! Allah is Forgiving, Merciful.**[34]

◆ ◆

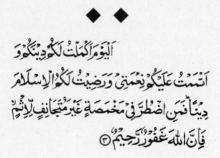

On the tenth day, proceeding to Mina, he cast the
accustomed stones at projecting eminences of the
narrow valley to drive away the devil, slew the vic-
tims brought for sacrifice, had his head shaved and
his nails pared, ordered the hair to be burned, and as
the ceremonies ended, laid aside his pilgrim garb.
Returning to Mecca, Muhammad once again made
the seven circuits of the Ka'bah and drank from the
sacred well, Zamzam. Then he took off his shoes and
went into the Ka'bah to pray. Having rigorously performed the ceremonies as a model for all time, he
returned to Medina.[35]

Sickness and Death

In the third month of the eleventh year of the
Hijra, Muhammad fell sick. The recent death of his
infant son, Ibrahim, weighed his spirits down, and
the poison he had consumed at Khaibar still both-
ered him. During a violent attack of fever, he called
his wives together and said: "You see that I am very

sick. I am not able to visit you in turn. If it be pleas-
ing to you, I will remain in the house of 'Ayisha."
They agreed.

After the fever had lasted nearly two weeks, his illness violently intensified on a Saturday night.
Racked and restless, he tossed on his bed. Replying
to one who tried to comfort him, Muhammad said,
"There is not upon earth a believer sore afflicted, but
the Lord causeth his sins to fall off from him even as
the leaves from off the trees in autumn."[36]

On Sunday he lay through the whole day in weak-
ness. When he swooned, his wives gave him some
medicine. Reviving, he asked what they had been
doing to him. On being told, he said that they had
given him medicine for another complaint, and he
ordered them all to partake of the medicine. So the
women arose and poured the medicine in the presence of the dying prophet into each other's mouths.

Monday morning brought relief with some return
of strength. Muhammad, leaning on an attendant,
entered the mosque and sat on the ground for the
service.

After a little conversation, he was helped back to
the chamber of 'Ayisha. Exhausted, he lay down
upon the bed. 'Ayisha, seeing him very low and
weak, raised his head from the pillow as she sat by
him on the ground, and placed his head on her
bosom. His strength soon rapidly sank. He called for
a pitcher of water and wetting his face from it,
prayed, "O Lord, I beseech Thee, assist me in the ag-
onies of death, come close, O Gabriel, to me." His
last words in a whisper were, "Lord grant me pardon; Eternity, in Paradise! Pardon. The blessed com-
panionship on high." He stretched himself gently,
and the prophet of Arabia was no more. It was a little after midday on the eighth of June 632.[37]

Burial

During the night his faithful followers laid out and washed his body. In the morning the people came in groups to gaze at his still form. His grave was dug on the spot where he had breathed his last. In the evening his red mantle was spread at the bottom of the grave, and his body was lowered into it. The vault was covered over with bricks, and the grave was made level with the floor.

The tomb is now close to the great mosque of Medina, which ranks in holiness next to that of Mecca. The present mosque, erected by a Mamaluke Sultan of Egypt in the sixteenth century, is the sixth which has stood on the spot.

The Khalifas

From 632 to 661, four Khalifs ruled from Medina, elected by the closest followers of the prophet. (Khalif means "a successor" in Arabic, but it became the title of the person who became the religious and political leader after Muhammad's death.)

Abu Bakr, the first Khalif, sent Khalid to subdue the tribes who rebelled immediately after the death of Muhammad. United by a military force of 18,000, they advanced on Palestine and Syria in 634 and defeated the Byzantine armies at Yarmouk River on August 26, 636.[38] Forty thousand more Muslims marched to conquer North Africa.

At the death of Abu Bakr, Umar ibn al Khattab was elected the second Khalif. It was Umar who accepted the peaceful surrender of Jerusalem. Umar was stabbed in the Medina Mosque in 646.

The next Khalif was Uthman ibn Affan, who spearheaded the revision of the Quran. He too was murdered when 80 years old while reading the Quran at his palace.

Muhammad's Family Tree
Quraysh of the Hollow

(Fihr is directly descended from Ishmael in the male line. The descendants of Fihr who came to be known as Quraysh of the Outskirts are not shown in the following tree.)

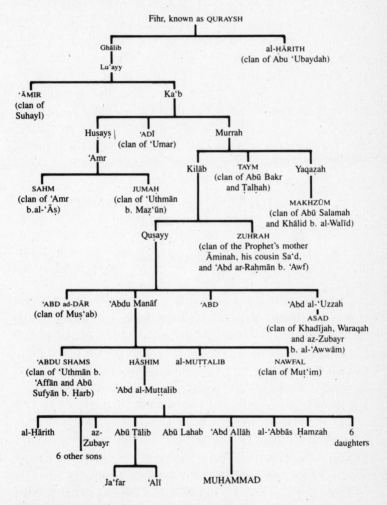

The names of founders of clans are given in small capitals. These are followed by the names of one or more of their descendants who were closely connected with the Prophet or else of historical importance.[40]

When Ali ibn Abu Talib was elected in 656, the governor of Syria, Muawiya, son of Abu Sufian, refused to recognize him. A civil war ensued, which ended five years later when Ali was assassinated.[39]

Muawiya became the next Khalif, ruling from Damascus. His Omayyid dynasty ruled the Muslim world for ninety years. The grandson of Muhammad, Husain, was brutally killed by the Omayyids in Kerbela in Iraq on October 10, 680. The feud between the Omayyids and Beni Hashim split the Muslim world and continues to this day. The Shi'ites are the ones who support the claims of the elected Khalif Ali because of Ali's blood relationship to the prophet. The other major sect is called Sunni, which supports the elected Khalif by majority vote.

IS MUHAMMAD MENTIONED IN THE BIBLE?

Is Muhammad Mentioned in the Old Testament?

Christ's coming is foretold in the Old Testament in many different places. If, therefore, the Most High God intended to send into the world a prophet far greater than Christ, we should find predictions concerning this future prophet in the Old Testament, and still more in the New Testament. It is natural, therefore, for Muslims to seek such prophecies in the Bible regarding the founder of their religion.

If Muhammad was the Seal of the Prophets—the person on whose account God created the universe—it would be very strange for God not to have told us to look for and obey the coming Prophet. Those who believe in Muhammad tell us that clear and unmistakable predictions regarding him are found in

the Bible. Muslims also say that other predictions of
Muhammad's coming were once there, but were removed by Jews and Christians.[41]

The appeal to the Bible in this matter implies that
the Bible is (1) divinely inspired, and (2) uncorrupt.
Otherwise, of what use would it be to refer to such a
book as authoritative? If our Muslim friends admit
these two points, then an inquiry into the alleged
biblical prophecies regarding Muhammad may be
very interesting and instructive. But if they do not
admit these points of fact, it is difficult to see what
use it is for them to refer to the Bible at all in seeking
proof of their prophet's mission. Of course, many
learned Muslims—all, in fact, who have carefully
studied the matter—do admit these two facts.[42]

Genesis 49:10

**The scepter shall not depart from Judah, nor a law-
giver from between his feet, until Shiloh comes; and
to Him shall be the obedience of the people.**

It is asserted that this passage refers to Muhammad, since "Judah" comes from a Hebrew verb
meaning "to praise," the same meaning for the Arabic name Muhammad. But the context of Genesis
shows that Shiloh was to be born among the descendants of Judah. Muhammad, however, came from
the Arabian tribe of the Quraish. He was not Jewish.
Moreover, the scepter departed from Judah more
than 550 years before Muhammad was born.

Deuteronomy 18:15, 18

**The Lord your God will raise up for you a Prophet
like me from your midst, from your brethren. Him
you shall hear, I will raise up for them a Prophet like
you from among their brethren, and will put My**

words in his mouth, and he shall speak to them all that I command him.

Muslims assert that the prophet predicted in Deuteronomy is Muhammad. Since "from your midst" does not appear in either the ancient Greek Old Testament (the Septuagint) or the Samaritan Pentateuch, the original text must state that the prophet would come from the relatives of the Israelites, the descendents of Ishmael, the Arabs.

However, there is earlier ancient Hebrew manuscript evidence supporting the customary reading. In addition, "brethren" naturally and commonly refers to one's closest relatives (e.g., the Israelite tribes). A qualifier would indicate less close relatives (e.g., the Ishmaelite tribes).

It is said that Muhammad was like Moses in many points. Both were brought up in their enemies' houses, appeared among idolaters, were at first rejected by their own people and afterward accepted by them, each gave a law, fled from their enemies (Moses to Midian, Muhammad to Medina, a name of a similar meaning), marched to battle against their enemies, wrought miracles, and enabled their followers to conquer Palestine. These correlations prove nothing.

God Himself has explained in the Gospels that this prophecy referred to Christ, not to Muhammad. Compare Deuteronomy 18:15, "Him you shall hear," with Matthew 17:5, ". . . This is My beloved Son, in whom I am well pleased. Hear Him!" (See also Mark 9:2 and Luke 9:35.) Jesus explains that this and other passages refer to Himself (John 5:46; Genesis 12:3; 24:4; 18:18; 22:28; 28:14). He was descended from Judah (Matthew 1:1–16; Luke 3:23–38; Hebrews 7:14), was born in Israel, and spent almost all of His life among the Jews. In Acts 3:25–26, this prophecy is cited as referring to Christ Jesus.

Psalm 45:3–5

**Gird Your Sword upon Your thigh, O Mighty One,
With Your glory and Your majesty.
And in Your majesty ride prosperously because of
truth, humility, and righteousness;
And Your right hand shall teach You awesome
things.
Your arrows are sharp in the heart of the King's ene-
mies;
The peoples fall under You.**

In Islam, Muhammad is called "the Prophet with the sword." However, a close study of the context of these verses easily refutes the claim that they refer to Muhammad. Verse six declares, "Your throne, O God, is forever and ever." Muslims never claim that Muhammad was God. Furthermore, Hebrews 1:8–9 clearly states that verse six is an address to Christ.

Isaiah 21:7

**And he saw a chariot with a pair of horsemen,
A chariot of donkeys, and a chariot of camels.**

Muslims think that the words "a chariot of donkeys" in this verse are a prediction of the coming of Christ, who entered Jerusalem riding on a donkey, and that "a chariot (or troop) of camels" refers to Muhammad, since he always rode on a camel. In fact, the context shows that this chapter refers to neither Christ nor Muhammad. It is a prophecy of the fall of Babylon, as we learn from verse 9, and tells how travellers bring word of the capture of the city and the destruction of its idols, which took place under Darius in 519 B.C. and again in 513 B.C.

Is Muhammad Mentioned in the New Testament?

Matthew 3:2

"Repent, for the kingdom of heaven is at hand!"

"The kingdom is at hand" is the call of John the Baptist, repeated by Jesus (Matthew 4:17), and said by Muslims to be a prediction of the establishment of the power of Islam, the Quran being the Law of the Kingdom. But "the kingdom of heaven," or as it is also called, "the kingdom of God," does not refer to the Islamic kingdom, since the heaven and God of Islam are not the heaven and God of the Bible.

The biblical kingdom of God has temporal and spiritual aspects, present and future implications. Long before the rise of Islamic power, Christ announced the presence of the kingdom, saying, "But if I cast out demons by the Spirit of God, surely the kingdom of God has come upon you" (Matthew 12:28). In Mark 9:1, Christ told His disciples that some of them would not taste death until they saw the kingdom of God present with power. Did they see Muhammad and the "kingdom" of Islam? Certainly not.

Mark 1:7

"There comes One after me who is mightier than I, whose sandal strap I am not worthy to stoop down and loose."

The Muslim Injil (gospel) of Jesus is not the same thing as the New Testament or the Gospels. Muslims maintain that the gospel of Jesus is the record of God's Word given through Jesus. The New Testament Gospels, they say, are the words of men—the recollections of Matthew, Mark, and those compiled by Luke and John. Only occasionally can we find Jesus' gospel buried in the midst of man's words and opinion. One of the preserved lines of Jesus' gospel, they say, is in Mark 1:7, where Jesus supposedly prophesied of Muhammad, "There cometh after Me he that is mightier than I."

This shows how hopelessly impossible it is for Muslims to find any prophecy regarding Muhammad, for verse six of this chapter tells us that these words were not spoken by Jesus but by John the Baptist. The context clearly shows this to be true (see also Matthew 3:11–14; Luke 3:16–17; and John 1:26–34). It will not do to say that Christ was already in the world, and that therefore He could not be said to come after John. Christ began to preach only after John had been cast into prison and beheaded (see Mark 1:14; also compare Matthew 4:12, 17), thus ending the forerunner's ministry.

John 4:21

Jesus said to her, "Woman, believe Me, the hour is coming when you will neither on this mountain, nor in Jerusalem, worship the Father."

This is supposed by some Muslims to be a declaration that Jerusalem would no longer be the Holy City and the "Qiblah" (focus of prayers), but that its place would be taken by another city, which, the Muslims say, must be Mecca.

Yet in verses 23–24, Christ Himself explained the meaning of His own words, saying that true and acceptable worship does not depend upon the place where it is offered but upon the state of the worshipper's heart. Hence, He does away with the possibility of there ever afterward being a need for any "Qiblah" on earth.

John 14:16, 17, 26

> "And I will pray the Father, and He will give you another Helper, that He may abide with you forever, even the Spirit of truth, whom the world cannot receive, because it neither sees Him nor knows Him; but you know Him, for He dwells with you and will be in you. But the Helper, the Holy Spirit, whom *the Father will send in My name,* He will teach you all things, and bring to your remembrance all things that I said to you."

Muslims assert that the Greek *paracleton* (helper) mentioned by Christ is Muhammad, whose name they believe to be a translation of the term. They contend that the prophecy in this passage was fulfilled in Muhammad, since he received the Quran from the angel Gabriel (whom Muslims believe to be the Holy Spirit) and bore witness to Christ (John 14:26), acknowledging Him as a prophet (John 16:14), as born of a virgin, as a worker of miracles, as having ascended up to Heaven without dying but not as God's Son (having never claimed to be such), and as having had the Gospel brought to Him.

But the Paracleton could not possibly refer to Muhammad for these reasons:

First of all, the word *paracleton* does not mean anything at all like Muhammad. Paracleton means helper, comforter, sustainer, and advocate. The first of these titles is clearly not suited to Muhammad, the "Prophet with the Sword," and the Quran itself denies the title of Advocate to all but God Himself.

Second, in the New Testament, the title Paracleton is directly applied only to the Holy Spirit (John 13:16, 17, 26; 15:26; 16:13) and by implication to

Christ (John 13:16; 1 John 2:1). The Paracleton of whom Christ speaks is not a man but the invisible Spirit of Truth, who was then dwelling with Christ's disciples and would soon be in their hearts (John 14:17; 16:14).

Third, the Paracleton was to be sent by Christ (John 15:26; 16:7), which Muslims cannot admit concerning Muhammad.

Fourth, the Paracleton's work was not to gather armies and gain victories with earthly weapons, but to convict men of sin, the very essence of sin being disbelief in Christ (John 16:9).

Fifth, His teaching was to glorify not Himself but Christ and to do the work Christ sent Him to do (John 16:14–15).

No!

These are some of the important biblical passages which Muslims emphasize contain prophecies concerning Muhammad. Quite clearly not a single one constitutes a prediction about him. Muhammad is not mentioned explicitly or implicitly in the Bible, God's oldest written revelation (and the only written revelation as far as Christians are concerned). But Christ Jesus is found in the Quran. And what it says about Him places Him far above the founder of Islam.

CHAPTER THREE

JESUS CHRIST ACCORDING TO ISLAM

❋ ❋ ❋

Islam recognizes Christ Jesus to be far more perfect and sinless than any human being ever has been or could be. The Quran itself does not give to any of the prophets, not even to Muhammad, any of those special characteristics pertaining to Christ.

'Isa is the name given to Jesus in the Quran. Both Christians and Muslims have wondered for centuries why He is not called Yesu' as the Gospels have it in Arabic. Here is the reason. Muhammad used the name "'Isa" in good faith after hearing it from the unbelieving Jews in Medina. In their hatred, the Jews ridiculed Jesus by calling him Esau, the rejected brother of Jacob who lost the blessing. They declared that the soul of Esau had been transformed into Jesus.[1] Muhammad picked up this name and put it in his Arabic tongue and applied it to Jesus without carrying with it the derogatory meaning given by the Jews.

A MIRACULOUS CONCEPTION

We read in the Surat al-Tahrim (Banning) 66:12,

And Mary, daughter of 'Imrān, whose body was chaste, therefore We breathed therein something of Our Spirit. And she put faith in the words of her Lord and His Scriptures, and was of the obedient.

◆ ◆

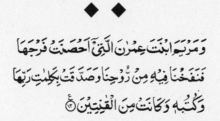

Al Saddi's version of the miracle states the following:

He took hold of her sleeve and breathed into her side, and it entered her breast and she conceived. Then Mary's sister, the wife of Zachariah, came to visit with and help her, and while she was assisting her she knew that Mary was pregnant and Mary mentioned her state to her.

The wife of Zachariah said, "I find the child in my womb worships that which is in yours." Another account relates that the breathing was in her mouth and reached her womb and immediately she conceived.[2]

A MIRACULOUS BIRTH

The Quran mentions a conversation between the Virgin Mary and the angel of the Lord in Surat Maryam (Mary) 19:19–21:

He said: I am only a messenger of thy Lord, that I may bestow on thee a faultless son.

She said: How can I have a son when no mortal

hath touched me, neither have I been unchaste?

He said: So (it will be). Thy Lord saith: It is easy for Me. And (it will be) that We may make of him a revelation for mankind and a mercy from Us, and it is a thing ordained.

◆ ◆

قَالَ إِنَّمَا أَنَا رَسُولُ رَبِّكِ لِأَهَبَ لَكِ غُلَامًا زَكِيًّا ۝

قَالَتْ أَنَّى يَكُونُ لِي غُلَامٌ وَلَمْ يَمْسَسْنِي بَشَرٌ وَلَمْ أَكُ بَغِيًّا ۝

قَالَ كَذَٰلِكِ قَالَ رَبُّكِ هُوَ عَلَيَّ هَيِّنٌ وَلِنَجْعَلَهُ آيَةً لِّلنَّاسِ وَرَحْمَةً مِّنَّا وَكَانَ أَمْرًا مَّقْضِيًّا ۝

Al Baidawi commented on the miraculous birth of Jesus, "That distinction sets Christ apart from other humans and messengers, because He was born without any human embrace or relationship."[3]

Al Fakhr el Razi also speaks of the miraculous birth of our Lord: "I bestow on thee a faultless boy." He explained that "faultless" means first that Christ was without sin; second, that He grew in integrity, as it is said that He who has no sin is chaste and in the growing plant there is purity; and third, he was above reproach and pure.

Furthermore, he expounded that the statement, "We may make of Him a revelation for mankind," means "we make His birth a sign to mankind, as He was born without a father"; and "a mercy from Us" means "mankind will be blessed by the manifestation of these signs for they will be overwhelming indications of His truthfulness and will make the acceptance of His word more likely."[4]

JESUS SPOKE AT HIS BIRTH

Here is a fantastic miracle the Quran attributes to our Lord Jesus Christ, yet it is not found in the New Testament:

Then she pointed to him. They said: How can we talk to one who is in the cradle, a young boy?
He spake: Lo! I am the slave of Allah. He hath given me the Scripture and hath appointed me a Prophet.

◆ ◆

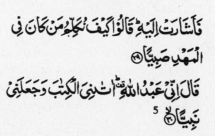

فَأَشَارَتْ إِلَيْهِ قَالُوا كَيْفَ نُكَلِّمُ مَن كَانَ فِي الْمَهْدِ صَبِيًّا ۝

قَالَ إِنِّي عَبْدُ اللَّهِ ءَاتَنِيَ الْكِتَابَ وَجَعَلَنِي نَبِيًّا ۝ [5]

Muslim scholars claim that when Mary's people went too far in reproaching her, she was silent and pointed to her child as if saying to them, "He will answer you."

Still another story, told by Al Razi, says Zachariah came to Mary during this debate among the Jews concerning mother and child, and said to 'Isa (Jesus), "Speak for yourself if you have been commanded so to do." And 'Isa said, "I am the Servant of Allah. He has given Me wisdom and made Me a Prophet."[6]

JESUS HAD SUPERNATURAL KNOWLEDGE

First, we look at Surat al-Imran (The Family of 'Imran) 3:49:

And I announce unto you what ye eat and what ye store up in your houses. Lo! herein verily is a portent for you, if ye are to be believers.

◆ ◆

بِمَا تَأْكُلُونَ وَمَاتَدَّخِرُونَ فِى بُيُوتِكُمْ ۚ إِنَّ فِى
ذَٰلِكَ لَآيَةً لَّكُمْ إِن كُنتُم مُّؤْمِنِينَ ۞

Muslim scholars take two positions on this passage. Some believe that from the beginning 'Isa (Jesus) learned hidden matters. Saddi relates that while 'Isa (Jesus) was playing with the children, He told them what their mothers and fathers did. He told one boy, "Your mother has hidden something for you," and the boy went home and cried until he received it.

Another scholarly opinion holds "discernment of hidden matters to be miraculous." Astrologers who tell the future and reveal hidden matters can only do so by questioning. They also confess that they often make mistakes. But knowledge of the unknown, without recourse to aids or previous knowledge, cannot be without inspiration.[7]

A second reference to Jesus' knowledge is in Surat Zukhruf (Ornaments of Gold) 43:57, 61:

And when the son of Mary is quoted as an example, behold! the folk laugh out. . . .

And lo! verily there is knowledge of the Hour. So doubt ye not concerning it, but follow Me. This is the right path.

◆ ◆

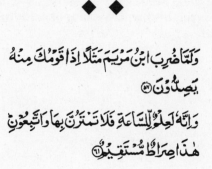

Al Jalalan explained the phrase "a knowledge of the Hour" as meaning that Jesus knew when the Day of Judgment would come. If you recognize Allah as separate from his creation, in that he alone knows the times to come, you can comprehend the measure of distinction to which the Quran assigns Christ.[8]

JESUS IS BLESSED

Surat Maryam (Mary) 19:31 gives us these words from Christ, "And hath made me blessed wheresoever I may be."

Al Tabari, quoting Unis ibn Abd al Ala and Sufyan, said that the explanation of "hath made me blessed" means "He hath made me a 'teacher of good.'"

JESUS IS ENDOWED WITH
THE HOLY SPIRIT

The Quran affirms that Jesus Christ was specially empowered by and endowed with the Holy Spirit.

And We gave Jesus, son of Mary, clear proofs (of Allah's sovereignty) and We supported him with the holy Spirit.

◆ ◆

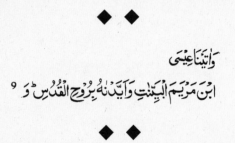

◆ ◆

The Messiah, Jesus son of Mary, was only a messenger of Allah, and His word which He conveyed unto Mary, and a spirit from Him. So believe in Allah and His messengers. . . .

◆ ◆

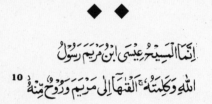

The substance of these verses, according to Muslims, is that Allah gave Jesus in His person a spirit, and this spirit supported Him in His personality. But Muslim scholars differ in their explanation of the Holy Spirit's supporting role.

Al Saddi and Kaab wrote, "The Holy Spirit is Gabriel, and his support of Jesus was by being His companion and friend, helping and accompanying Him wherever He went, until He was taken up into heaven."

Ibn Jubair explained, "Spirit of the Holy is the supreme name for Allah and by it Jesus was raising the dead."

Ibn Abbas announced, "As it was the spirit which was breathed into Him and the Holy One is Allah so He is the Spirit of Allah."[11]

JESUS IS SINLESS

Some scholars link infallibility of message with infallibility of conduct, but the Quran contradicts this idea. Many verses in the Quran make clear that the prophets were not without blame before or after giving their messages. But the Quran claims Christ's life was as infallible as His message. The angel witnessed to that when he said to His mother, "I am only a messenger of thy Lord and I may bestow on thee a faultless son." Therefore, the very angel of God attests to the sinless conduct of Jesus, the son of Mary.

JESUS IS THE WORD OF GOD

The Quran testifies very clearly that Jesus is the Word of God. Surat al-Nisa (Women) 4:171 says,

The Messiah, Jesus son of Mary, was only a messenger of Allah, and His word which He conveyed unto Mary, and a spirit from Him.

Surat al-Imran (The Family of 'Imran) 3:39 says,

> **Allah giveth thee glad tidings of (a son whose name
> is) John, (who cometh) to confirm a word from Allah,
> lordly, chaste, a Prophet of the righteous.**

◆ ◆

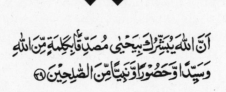

The Imam Abu Al Su'ud commented on the phrase
"confirm a word from Allah," stating that John the
Baptist was the first to believe in Jesus and to support His being the Word of God and a spirit from
Him.

Al Saddi writes that the mother of Yahya (John)
inquired of the mother of 'Isa (Jesus), "Mary, have
you felt my pregnancy?" Mary answered, "I too am
pregnant." John's mother then replied, "I find that
what is in my belly worships what is in your belly."[12]
Surat al-Imran (The Family of 'Imram) 3:45 adds,

> **(And remember) when the angels said: O Mary!
> Lo! Allah giveth thee glad tidings of a word from
> Him, whose name is the Messiah, Jesus, son of Mary,
> illustrious in the world and the Hereafter, and one of
> those brought near (unto Allah).**

◆ ◆

اِذْ قَالَتِ الْمَلَٰئِكَةُ يٰمَرْيَمُ اِنَّ اللّٰهَ يُبَشِّرُكِ بِكَلِمَةٍ
مِّنْهُ ۖ اسْمُهُ الْمَسِيحُ عِيسَى ابْنُ مَرْيَمَ وَجِيهًا
فِى الدُّنْيَا وَالْاٰخِرَةِ وَمِنَ الْمُقَرَّبِيْنَ ۝

This is clarified in the saying of the Muslim scholar, Al Sheikh Muhyi Al Din Al Arabi, "The word is Allah in theophany . . . and is the one divine person, not any other." He also said that the word is a divine person on page 13 of his book, *Fusus al Hugm*, Part 2. Actually, the Quran agrees completely with John 1:1, 14: "In the beginning was the Word, and the Word was with God, and the Word was God. . . . And the Word became flesh."

JESUS IS ALLAH'S MEDIATOR AND MESSIAH

In Surat al-Zumar (The Troops) 39:44, the Quran confines the work of intercession to Allah alone, "Unto Allah belongeth all intercession. . . ." Extraordinarily, the Quran hints that intercession is also one of the privileges of the Messiah, as in Surat al-Imran (The Family of 'Imran) 3:45.

> **(And remember) when the angels said: O Mary! Lo! Allah giveth thee glad tidings of a word from Him, whose name is the Messiah, Jesus, son of Mary, illustrious in the world and the Hereafter, and one of those brought near (unto Allah).**

Messiah is the Hebrew title for God's anointed Savior. "Christ" is the Greek equivalent. "Almasseh" is the Arabic term. The Quran acknowledges Jesus of Nazareth as the only Messiah of God.

Al Jalalan observed, "Illustrious in the world by the ministry of prophecy and in the hereafter by intercession and position and being one of those brought near unto Allah."[13] Badawi contended that "According to some, what was intended here was the high place that Jesus was to have in Paradise . . . and in the Society of Angels."[14]

JESUS IS LIKE ADAM

The Quran states in Surat al-Imran (The Family of 'Imran) 3:59:

> Lo! the likeness of Jesus with Allah is as the likeness of Adam. He created him of dust, then He said unto him: Be! and he is.

◆ ◆

اِنَّ مَثَلَ عِيْسٰى عِنْدَاللّٰهِ كَمَثَلِ اٰدَمَ خَلَقَهُ مِنْ
تُرَابٍ ثُمَّ قَالَ لَهُ كُنْ فَيَكُونُ ۞ [1]

Despite this reading, we must never overlook the fact that Adam was created fully grown, but Jesus was born the infant of a virgin.

Al Qisam, Ibn Jaraij, and A'krama report,

> We heard that the Christians of Najran sent a deputation to Muhammad, among them Al Aquib and As Sayyid, who said, "O Muhammad, why do you revile our Friend?" He replied, "Who is your Friend?" They said, "'Isa (Jesus), Son of Mary. You allege He is a servant," to which Muhammad replied, "Truly, He is a servant of Allah and His Word, bestowed on Mary and a Spirit from Him."
>
> Then they were angry with him and said, "If you are truthful show us a servant who can raise the dead and heal the blind and the leper and who, creating from clay the form of a bird, will breathe into it so that it becomes a bird—isn't He Allah?" Muhammad said nothing until Gabriel came to him and said, "O

Muhammad! They have blasphemed who said that
Allah is Christ the Son of Mary." Then Muhammad
replied, "O Gabriel! They asked me to tell them to
whom 'Isa (Jesus) is similar," and Gabriel said, "'Isa
is just as Adam."[15]

JESUS IS A SERVANT

He spake: Lo! I am the slave of Allah. He hath
given me the Scripture and hath appointed me a
Prophet, and hath made me blessed wheresoever I
may be, and hath enjoined upon me prayer and almsgiving so long as I remain alive, and (hath made me)
dutiful toward her who bore me, and hath not made
me arrogant, unblest.

◆ ◆

قَالَ اِنِّى عَبْدُ اللهِ ۖ اٰتٰىنِىَ الْكِتٰبَ وَجَعَلَنِى
نَبِيًّا ۞

وَّجَعَلَنِى مُبٰرَكًا اَيْنَ مَا كُنْتُ وَاَوْصٰنِى بِالصَّلٰوةِ
وَالزَّكٰوةِ مَا دُمْتُ حَيًّا ۞

وَّبَرًّا بِوَالِدَتِى ۖ وَلَمْ يَجْعَلْنِى جَبَّارًا شَقِيًّا ۞

In this phrase "slave of Allah," there are four
points to note from the above Surat Maryam (Mary)
19:30–32.

The first, that it does away with the erroneous belief of the Christians that 'Isa (Jesus) is God.

The second, if Christ, when He confessed His servitude was truthful in His statement then truly He

was Allah's slave. If He was lying, the power He used would not have been divine, but satanic, and both suppositions would render void His being a God.

The third, that which was the pressing need for Him at that time was to remove the accusation of adultery from His mother Mary. However, 'Isa (Jesus) did not clearly deny that, but laid emphasis on the fact of His servitude as if He made the removal of the accusation that He was equal with Allah more important than removing the accusation from His mother.

The fourth, the removal of this accusation from Allah assists the removal of the accusation from His mother, because Allah would not choose an adulteress to bear a child for this great and high position.[16]

The Quran's concept regarding the person of Jesus Christ is based upon the truth that Jesus, the Son of Mary, was the Servant of God, as predicted by Isaiah 52:13 and 43:11:

Behold, My Servant shall deal prudently, He shall be exalted and extolled and be very high. . . . By His knowledge My righteous Servant shall justify many, for He shall bear their iniquities.

JESUS CREATES

In the Surat al-Ma'idah (The Table Spread) 5:110 we read,

When Allah saith: O Jesus, son of Mary! Remember My favour unto thee and unto thy mother; how I strengthened thee with the holy Spirit, so that thou speakest unto mankind in the cradle as in maturity; and how I taught thee the Scripture and Wisdom and the Torah and the Gospel; and how thou

**didst shape of clay as it were the likeness of a bird by
My permission. . . .**

◆ ◆

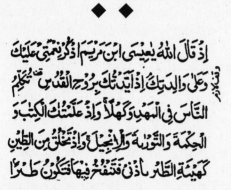

To none other than 'Isa has God given this power
to impart life. Even the New Testament Gospels do
not record such creative acts of Jesus as turning clay
birds into live ones.

JESUS HEALS AND RAISES
FROM THE DEAD

Surat al-Imran (The Family of 'Imran) 3:49 states,

**I heal him who was born blind, and the leper, and I
raise the dead, by Allah's leave.**

◆ ◆

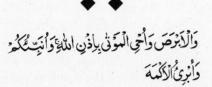

Baidawi tells us that thousands gathered around
Jesus. Those who were able came to him, while to

those who were unable, Jesus went himself. Moreover, Jesus always healed through prayer.

Concerning the phrase "I raise the dead," Wahab ibn Minabbeh relates that while 'Isa was playing with boys, a youth sprang on one and killed him, then threw him bleeding into the arms of 'Isa. Onlookers accused 'Isa, then seized him, took him to a judge, and said, "This boy 'Isa has killed another boy." The judge questioned him and 'Isa replied, "I do not know the one who killed him, neither am I one of his friends." When they wanted to strike 'Isa, He said to them, "Bring the boy to Me," and they asked Him, "Why?" He replied, "I will ask him who killed him." They asked, "How can he speak to you if he is dead?" Then they took Him to the dead boy and 'Isa began to pray for him, and Allah restored him to life.[17]

The above story can be traced to the *Infancy of Jesus Christ*, an early pseudo-gospel rejected as untrue and counterfeit by the Christian Church from the earliest times.

JESUS DIED

We come now to one of the most controversial subjects among Muslims and Christians in the entire theological debate. It is necessary to affirm that Surat al-Nisa (Women) 4:157, 158; Surat Maryam (Mary) 19:33; Surat al-Ma'idah (The Table Spread) 5:116, 117; Surat al-Baqarah (The Cow) 2:87; and Surat al-Imran (The Family of 'Imran) 3:55, all support the fact that Jesus truly died.

One of the most crucial statements comes from Surat al-Imran (The Family of 'Imran) 3:55:

(And remember) when Allah said: O Jesus! Lo! I
am gathering thee and causing thee to ascend unto
Me, and am cleansing thee of those who disbelieve
and am setting those who follow thee above those
who disbelieve until the Day of Resurrection. Then
unto Me ye will (all) return, and I shall judge between you as to that wherein ye used to differ.

◆ ◆

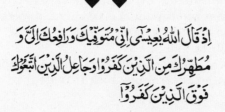

This phrase in the Arabic language, "Inni muta-
waf-feeka," is translated as "I am gathering thee."
Some say the word does not indicate death, while
others affirm that Christ did actually die. As an
Arab, I have never known of any other meaning than
death for this expression, within or without the
Quran.

The many versions of this phrase by imminent
Muslim scholars make its meaning confusing. Some
say it refers only to sleep. Al Muthanna relates, "I
was told by Ishaq that 'Inni mutawaffeeka' means a
death of sleep and God took him in his sleep."[18]

No Muslim scholar will deny that John the Baptist
was born, died, and will be raised up. Here is the
Quranic passage in Surat Maryam (Mary) 19:15:

Peace on him the day he was born, and the day he
dieth and the day he shall be raised alive!

◆ ◆

وَسَلَمٌ عَلَيْهِ يَوْمَ وُلِدَ وَيَوْمَ يَمُوتُ وَيَوْمَ
يُبْعَثُ حَيًّا ۝

However, practically the same wording is given about Jesus in Surat Maryam (Mary) 19:32–34:

> And (hath made me) dutiful toward her who bore me, and hath not made me arrogant, unblest. Peace on me the day I was born, and the day I die, and the day I shall be raised alive!
> Such was Jesus, son of Mary, (this is) a statement of the truth concerning which they doubt.

◆ ◆

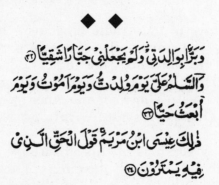

وَبَرًّا بِوَالِدَتِيْ وَلَمْ يَجْعَلْنِيْ جَبَّارًا شَقِيًّا ۝
وَالسَّلَامُ عَلَيَّ يَوْمَ وُلِدْتُ وَيَوْمَ أَمُوتُ وَيَوْمَ
أُبْعَثُ حَيًّا ۝
ذٰلِكَ عِيْسَى ابْنُ مَرْيَمَ قَوْلَ الْحَقِّ الَّذِيْ
فِيْهِ يَمْتَرُوْنَ ۝

Surat al-Ma'idah (The Table Spread) 5:117 says,

> I spake unto them only that which Thou commandedst me, (saying): Worship Allah, my Lord and your Lord. I was a witness of them while I dwelt among them, and when Thou tookest me Thou wast the Watcher over them. Thou art Witness over all things.

◆ ◆

مَاقُلْتُ لَهُمْ إِلَّامَا أَمَرْتَنِي بِهِ أَنِ اعْبُدُوااللّهَ
رَبِّي وَرَبَّكُمْ وَكُنْتُ عَلَيْهِمْ شَهِيدًا مَا دُمْتُ
فِيهِمْ فَلَمَّا تَوَفَّيْتَنِي كُنْتَ أَنْتَ الرَّقِيبَ عَلَيْهِمْ
وَأَنْتَ عَلَى كُلِّ شَيْءٍ شَهِيدٌ ۝

Al Muthanna says, quoting Abd Allah Ibn Salih, Muawiheh, and Ali Ibn Abbas, that "Inni mutawaffeeka" means "I cause you to die."[19]

These differences of opinion and contradictions among Muslim scholars ignore the plain truth that is in the New Testament Gospels. There are no contradictions in the Gospels. Every Gospel writer tells in great detail of the death of Christ, His resurrection, and His ascension.

JESUS ASCENDED AND WILL RETURN

Surat al-Imran (The Family of 'Imran) 3, verse 55 says,

(And remember) when Allah said: O Jesus! Lo! I am gathering thee and causing thee to ascend unto Me, and am cleansing thee of those who disbelieve and am setting those who follow thee above those who disbelieve.

There are many interpretations of this significant verse. Al Fakhri al Razi said, "The meaning of 'I am gathering thee' is that Allah was specifically exalting him to a place of honor. Furthermore," Razi declares:

> The interpretation of 'causing thee to ascend unto me' means that Allah was raising Him to a place where no one could judge Him, for on earth men pass various kinds of judgment on one another, but in Heaven there is no true omniscient Judge except Allah.[20]

I believe, however, that this Quranic reference is borrowed from the words of Jesus quoted in John 20:17, ". . . I am ascending to my Father and your Father, and to my God and your God."

I suppose one of the most famous verses in all the Quran, as far as Christians are concerned, is from Surat Maryam (Mary) 19:33–34:

> Peace on me the day I was born, and the day I die, and the day I shall be raised alive!
> Such was Jesus, son of Mary, (this is) a statement of the truth concerning which they doubt.

◆ ◆

وَالسَّلَامُ عَلَيَّ يَوْمَ وُلِدْتُّ وَيَوْمَ أَمُوتُ وَيَوْمَ
أُبْعَثُ حَيًّا ۝
ذَٰلِكَ عِيسَى ابْنُ مَرْيَمَ قَوْلَ الْحَقِّ الَّذِي
فِيهِ يَمْتَرُونَ ۝

Almost all Muslim scholars declare that Jesus will come again and defeat the anti-Christ, then die and be raised up. Whatever the interpretation is, one must still understand from this passage that Jesus Christ is coming again.

A similar statement is found in Surat Zukhruf (Ornaments of Gold) 43:61: "And lo! verily there is knowledge of the Hour. . . ." Jesus himself enunciated this truth when he declared in John 5:25, "Most assuredly, I say to you, the hour is coming, and now is, when the dead will hear the voice of the Son of God; and those who hear will live."

Every scholar of the Quran perceives that "the Hour" is a reference to the hour of judgment. Jesus is also recognized as the one who knows "the Hour," and therefore will be present at the final judgment. In other words, He will be coming again.

In Mishkat Al Masabih, several authorities are quoted as saying that Muhammad announced that there will be ten signs before the "last hour." Interestingly enough, Muhammad announced that the coming of the Anti-christ, "Dajjal," is one, and the return of Jesus the Christ is another.[21]

Jesus ('Isa) is mentioned ninety-seven times in ninety-three verses of the Quran. He is called the Spirit of God seven different times.[22]

Christ Jesus, according to Islam, is one of the six prophets with special titles, listed chronologically below:

Adam, the Chosen of God
Noah, the Preacher for God
Abraham, the Friend of God
Moses, the Speaker with God
Jesus, the Word of God
Muhammad, the Apostle of God.[23]

It is obvious from the above references that Jesus Christ emerges from the Quranic passages, as well as the Hadith's pages, as a very formidable, fascinating, and divine figure indeed. In fact, the Quranic description of Jesus of Nazareth stands second only to the Bible.

The major problem in Muhammad's misunder-

standing of the full truth of who Jesus is could be
related to the fact that Muhammad's information
came neither from true Christian believers, nor the
New Testament Gospels. Rather, it was acquired
from Jewish fables as well as from local heretical
Christian sects. Still, one is profoundly amazed at
how close a figure the Quran presents of the true
Christ of the Gospels, our Savior and Lord. He is ab-
solutely more than a prophet!

JESUS AND MUHAMMAD

JESUS	MUHAMMAD
His name means Savior	His name means praised one
Born of the Virgin Mary	Born of Aminah
No earthly father	Abd Allah was his father
Born about 4 B.C. in Bethlehem	Born A.D. 570 in Mecca
Raised by Mary, His mother and Joseph, His adopted father	Raised by his mother, Halima the nurse, then his uncle and grandfather
Labored as a carpenter in Nazareth	Started as a shepherd then became a camel-caravan leader
Spoke in Hebrew, Aramaic, and probably Greek	Spoke only Arabic
Was literate; wrote no books	Was literate; wrote the Quran
Attracted multitudes by His miracles and teachings	Attracted multitudes by his teaching and sword
Had to move to Capernaum because of rejection by His townspeople	Had to move to Medina because of rejection by his townspeople
Was never married	Married to fifteen wives
Lived a sinless life	Prayed earnestly and fre-

Did not pray for forgiveness of His sins	quently for forgiveness of his sins
Waged no war	Waged war by fighting or leading in sixty-six battles
Ordered the death of no one	Ordered the death of many men and women (the first was a poetess)
Established a religion of mercy and love even for enemies	Established a religion of no mercy and the sword
Established a spiritual kingdom	Established an earthly empire
Died by crucifixion in Jerusalem at age 33	Died in Medina due to effects of pneumonia and poisoning at age 62
Arose the third day, emptying His tomb	Lingers still in his grave awaiting the Day of Judgment
Old Testament predicted His coming	No scripture predicted his coming
Mentioned in the Quran ninety-seven times	Mentioned in the Quran twenty-five times
1,500,000,000 claim to be His followers	800,000,000 claim to be his followers
Many of His followers (Christians) are known for their dedication, love, and caring for others	Many of his followers (Muslims) are known for their fanatic dedication to war and vengeance, even for killing other Muslims

JESUS IS SPOKEN OF AS:	MUHAMMAD IS SPOKEN OF AS:
Alpha and Omega	A Messenger
Amen	A Preacher
Ancient of Days	A Warner
Bread of Life	Son of Abd Allah

Conqueror   Evangelist
Counselor   An Apostle
David's Son
Door to Heaven
Dayspring
Eternal Life
Friend of Sinners
First and Last
God our Savior
Good Shepherd
Holy One of God
Hope of Glory
I AM
Image of the Invisible God
Judge of Living and Dead
King Eternal
Life
Light
Living Bread
Lord
Mediator
Messiah
Mighty God
Only Begotten of the Father
Our Passover
Our Peace
Prince of Peace
Prophet
Priest
Redeemer
Righteous Judge
Rose of Sharon
Savior
Second Adam
Son of God
Teacher from God
Truth and Grace
Unspeakable Gift

Way
Word of God
Word Made Flesh

The Power of Jesus

I had an intriguing experience in Deraa', Syria, in
1966. A pastor from that area had invited me to lead
a series of meetings because I had just surrendered
to the evangelistic ministry. Alas! The series had to
be cut short due to a political coup by the Air Force
General, Mr. Hafez al-Assad, the current President of
Syria. To complicate matters, the Syrian-Jordanian
borders were sealed off until things settled down in
Damascus. The Muslim neighbor of the pastor, realizing I could not go back to my home in Jerusalem
for a while, reminded the pastor that he had invited
him several times for dinner. Now was the time for
him to be my host as well as the pastor's host. In
typical Arab fashion, the neighbors filed into the
Muslim house to welcome us as the honored guests.
Naturally, our host invited them to stay for the big
dinner.

Happily, the conversation gravitated toward who
Jesus Christ was. Our new Muslim friends were very
impressed when they learned that there are Quranic
passages affirming the Virgin Birth, the Divinity, the
Death, and the Resurrection of Jesus Christ.

But before dinner was served, one by one they got
up and left. Surprised and puzzled at their activity, I
sat wondering. In a few moments, our gracious host
came into the room with a strange grin on his face.
He announced, "Don't worry, they will return. But
they declared to me that if they had lingered another
hour, they would no longer remain Muslims."

Sure enough, as soon as the huge platter of rice,

covered with lamb's meat cooked in yogurt, with roasted almonds and pinola nuts, was brought in, they came right back.

When the truth is presented in the power of the Holy Spirit, no one can be neutral!

_____

CHAPTER FOUR

THE CRUCIFIXION: FACT OR FICTION?

❋ ❋ ❋

Moreover, brethren, I declare to you the gospel which I preached to you, which also you received and in which you stand, by which also you are saved, if you hold fast that word which I preached to you— unless you believed in vain.

For I delivered to you first of all that which I also received: that Christ died for our sins according to the Scriptures, and that He was buried, and that He rose again the third day according to the Scriptures.[1]

THE RECORD OF THE QURAN

From the dawn of Christianity, many people have received and accepted the crucifixion of Christ, by which they are saved and forgiven. Islam as a whole, however, denies the crucifixion of Christ. Before we deal with the verse that presents this, we must ask why this denial is recorded in the Quran and how such a doctrine seeped into the book.

Even during Christ's lifetime there were those who objected to the idea that the Christ would be crucified. We read in John 12:34:

The people answered Him, "We have heard from the law that the Christ remains forever, and how can

You say, 'The Son of Man must be lifted up'? Who is this Son of Man?"

Historians tell us that this heresy was later wide-spread among the early Christians of the Arabian Peninsula.

Additionally, a great number of Jewish converts in Arabia during Muhammad's time believed that Christ was able to transform himself from one form to another. Therefore, they advanced the idea that when His enemies came to arrest Him, He cast His likeness onto another man, and that man was crucified instead of Jesus. To explain what happened to Christ, they said He was lifted up to God. This explains the pseudo-Christian and Jewish influence on the Quran.[2]

Surat al-Nisa (Women) 4:157–158

And because of their saying: We slew the Messiah Jesus son of Mary, Allah's messenger—They slew him not nor crucified, but it appeared so unto them; and lo! those who disagree concerning it are in doubt thereof; they have no knowledge thereof save pursuit of a conjecture; they slew him not for certain.

But Allah took him up unto Himself. Allah was ever Mighty, Wise.

◆ ◆

وَقَوْلِهِمْ إِنَّا قَتَلْنَا الْمَسِيحَ عِيسَى ابْنَ مَرْيَمَ
رَسُولَ اللّٰهِ وَمَا قَتَلُوهُ وَمَا صَلَبُوهُ وَلَكِنْ شُبِّهَ
لَهُمْ وَإِنَّ الَّذِينَ اخْتَلَفُوا فِيهِ لَفِى شَكٍّ مِنْهُ مَا
لَهُمْ بِهِ مِنْ عِلْمٍ إِلَّا اتِّبَاعَ الظَّنِّ وَمَا قَتَلُوهُ
يَقِينًا ۝
بَلْ رَفَعَهُ اللّٰهُ إِلَيْهِ وَكَانَ اللّٰهُ عَزِيزًا حَكِيمًا ۝

The Cross, in Islam's estimation, was not a historical event or the basis for a doctrine of redemption. Rather it was a symbol or a sign, like the star which guided the Magi to the cradle of the child in Bethlehem, or like the appearance of the Holy Spirit as a dove descending upon Christ at His baptism in the Jordan. But the heavy cross on which Christ was hanged, which is the altar of redemption, where the Lamb of God was sacrificed to take away the sin of the world, is of no real importance to Muslims.

Muslim theologians disagree on the matter of how another took the place of Christ. Many stories have arisen about it. One is that when the Jews determined to kill Christ, God took Him to heaven. Because leaders feared an uprising of the people, they killed a man by crucifixion and sought to deceive the people by saying he was Christ.

One other explanation is that God cast Christ's likeness onto another man who died instead of Him. This story has many versions.

(1) A Jew named Judas entered a house where Christ was with the purpose of arresting Him, but did not find Him. God caused the likeness of Christ (A'isa) to be on Judas. When he came out of the house, people thought he was A'isa and took him and crucified him.

(2) The Jews, when they arrested A'isa, set over Him a watchman. However A'isa was taken up to God by a miracle and God caused A'isa's likeness to rest on the watchman, whom they took and crucified, while he cried out, "I am not A'isa."

(3) One of A'isa's friends was promised Paradise, and volunteered to die in His place. God caused him to resemble A'isa, and he was taken and crucified, but A'isa was taken up to heaven.

(4) One of A'isa's followers, Judas, sought to betray A'isa by guiding the Jews to Him. He went with

them to arrest A'isa, but God caused Judas to appear like A'isa so Judas was taken and crucified instead.

> **Few commentators on the Quran agree. Al Jalalan in his interpretation of the Quranic phrase, "it appeared so unto them" (Shubbiha Lahum), says that Allah caused the likeness of A'isa to be upon the dead man. Because they thought he was A'isa, they killed and crucified him. The phrase, "those who disagree and are in doubt about Him" (that is, about A'isa, regarding his death), means that some of them, when they saw the dead man, said, "The face is the face of A'isa, but the body is not His body." Others said, "It is He."[3]**

Al Baidawi said, "It is related that a group of Jews captured A'isa and His mother. He cursed them and they were changed into apes and pigs! The Jews met together to kill Him, but God told Him He would take Him to heaven. He said to His friends, 'Who is ready to take my likeness upon him and be killed and crucified and enter Paradise?' One of them responded and God cast the likeness of A'isa upon him. He was killed by crucifixion."[4]

Al Zmakhashri said, "The words, 'it appeared so unto them' mean they imagined it to be so or they presumed that they killed and crucified him—so He is dead and not alive. But He is alive because God took Him to Himself."[5]

Surat al-Imran (The Family of 'Imran) 3:55

> **(And remember) when Allah said: O Jesus! Lo! I am gathering thee and causing thee to ascend unto Me, and am cleansing thee of those who disbelieve and am setting those who follow thee above those who disbelieve until the Day of Resurrection. Then**

**unto Me ye will (all) return, and I shall judge be-
tween you as to that wherein ye used to differ.**

إِذْ قَالَ اللهُ يَعِيسَى إِنِّى مُتَوَفِّيكَ وَرَافِعُكَ إِلَىَّ وَ
مُطَهِّرُكَ مِنَ الَّذِينَ كَفَرُوا وَجَاعِلُ الَّذِينَ اتَّبَعُوكَ
فَوْقَ الَّذِينَ كَفَرُوا إِلَى يَوْمِ الْقِيَمَةِ ثُمَّ إِلَىَّ
مَرْجِعُكُمْ فَأَحْكُمُ بَيْنَكُمْ فِيمَا كُنْتُمْ فِيهِ تَخْتَلِفُونَ ۝

The variety of versions of the previous story re-
sulted from the lack of clear wording in the Quran
with regard to the last days of Christ's human life on
earth. This disparity opened the door to many different and opposing opinions. One of the most famous is by Imam Fakhr ed Din ar Razi. He explains
the matter of the transfer of Christ's likeness to another man in a variety of ways.[6]

(1) If it is permissable to assert that Allah casts the
resemblance of one person onto another, then the
door is open to calumny. In time this allows subtle
reasoning which invalidates prophecies.

(2) God supported Him (A'isa) with His Holy
Spirit. Was God in this case not able to do so? He
(A'isa) was able to raise the dead—was He not able
to protect Himself?

(3) God was able to rescue Him by raising Him to
heaven, therefore what use was it to cause another to
bear His likeness?

(4) By so doing—that is, by causing another to resemble Him—they were made to believe that this
other was A'isa, although he was not. This was a de-

ception and not in keeping with the integrity of God.

(5) The majority of Christians from East to West, with their intense love for Christ and extreme zeal for His cause, witnessed His crucifixion. Therefore, if we deny this, we discredit the historicity (chronology) of events and the prophecy of Muhammad, A'isa, and the rest of the prophets.

(6) The logical (normal) thing would be that the "other man" would be able to defend himself by saying he was not A'isa. That is what he would have done. As he did not do so, we understand the matter was not as reported. If the sayings of the Quran do repudiate the crucifixion of Christ, they certainly do not repudiate His death before He was taken to heaven.

As an Arab who has been raised in a Muslim culture, Arabic is my native language. The critical word *mutawafika* means "cause you to die." Confusion arising from various interpretations of this word has cast a shadow over the truth of the death of Christ. Even until this day, fourteen hundred years after the appearance of the Quran, you can ask any Arab about what happened to his uncle who passed away last week and he will use the same word as a past tense, "Tawafa," which means he died. Since that term is used of Jesus, he must have died.

Surat Maryam (Mary) 19:33

Peace on me the day I was born, and the day I die, and the day I shall be raised alive!

◆ ◆

وَالسَّلَـٰمُ عَلَىَّ يَوْمَ وُلِدتُّ وَيَوْمَ أَمُوتُ وَيَوْمَ أُبْعَثُ حَيًّا ۝

This verse is a clear confession that Christ became incarnate, died, and was raised from the dead. Moreover, this was done according to prophecy and based on miracles. This is one of the clearest passages in the Quran on this subject, and it agrees with the Gospel narratives.

I was in the audience on July 7, 1985, when Mr. Ahmed Deedat was debating Dr. Floyd Clark of Tennessee in London's Royal Albert Hall. During the question and answer period, I asked Mr. Deedat if he believed that the Quran contradicted itself or not? The question was related to this very verse, as I quoted it in Arabic before the entire crowd of people in that gigantic hall. To my utter astonishment, Mr. Deedat responded, "The first part of the sentence was in the past tense—'Peace on me the day I was born.'" Then he went on to say, "'The day I die and the day I shall be raised alive' is a future tense, it has not happened yet." There was no more opportunity for a rebuttal, but it was a revelation to me of how clever and artful a person can be in explaining away what he does not want to believe. The reason Jesus used future tense is very simple. He was alive when He said these words and neither death nor resurrection had yet taken place. But both events did occur when He was 33 years old.

What a contradiction Mr. Deedat presented in the debate! He accepted the crucifixion but not the death of Christ. Can you imagine such a thing when he, as a spokesman, a theologian, and a debater for the Muslim faith disputes his own holy book's statement about the crucifixion? He does this by stating that Christ came out of the grave after having swooned and experienced resuscitation!

Surat al-Ma'idah (The Table Spread)
5:116–117

And when Allah saith: O Jesus, son of Mary! Didst thou say unto mankind: Take me and my mother for two gods beside Allah? he saith: Be glorified! It was not mine to utter that to which I had no right. If I used to say it, then Thou knewest it. Thou knowest what is in my mind, and I know not what is in Thy mind. Lo! Thou, only Thou art the Knower of Things Hidden.

I spake unto them only that which Thou commandedst me, (saying): Worship Allah, my Lord and your Lord. I was a witness of them while I dwelt among them, and when Thou tookest me Thou wast the Watcher over them. Thou art Witness over all things.

◆ ◆

وَإِذْ قَالَ اللّهُ يَعِيسَى ابْنَ مَرْيَمَ ءَأَنتَ قُلْتَ
لِلنَّاسِ اتَّخِذُونِى وَأُمِّى إِلَهَيْنِ مِن دُونِ اللّهِ قَالَ
سُبْحَانَكَ مَا يَكُونُ لِى أَنْ أَقُولَ مَا لَيْسَ لِى بِحَقٍّ إِن
كُنتُ قُلْتُهُ فَقَدْ عَلِمْتَهُ تَعْلَمُ مَا فِى نَفْسِى وَلَا
أَعْلَمُ مَا فِى نَفْسِكَ إِنَّكَ أَنتَ عَلَّامُ الْغُيُوبِ ۝
مَا قُلْتُ لَهُمْ إِلَّا مَا أَمَرْتَنِى بِهِ أَنِ اعْبُدُوا اللّهَ
رَبِّى وَرَبَّكُمْ وَكُنتُ عَلَيْهِمْ شَهِيدًا مَا دُمْتُ
فِيهِمْ فَلَمَّا تَوَفَّيْتَنِى كُنتَ أَنتَ الرَّقِيبَ عَلَيْهِمْ
وَأَنتَ عَلَى كُلِّ شَىْءٍ شَهِيدٌ ۝

This particular passage is certainly a powerful one against the heretic Miriamites, who had made Mary a goddess, Jesus her son, and God Almighty her husband. This definitely is blasphemy and certainly is not accepted by true Christians who believe in the

Holy Bible. So we have no argument with this particular verse at all once it is understood clearly and
correctly. However, "thou tookest me" is "Tawafay-
tani" in Arabic and means "caused me to die." It is
another verse acknowledging the death of Jesus.

Surat al-Baqarah (The Cow) 2:87

**And verily We gave unto Moses the Scripture and
We caused a train of messengers to follow after him,
and We gave unto Jesus, son of Mary, clear proofs (of
Allah's sovereignty), and We supported him with the
Holy Spirit. Is it ever so, that, when there cometh
unto you a messenger (from Allah) with that which
ye yourselves desire not, ye grow arrogant, and some
ye disbelieve and some ye slay?**

◆ ◆

وَلَقَدْ ءَاتَيْنَا مُوسَى الْكِتَبَ وَقَفَّيْنَا مِنْ بَعْدِهِ بِالرُّسُلِ
وَءَاتَيْنَا عِيسَى ابْنَ مَرْيَمَ الْبَيِّنَتِ وَأَيَّدْنَهُ بِرُوحِ الْقُدُسِ
أَفَكُلَّمَا جَاءَكُمْ رَسُولٌ بِمَا لَا تَهْوَى أَنْفُسُكُمُ اسْتَكْبَرْتُمْ
فَفَرِيقًا كَذَّبْتُمْ وَفَرِيقًا تَقْتُلُونَ ۝

The Arabic word for "slay" here is very clear and
can only be translated as "killing." Since the Quran
does not mention how the killing of Jesus took place,
the Gospels are the original and only authentic
sources on this subject.

Let us consider, please, Surat al-Nisa (Women)
4:157–158 and compare it with Surat al-Baqarah
(The Cow) 2:87. The question before us is what was
the Jewish leaders' purpose in killing Jesus? We discover the answer in John 11:47–50:

> **Then the chief priests and the Pharisees gathered a council and said, "What shall we do? For this Man works many signs. If we let Him alone like this, everyone will believe in Him, and the Romans will come and take away both our place and nation."**
>
> **And one of them, Caiaphas, being high priest that year, said to them, "You know nothing at all, nor do you consider that it is expedient for us that one man should die for the people, and not that the whole nation should perish."**

When the Jews hung Jesus upon the cross and He died, He was put in the tomb of Joseph of Arimathea. A stone was rolled over the entrance of the tomb and, following Pilate's orders, it was sealed. The Jews rejoiced, thinking that they were finally saved from His teaching and miracles. It was their hope that His cruel death was enough to prevent His followers from any further activity. But it was not to be so. Jesus' atoning death on the cross and subsequent resurrection has attracted thousands of believers in Jerusalem itself and millions more from all over the world. Today the largest number of followers of any religion are the followers of Jesus Christ. Throughout the 215 countries of the world 1,563,000,000 people pay allegiance to Him.[7] In John 12:32, Jesus Himself affirmed, "And I, if I am lifted up from the earth, will draw all peoples to Myself."

Once again we look at this passage from Surat al-Nisa (Women) 4:157, ". . . Those who disagree concerning it are in doubt thereof; they have no knowledge thereof save pursuit of a conjecture; they slew him not for certain." The contemporaries of Jesus confidently tell us that He did die and rose the third day, and during the forty days after that appeared to as many as five hundred people at one time (1 Corinthians 15:6; see also Matthew 28:11–15). Then He ascended to heaven and sat at the right hand of God—in keeping with the Quranic statement, in Surat al-Imran (The Family of 'Imran) 3:55, "Lo! I am gathering thee and causing thee to ascend unto Me." Isn't it marvelous to recognize the truth when it is investigated thoroughly rather than interpreted according to one's own biased opinion?

THE RECORD OF THE OLD TESTAMENT

Now let us examine what the Scriptures stated as prophecies many centuries before Christ.

Genesis 3:15

**"And I will put enmity
Between you and the woman,
And between your seed and her Seed;
He shall bruise your head,
And you shall bruise His heel."**

Here at the dawn of man's history is a promise of the Almighty God concerning the Savior. These words are spoken to Satan, the serpent, after he tempted Adam and Eve to sin against God. For centuries the church has understood this text to point to the Seed of the woman, Jesus Christ. Matthew Poole wrote,

"Her seed" is first and principally the Lord Jesus Christ, who with respect to this text, and promise, is called by way of eminency, *the seed*, whose work only is to break the serpent's head. . . . The head and the mind is the principal instrument both of the serpent's fury and mischief, and of his defense, and the principal seat of the serpent's life, which therefore

men chiefly strike at. . . . In the devil, this denotes
his power and authority over men, the strength
whereof consists in death, which Christ, the blessed
seed of the woman, overthrew by taking away the
sting of death which is sin, and destroying him that
had the power of death, that is the devil.[8]

Psalm 22

In the Psalms of David, the following was predicted a thousand years before the event took place
in actual history.

My God, My God, why have You forsaken Me?
Why are You so far from helping Me,
And from the words of My groaning?
But I am a worm, and no man;
A reproach of men, and despised of the people.
All those who see Me laugh Me to scorn;
They shoot out the lip, they shake the head, saying,
"He trusted in the LORD, let Him rescue Him;
Let Him deliver Him, since He delights in Him!"
For dogs have surrounded Me;
The assembly of the wicked has enclosed Me.
They pierced My hands and My feet;
I can count all My bones.
They look and stare at Me.
They divide My garments among them,
And for My clothing they cast lots (vv. 1, 6–8, 16–18).

"My God, My God, why have You forsaken Me?"
were the very words Jesus uttered on the cross (Mark
15:34). "They pierced My hands and My feet" accurately describes the wounds Jesus suffered when
crucified (John 19:17–18). And finally, "They divide
My garments among them, and for My clothing they
cast lots" was fulfilled to the letter (Mark 14:24). A

thousand years before Christ was born these Scriptures were written![9]

Isaiah 53

Another historical prophecy made many centuries before the crucifixion is Isaiah 53. This chapter, along with other fascinating passages in this incredible book, have caused biblical scholars to call Isaiah "The Fifth Gospel." Isaiah 53:5 states,

> **But He was wounded for our transgressions,**
> **He was bruised for our iniquities;**
> **The chastisement for our peace was upon Him,**
> **And by His stripes we are healed.**

In verse 7 we read some very remarkable prophetic statements:

> **He was oppressed and He was afflicted,**
> **Yet He opened not His mouth;**
> **He was led as a lamb to the slaughter,**
> **And as a sheep before its shearers is silent,**
> **So He opened not His mouth.**

The fulfillment is seen 1 Peter 2:23–24:

> **. . . who, when He was reviled, did not revile in return; when He suffered, He did not threaten, but committed Himself to Him who judges righteously; who Himself bore our sins in His own body on the tree, that we, having died to sins, might live for righteousness—by whose stripes you were healed.**

Isaiah 53:9 reads,

> **And they made His grave with the wicked—**
> **But with the rich at His death,**

Because He had done no violence,
Nor was any deceit in His mouth.

Its fulfillment is recorded in Mark 15:42–47:

Now when evening had come, because it was the
Preparation Day, that is, the day before the Sabbath,
Joseph of Arimathea, a prominent council member,
who was himself waiting for the kingdom of God,
coming and taking courage, went in to Pilate and
asked for the body of Jesus. Pilate marveled that He
was already dead; and summoning the centurion, he
asked him if He had been dead for some time. And
when he found out from the centurion, he granted
the body to Joseph.

Then he brought fine linen, took Him down, and
wrapped Him in the linen. And he laid Him in a
tomb which had been hewn out of the rock, and
rolled a stone against the door of the tomb. And
Mary Magdalene and Mary the mother of Joses observed where He was laid.

Zechariah 11:12–13

Then I said to them, "If it is agreeable to you, give
me my wages; and if not, refrain." So they weighed
out for my wages thirty pieces of silver.

And the LORD said to me, "Throw it to the potter"—that princely price they set on me. So I took
the thirty pieces of silver and threw them into the
house of the LORD for the potter.

Its fulfillment is noted in Matthew 26:14–15:

Then one of the twelve, called Judas Iscariot, went
to the chief priests and said, "What are you willing to
give me if I deliver Him to you?" And they counted
out to him thirty pieces of silver.

Verse 13 is also fulfilled in Matthew 27:3–8:

> Then Judas, His betrayer, seeing that He had been condemned, was remorseful and brought back the thirty pieces of silver to the chief priests and elders, saying, "I have sinned by betraying innocent blood." And they said, "What is that to us? You see to it!" Then he threw down the pieces of silver in the temple and departed, and went and hanged himself.
>
> But the chief priests took the silver pieces and said, "It is not lawful to put them into the treasury, because they are the price of blood." And they took counsel and bought with them the potter's field, to bury strangers in. Therefore that field has been called the Field of Blood to this day.

We can see this same "field of blood" in Jerusalem to this very day! It is a well-attested historical site! Zechariah 12:10 reads,

> "And I will pour on the house of David and on the inhabitants of Jerusalem the Spirit of grace and supplication; then they will look on Me whom they have pierced; they will mourn for Him as one mourns for his only son, and grieve for Him as one grieves for a firstborn."

This passage speaks of both the first and second advents of our Lord. "Then they will look on Me whom they have pierced" indicates Jesus' first coming. The verse predicted that the Jews at some time will repent of their rejection of their Messiah and "mourn for Him as one mourns for his only son," as they realize He is the Heavenly Father's "only Son." Zechariah thus sees beyond the first coming to the future, when the Jews have been gathered again in the land.

This return to Jerusalem occurred in 1967, when the Jewish government assumed control over the city. Now we wait patiently for the time when Jews will believe in the Lord Jesus Christ as the Messiah. I am convinced beyond any doubt, that the conversion of the Jews will happen in our lifetime.[10]

Micah 5:2

"But you, Bethlehem Ephrathah,
Though you are little among the thousands of Judah,
Yet out of you shall come forth to Me
The One to be ruler in Israel,
Whose goings forth have been from of old,
From everlasting."

Since Micah lived in the time of King Hezekiah, he made this prophecy some eight centuries before Jesus. The fulfillment is recorded in Matthew 2:1–9, "Now after Jesus was born in Bethlehem of Judea. . . ."

Malachi 3:1

"Behold, I send My messenger,
And he will prepare the way before Me.
And the Lord, whom you seek,
Will suddenly come to His temple,
Even the Messenger of the covenant,
In whom you delight.
Behold, He is coming,"
Says the LORD of hosts.

This is really a double prophecy. The first part deals with John the Baptist, and we note the fulfillment of that in Matthew 11:10–13:

"For this is he of whom it is written:
'Behold, I send My messenger before Your face,
Who will prepare Your way before You.'
Assuredly, I say to you, among those born of women
there has not risen one greater than John the Baptist;
but he who is least in the kingdom of heaven is
greater than he. And from the days of John the Bap-
tist until now the kingdom of heaven suffers vio-
lence, and the violent take it by force.

   For all the prophets and the law prophesied until
John."

The second part of Malachi 3:1 deals with Jesus.
In John 1:15, we read, "John bore witness of Him and
cried out, saying, 'This was He of whom I said, "He
who comes after me is preferred before me, for He
was before me."'"
Numerous other Old Testament passages foretell
the events of the crucifixion. Psalm 34:20 says, "He
guards all his bones; Not one of them is broken."
This was fulfilled according to John 19:32–33:

Then the soldiers came and broke the legs of the first
and of the other who was crucified with Him. But
when they came to Jesus and saw that He was al-
ready dead, they did not break His legs.

Another passage is Psalm 69:21:

They also gave me gall for my food,
And for my thirst they gave me vinegar to drink.

Its fulfillment is in Matthew 27:34 and 48:

. . . they gave Him sour wine mingled with gall to
drink. But when He had tasted it, He would not

drink. Immediately one of them ran and took a sponge, filled it with sour wine and put it on a reed, and gave it to Him to drink.

THE RECORD OF CHRIST'S OWN PREDICTIONS

Unless it can be proven that Jesus did not make the following unique claims, we must, in all honesty, accept and believe them to be authentic.

Matthew 16:21–23

From that time Jesus began to show to His disciples that He must go to Jerusalem, and suffer many things from the elders and chief priests and scribes, and be killed, and be raised again the third day. Then Peter took Him aside and began to rebuke Him, saying, "Far be it from You, Lord; this shall not happen to You!" But He turned and said to Peter, "Get behind Me, Satan! You are an offense to Me, for you are not mindful of the things of God, but the things of men."

Jesus repeatedly foretold His redemptive work on the cross, yet the disciples did not comprehend it completely.

Mark 8:31

And He began to teach them that the Son of Man must suffer many things, and be rejected by the elders and chief priests and scribes, and be killed, and after three days rise again.

Luke 9:22

The Son of Man must suffer many things, and be rejected by the elders and chief priests and scribes, and be killed, and be raised the third day.

The declaration of Peter that Jesus was the Christ, the Son of God, is followed by this humbling and overwhelming statement that Jesus would be killed and would rise the third day.

John 3:14–16

"And as Moses lifted up the serpent in the wilderness, even so must the Son of Man be lifted up, that whoever believes in Him should not perish but have eternal life. For God so loved the world that He gave His only begotten Son, that whoever believes in Him should not perish but have everlasting life."

Here is one of the most glorious statements in the entire Bible. In the first part, we are reminded of what Moses did to save his people in the wilderness. The salvation from the biting serpents was by faith in looking up to the brass serpent. This was symbolic of Jesus, who knew no sin, but who became sin for us, nailing sin and Satan's power to the cross.

The unfathomable love of God is demonstrated by Christ's unconditional love for all sinners who believe, repent, and trust Him as the one who paid for our sins. The entire Christian faith can be summarized in this one verse, John 3:16, "For God so loved the world that He gave His only begotten Son, that whoever believes in Him should not perish but have everlasting life."

THE RECORD OF THE
SYNOPTIC GOSPELS

Matthew 17:22–23

Now while they were staying in Galilee, Jesus said to them, "The Son of Man is about to be betrayed into the hands of men, and they will kill Him, and the third day He will be raised up." And they were exceedingly sorrowful.

Here once again is the fact that Jesus had to be crucified, die, and be raised the third day.

Mark 15:1–43

All three of the synoptic (chronologically arranged) New Testament Gospels—Matthew, Mark, and Luke—recount the death and resurrection of Jesus Christ. Mark's Gospel provides one of the most succinct accounts of the trial and crucifixion of Christ. (To conserve space we will reproduce here only those specific verses from the passage dealing directly with His death. Refer to the entire passage in a Bible for the context.)

Then Pilate said to them, "Why, what evil has He done?" And they cried out more exceedingly, "Crucify Him!" So Pilate, wanting to gratify the crowd, released Barabbas to them; and he delivered Jesus, after he had scourged Him, to be crucified. . . .

And when they crucified Him, they divided His garments, casting lots for them to determine what every man should take. Now it was the third hour and they crucified Him. And the inscription of His accusation was written above: With Him they also crucified two robbers, one on His right and the other on His left. . . .

And at the ninth hour Jesus cried out with a loud voice, saying, "Eloi, Eloi, lama sabachthani?" which is translated, "My God, My God, why have You forsaken Me?" . . .

And Jesus cried out with a loud voice, and breathed His last. Then the veil of the temple was torn in two from top to bottom. Now when the centurion, who stood opposite Him, saw that He cried out like this and breathed His last, he said, "Truly this Man was the Son of God!" . . .

Joseph of Arimathea, a prominent council member, who was himself waiting for the kingdom of God, coming and taking courage, went in to Pilate and asked for the body of Jesus. Pilate marveled that He was already dead; and summoning the centurion, he asked him if He had been dead for some time. And when he found out from the centurion, he granted the body to Joseph.

Then he bought fine linen, took Him down, and wrapped Him in the linen. And he laid Him in a tomb which had been hewn out of the rock, and rolled a stone against the door of the tomb. And Mary Magdalene and Mary the mother of Joses observed where He was laid.

Luke 22:66–23:43

Luke, the Greek physician turned gospel writer and missionary, clearly asserted that Jesus Christ was crucified and died. Here are some of the most significant verses:

But they were insistent, demanding with loud voices that He be crucified. And the voices of these men and of the chief priests prevailed. So Pilate gave sentence that it should be as they requested. And he released to them the one they requested, who for insurrection and murder had been thrown into prison; but he delivered Jesus to their will. . . .

There were also two others, criminals, led with Him to be put to death. And when they had come to the place called Calvary, there they crucified Him, and the criminals, one on the right hand and the other on the left. . . .

And when Jesus had cried out with a loud voice, He said, "Father, 'into your hands I commend My spirit.'" And having said this, He breathed His last.

Matthew's account parallels these passages in Mark and Luke (see Matthew 27:1–60).

THE RECORD OF THE APOSTLE JOHN

John wrote the Fourth Gospel, the three letters which bear his name, and the book of Revelation. Let us examine excerpts from his writings concerning this very significant subject.

John 19:30–42

So when Jesus had received the sour wine, He said, "It is finished!" And bowing His head, He gave up His spirit.

Therefore, because it was the Preparation Day, that the bodies should not remain on the cross on the Sabbath (for that Sabbath was a high day) the Jews asked Pilate that their legs might be broken, and that they might be taken away. Then the soldiers came and broke the legs of the first and of the other who was crucified with Him. But when they came to Jesus and saw that He was already dead, they did not break His legs. But one of the soldiers pierced His side with a spear, and immediately blood and water came out. And he who has seen has testified, and his testimony is true; and he knows that he is telling the truth, so that you may believe. . . .

Then they took the body of Jesus, and bound it in strips of linen with the spices, as the custom of the Jews is to bury.

Revelation 1:17–18

And when I saw Him, I fell at His feet as dead. But He laid His right hand on me, saying to me, "Do not be afraid; I am the First and the Last. I am He who lives, and was dead, and behold, I am alive forevermore. Amen. And I have the keys of Hades and of Death."

The Apostle John recorded his prophetic revelation under the inspiration of the Holy Spirit. This book, Revelation, contains more information about God's plans for the future of our world than any other book of the Bible. And yet, for all of this focus on the future, Revelation consistently centers God's redemptive and transforming power on His only Son, Jesus Christ. At the very beginning of this book, John records the words of Jesus, "Do not be afraid. . . . I am He who lives, and was dead, and behold, I am alive forevermore."

The Writings of the Apostle Paul

No figure in Christian history stands so tall or has had such a tremendous influence as has Saul of Tarsus, who later became the Apostle Paul. The passing of centuries has not dimmed the luster of his personality nor altered the significance of his incredible insight into the Christian message. From the day of his conversion on the road to Damascus until his martyrdom thirty years later, Paul found love, life, liberty, and light as a bond-slave of Christ Jesus.

I feel that if Muhammad had experienced Christ as Paul did on the road to Damascus, he would have become another Paul.

At any rate, since Paul understood the death, resurrection, and atonement of Christ so well, his writings, preserved in the New Testament, are full of such references. The Christ-centered labors of this dedicated missionary-evangelist so deeply rooted the faith that within three centuries the Roman Empire adopted Christianity as the state religion.

The writings of Paul contain the most comprehensive theology (teaching) about the person, nature, and mission of Jesus Christ. John 1:1, 8:58, and 20:28, Titus 2:13, and Romans 9:5 are just a few of the verses which confirm that Jesus Christ is truly God, of the same nature as His heavenly Father.

Romans 1:3–4, and Philippians 2:5–11 are two Pauline passages affirming that the divine Son of God also became man. First Timothy 2:5 points out the importance of the Incarnation, that is, that God became man: "There is one God and one Mediator between God and men, the Man Christ Jesus."

Christ's incarnation, death, resurrection, and exaltation are eloquently summarized in Philippians 2:8–11:

And being found in appearance as a man, He humbled Himself and became obedient to the point of death, even the death on the cross. Therefore God also has highly exalted Him and given Him the name which is above every name, that at the name of Jesus every knee should bow, of those in heaven, and of those on earth, and of those under the earth, and that every tongue should confess that Jesus Christ is Lord, to the glory of God the Father.

The Apostle Paul considered the crucifixion, resurrection, and the return of Jesus Christ as the most central doctrines of the Christian faith. The biblical and historical evidence overwhelmingly outweighs the meager Quranic verses that deny these truths.

THE TESTIMONY OF SECULAR HISTORY

Sacred history in the New Testament documents has shown us ample evidence of the historicity of Christ's death and resurrection. Not surprisingly, secular history has far less concerning the traveling preacher from an obscure Empire outpost. However, even secular history is not silent concerning Christ.

Flavius Josephus

Now, there was about this time, Jesus, a wise man, if it be lawful to call him a man, for he was a doer of wonderful works,—a teacher of such men as receive the truth with pleasure. He drew over to him both many of the Jews, and many of the Gentiles. He was (the) Christ; and when Pilate, at the suggestion of the principal men amongst us, had condemned him to the cross, those that loved him at the first did not forsake him, for he appeared to them alive again the third day, as the divine prophets had foretold these and ten thousand other wonderful things concerning him; and the tribe of Christians, so named from him, are not extinct at this day.[11]

The Jewish Talmud

The Talmud is a holy book of tradition and commentary in Jewish eyes. It has been collected in huge volumes, which anyone interested can see. In the

copy published in 1943 in Amsterdam, one can read
on page 42:

> **Jesus was crucified one day before the Passover. We
> warned Him for 40 days that He would be killed be-
> cause He was a magician and planned to deceive Is-
> rael with His delusions. Whoever wished to do so
> was asked to defend him, and when none did, He was
> crucified on the eve of the Passover. Does anyone
> dare to defend Him? Was He not a stirrer up of evil?
> It is said in the prophets, Deuteronomy chapter 13,
> verses 8–9, "You shalt not consent to him or listen
> to him, nor shall your eye pity him, nor shall you
> spare him or conceal him; but you shall surely kill
> him. . . ."**

Roman and Greek Historians

The death of Christ on the cross is confirmed by
early historians, heathen and Jewish.

Tacitus, the historian who was a heathen, wrote in
the year A.D. 55, detailing passages about the crucifixion of Christ and his sufferings. Furthermore,
the Roman historians Pliny the Younger and Seuto-
nius, along with non-Roman historians Thallus, Phle-
gon, and the satirist Lucian of Samsota, refer to the
crucifixion of Jesus in their writings. (Martin Hengel's
book, *Crucifixion in the Ancient World,* gives more
details.)

The Greek historian, Lucien, who lived around
A.D. 100, was an outstanding writer. He told of the
death of Christ and the growing group of Christians.
He was an Epicurean who could not understand the
faith of Christians and their readiness to die for
Christ. In his writings he ridiculed the Christians'
belief in the immortality of the soul and their long-

ing for heaven. He looked on them as a deceived people clinging to uncertainties after death rather than living for the present. One of the most significant allusions to the subject of Christ in his writings is this: "The Christians continue to worship that great man who was crucified in Palestine because he brought a new religion to the world."[12]

A MODERN DOCTOR LOOKS AT THE CRUCIFIXION

In the *Journal of the American Medical Association,* March 21, 1986 (p. 1455 ff.), readers were treated to an astonishing nine-page essay entitled "On the Physical Death of Jesus Christ." The extensive, investigative, and extraordinary material was written by William D. Edwards, M.D., Wesley J. Gabel, M. Div., and Floyd E. Hosmer, M.S., AMI. I would recommend reading the entire article. However, here is the summary:

> Jesus of Nazareth underwent Jewish and Roman trials, was flogged, and was sentenced to death by crucifixion. The scourging produced deep stripelike lacerations and appreciable blood loss, and it probably set the stage for hypovolemic shock, as evidenced by the fact that Jesus was too weakened to carry the crossbar (patibulum) to Golgotha. At the site of crucifixion, his wrists were nailed to the patibulum and, after the patibulum was lifted onto the upright post (stipes), his feet were nailed to the stipes. The major pathophysiologic effect of crucifixion was an interference with normal respirations. Accordingly, death resulted primarily from hypovolemic shock and exhaustion asphyxia. Jesus' death was ensured by the thrust of a soldier's spear into his side. Modern medical interpretation of the historical evidence indicates

that Jesus was dead when taken down from the cross.

THE NECESSITY OF THE CROSS

All men are in desperate need of salvation. The reason is revealed in Romans 3:23, "For all have sinned and fall short of the glory of God." Sin is found in every human heart.

Isaiah 53:6 tells us the truth of our state of affairs:

All we like sheep have gone astray;
We have turned, every one, to his own way;
And the Lord has laid on Him the iniquity of us all.

In 1 John 1:8–10, the nature of sin is acknowledged clearly:

If we say that we have no sin, we deceive ourselves, and the truth is not in us. If we confess our sins, He is faithful and just to forgive us our sins and to cleanse us from all unrighteousness. If we say that we have not sinned, we make Him a liar, and His word is not in us.

The awareness that repentance alone cannot remove the debt of past sins is in the heart of every man everywhere. Our Muslim friends declare that their salvation is by works and repentance from sin. However, the fact is there must be a more effective means of obtaining forgiveness than just that. The good acts of sinful men do not change the men's inner sinful nature—only their outward appearances. There must be atonement. A sinless sacrifice must be presented to a just God.

"The payment for sin is death but the gift of God is eternal life through Jesus Christ our Lord" (Romans 6:23). Hebrews 9:22 affirms, "And according to the law almost all things are purged with blood, and without shedding of blood there is no remission."

Sin is an insult to the name of God and destructive to man, who is created in the image of God. Therefore, sinful man deserves just judgment.

God can never be just unless He punishes the sinner. Repentance, which is but merely the return to the place of obedience, cannot bring the justification sought for the sins committed. In other words, if a murderer tells the court that he is sorry for his terrible deed, such a confession does not mean that he goes free. The court will still give him a sentence of death or life-imprisonment, as his payment for his disobedience. There is nothing of atonement in confession and repentance. Atonement for past sins is necessary because the honor, justice, holiness, and righteousness of God cannot be satisfied by mere repentance. Who is going to pay for our sins? How can we resolve the sin problem?

The blessing for all humanity is that this atonement of Christ covers all kinds of people, not just Jewish people. He came for the Jew, the Gentile, and the Muslim. Romans 3:29–30 promises,

Or is He the God of the Jews only? Is He not also the God of the Gentiles? Yes, of the Gentiles also, since there is one God who will justify the circumcised by faith and the uncircumcised through faith.

Through the atoning sacrifice of Jesus Christ on the cross, salvation comes to all who believe, and all become spiritual children of Abraham:

There is neither Jew nor Greek, there is neither slave nor free, there is neither male nor female; for you are all one in Christ Jesus. And if you are Christ's, then you are Abraham's seed, and heirs according to the promise.[13]

Summary

Humans, in spite of their downfall into sin, have not totally lost their consciences. This small power which remains in us can discern right from wrong and understand punishment and reward. This power is an echo of the grace of God, who created our consciences. However, this power, important as it is, cannot save us from judgment. It can influence our leanings toward or away from sin, but it cannot justify us or loose us from sin's bondage.

The Law cannot justify the sinner either. According to Paul, the Law leads us to Christ Jesus, because there is no other way to salvation. But with all the importance of this truth, most people attempt to solve the problem of conscience by doing works of self-righteousness. Seemingly, many think that good works are comparable with earning the mercy of God. But the Old Testament says that our good works are nothing more than filthy, dirty rags. In the New Testament, we are challenged to recognize that salvation is by grace, not by works, lest any man should be proud or boastful (Ephesians 2:8–9).

God loves us with a wonderful love which is full of mercy. This love became incarnate in Jesus Christ, who expressed it to the fullest by dying for our redemption on the cross. Jesus declared, "And I, if I am lifted up from the earth, will draw all peoples to Myself" (John 12:32). John the Baptist announced,

"Behold! The Lamb of God who takes away the sin of the world!" (John 1:29).

The cross, a symbol of shame, became through Christ the symbol of challenge. The cross, a symbol of death, became through Christ the symbol of life. The crucifixion of Christ was not a tragedy; it was the triumph of the ages. It was the reconciliation of love and truth. The empty tomb is a guarantee that we will triumph over death also and spend eternity with the risen Redeemer, Christ Jesus.

CHAPTER FIVE

ISLAM UNVEILED

❈ ❈ ❈

**And they say: Fables of the men of old which he
hath had written down so that they are dictated to
him morn and evening.**

◆ ◆

¹

**"And you shall know the truth, and the truth shall
make you free."²**

THE TRUE SOURCES OF ISLAM

E. Stanley Jones, the famed Christian apostle to
India for sixty years, explained the types of religion
in the world. Dr. Jones declared that the first type of
religion is the word made word—God revealing
himself primarily through a written revelation in a
holy book. The second type is the word made law, in

which God is viewed as revealing Himself primarily
in a set of rules to follow. The third is the word made
flesh. If humans were libraries, the best way to com-
municate with them would be through a book. If humans were constitutions and by-laws, they would
respond best to a set of laws. Because we are human,
God chose to make the word flesh.[3]

The Muslims seem to believe that in the beginning
was the "Word" and the "Word" became a "Book"!
Muslims assert that Allah has revealed himself most
clearly in a book, not in Muhammad the person. Indeed, according to my count, the word *book* occurs
259 times in the Quran. In contradistinction, Christians believe that in the beginning was the "Word"
and the "Word" became a human being![4] Here are
some verses worth our consideration:

> **That (this) is indeed a noble Qur'ān in a Book kept
> hidden which none toucheth save the purified, a rev-
> elation from the Lord of the Worlds. It is this State-
> ment that ye scorn. . . .**

◆ ◆

إِنَّهُۥ لَقُرْءَانٌ كَرِيمٌ ۝

فِى كِتَٰبٍ مَّكْنُونٍ ۝

لَّا يَمَسُّهُۥٓ إِلَّا ٱلْمُطَهَّرُونَ ۝

تَنزِيلٌ مِّن رَّبِّ ٱلْعَٰلَمِينَ ۝

أَفَبِهَٰذَا ٱلْحَدِيثِ أَنتُم مُّدْهِنُونَ ۝ [5]

> **And they say: If only he would bring us a miracle
> from his Lord! Hath there not come unto them the
> proof of what is in the former Scriptures? . . .**

◆ ◆

وَقَالُوا لَوْلَا يَأْتِينَا بِآيَةٍ مِّن رَّبِّهِ أَوَلَمْ تَأْتِهِم
بَيِّنَةُ مَا فِي الصُّحُفِ الْأُولَى ﴿٦﴾ [6]

**. . . And thou (O Muhammad) wast not a reader of
any Scripture before it, nor didst thou write it with
thy right hand, for then might those have doubted
who follow falsehood.**

◆ ◆

وَمَا كُنتَ تَتْلُو مِن قَبْلِهِ مِن كِتَابٍ وَلَا تَخُطُّهُ
بِيَمِينِكَ إِذًا لَّارْتَابَ الْمُبْطِلُونَ ﴿٤٨﴾ [7]

In contrast, we must study John 1:1–15, especially
verse 14 which is among the most unique statements
to be found in all of literature: "And the Word became flesh and dwelt among us, and we beheld His
glory, the glory as of the only begotten of the Father,
full of grace and truth."

THE OLD TESTAMENT

Any reader of the Quran familiar with the Old Testament discovers that the names and events of Old
Testament books and prophets are very definitely
copied in the Quran. However, often the stories in
the Quran are garbled and confused. Muhammad
must have heard these stories from his Jewish
friends in Medina, where he lived during the time he
said he received most of the revelations which became the Quran. His seventh wife, Raihana, and

ninth, Safiyya, were Jewesses. His first wife, Khadija, had a Christian background. The eighth wife, Maryam, was part of a Christian sect. They undoubtedly shared with him much of the Old and New Testament literature, drama, and prophetic stories.

The Quran singles out the following Old Testament names from among the twenty-eight authentic prophets: Adam, Noah, Abraham, Moses, Isaac, Jacob, Ishmael, Joseph, David, Solomon, Elijah, Elisha, and Jonah.[8]

Compare Genesis 4:1–16 and Surat al-Ma'idah (The Table Spread) 5:27–32.

Genesis 4:1–16

Now Adam knew Eve his wife, and she conceived and bore Cain, and said, "I have gotten a man from the LORD." Then she bore again, this time his brother Abel. Now Abel was a keeper of sheep, but Cain was a tiller of the ground.

And in the process of time it came to pass that Cain brought an offering of the fruit of the ground to the LORD. Abel also brought of the firstlings of his flock and of their fat. And the LORD respected Abel and his offering, but He did not respect Cain and his offering. And Cain was very angry, and his countenance fell.

So the LORD said to Cain, "Why are you angry? And why has your countenance fallen? If you do well, will you not be accepted? And if you do not do well, sin lies at the door. And its desire is for you, but you should rule over it."

Now Cain talked with Abel his brother; and it came to pass, when they were in the field, that Cain rose against Abel his brother and killed him.

Then the LORD said to Cain, "Where is Abel your brother?"

And he said, "I do not know. Am I my brother's keeper?"

And He said, "What have you done? The voice of your brother's blood cries out to Me from the ground."

Surat al-Ma'idah (The Table Spread) 5:27–32

But recite unto them with truth the tale of the two sons of Adam, how they offered each a sacrifice, and it was accepted from the one of them and it was not accepted from the other. (The one) said: I will surely kill thee. (The other) answered: Allah accepteth only from those who ward off (evil). Even if thou stretch out thy hand against me to kill me, I shall not stretch out my hand against thee to kill thee, lo! I fear Allah, the Lord of the Worlds. Lo! I would rather thou shouldst bear the punishment of the sin against me and thine own sin and become one of the owners of the Fire. That is the reward of evil-doers.

But (the other's) mind imposed on him the killing of his brother, so he slew him and became one of the losers.

Then Allah sent a raven scratching up the ground, to show him how to hide his brother's naked corpse. He said: Woe unto me! Am I not able to be as this raven and so hide my brother's naked corpse? And he became repentant.

For that cause We decreed for the Children of Israel that whosoever killeth a human being for other than manslaughter or corruption in the earth, it shall be as if he had killed all mankind, and *whoso saveth the life of one, it shall be as if he had saved the life of all mankind.* Our messengers came unto them of old with clear proofs (of Allah's sovereignty), but afterwards, lo! many of them became prodigals in the earth.

وَاتْلُ عَلَيْهِمْ نَبَأَ ابْنَىْ ادَمَ بِالْحَقِّ اِذْ قَرَّبَا قُرْبَانًا

فَتُقُبِّلَ مِنْ اَحَدِهِمَا وَلَمْ يُتَقَبَّلْ مِنَ الْاٰخَرِ قَالَ

لَاَقْتُلَنَّكَ قَالَ اِنَّمَا يَتَقَبَّلُ اللهُ مِنَ الْمُتَّقِيْنَ ۝

لَئِنْ بَسَطْتَّ اِلَىَّ يَدَكَ لِتَقْتُلَنِيْ مَاۤ اَنَا بِبَاسِطٍ يَّدِيَ

اِلَيْكَ لِاَقْتُلَكَ اِنِّيۤ اَخَافُ اللهَ رَبَّ الْعٰلَمِيْنَ ۝

اِنِّيۤ اُرِيْدُ اَنْ تَبُوۤأَ بِاِثْمِيْ وَ اِثْمِكَ فَتَكُوْنَ مِنْ

اَصْحٰبِ النَّارِ ۚ وَ ذٰلِكَ جَزٰٓؤُا الظّٰلِمِيْنَ ۝

فَطَوَّعَتْ لَهُ نَفْسُهُ قَتْلَ اَخِيْهِ فَقَتَلَهُ فَاَصْبَحَ

مِنَ الْخٰسِرِيْنَ ۝

فَبَعَثَ اللهُ غُرَابًا يَّبْحَثُ فِى الْاَرْضِ لِيُرِيَهُ كَيْفَ

يُوَارِيْ سَوْءَةَ اَخِيْهِ ۚ قَالَ يٰوَيْلَتٰۤى اَعَجَزْتُ اَنْ

اَكُوْنَ مِثْلَ هٰذَا الْغُرَابِ فَاُوَارِيَ سَوْءَةَ اَخِيْ ۚ

فَاَصْبَحَ مِنَ النّٰدِمِيْنَ ۝

مِنْ اَجْلِ ذٰلِكَ ۛ كَتَبْنَا عَلٰى بَنِيْۤ اِسْرَآءِيْلَ اَنَّهُ مَنْ

قَتَلَ نَفْسًۢا بِغَيْرِ نَفْسٍ اَوْ فَسَادٍ فِى الْاَرْضِ فَكَاَنَّمَا

قَتَلَ النَّاسَ جَمِيْعًا ۗ وَ مَنْ اَحْيَاهَا فَكَاَنَّمَاۤ اَحْيَا النَّاسَ

جَمِيْعًا ۗ وَ لَقَدْ جَآءَتْهُمْ رُسُلُنَا بِالْبَيِّنٰتِ ثُمَّ اِنَّ كَثِيْرًا

مِّنْهُمْ بَعْدَ ذٰلِكَ فِى الْاَرْضِ لَمُسْرِفُوْنَ ۝

The italicized words above support the basis of the Old Testament hope for the finished work of Jesus, who was to take away the sins of the world (see John 1:29).

The passage above echoes an ancient Jewish tradition (c. A.D. 150–200), preserved by Pirke Rabbi Eleazer:

> **Adam and Eve, sitting by the corpse (of Abel) wept not knowing what to do, for they had as yet no knowledge of burial. A Raven coming up, took the dead body of its fellow (mate), and having scratched up the earth, buried it thus before their eyes. Adam said, "Let us follow the example of the Raven," and so taking up Abel's body buried it at once.[9]**

The Quranic text also reflects its source in the second-century Jewish Mishnah Sanhedrin 4:5:

> **We find in the case of Cain who murdered his brother, the voice of thy brother's blood cries (Genesis 4:10). It is not said here blood in the singular, but bloods in the plural. That is, his own blood and the blood of his seed. Man was created single in order to show that to him who kills a single individual (a human being) it shall be reckoned (counted) that he has slain the whole race; but to him who preserves the life of a single individual, it is counted that he has preserved the whole race.[10]**

If Islam could trace its origin and prophecy to Abraham, then we would expect to find Old Testament references to Allah, Muhammad, Mecca, the black stone of the Ka'bah, and the many ceremonies and practices of Islam. We have already seen that the Holy Bible is devoid of references to Muhammad, and there are no biblical references to anything else Islamic.

It is much more reasonable to conclude that Islam grew from the polytheistic and animistic culture of Muhammad's tribe. In fact, the people of Mecca worshipped 360 idols, one of whom was named Al-ilah!

That being the case, however, there are numerous passages in the so-called inspired Quran which originally appeared in the Old Testament more than one thousand years before the prophet of Arabia was even born. Though the Quranic and biblical passages are not identical, they are similar enough to show Muhammad's dependence on some of the Holy Bible's teaching for his "revelations." Here are a select few of the many texts that could be cited:

- The Night of Power is better than a thousand months. (Surat al-Qadr [The Power] 97:3)
  For a day in Your courts is better than a thousand. (Ps. 84:10)

- Show us the straight path. (Surat al-Fatihah [The Opening] 1:6)
  Teach me Your way, O Lord, And lead me in a straight path. (Ps. 27:11)

- We have written in the Scripture, after the Reminder My righteous slaves will inherit the earth. (Surat al-Anbiya' [The Prophets] 21:105)
  The righteous shall inherit the land, And dwell in it forever. (Ps. 37:29)

- He it is Who sendeth down water from the sky, whence ye have drink, and whence are trees . . . He causeth crops to grow for you, and the olive and the date-palm and grapes and all kind of fruit. Lo! herein is indeed a portent for people who reflect. And he hath constrained the night and the day and the sun and the moon to be of service unto you, and the stars are made subservient by His command . . . And He hath cast into the earth firm hills that it quake not with you,

and streams and roads that ye may find a way.
And landmarks (too), and by the star they find a
way. (Surat al-Nahl [The Bee] 16:10–12, 15, 16)
He sends the springs into the valleys, Which flow
among the hills . . . He causes the grass to grow
for the cattle, And vegetation for the service of
man, That he may bring forth food from the
earth . . . He appointed the moon for seasons;
The sun knows its going down. You make
darkness, and it is night, In which all the beasts
of the forest creep about. (Ps. 104:10, 14, 19, 20)

• . . . having hearts wherewith they understand not, and having eyes wherewith they
  see not, and having ears wherewith they hear
  not. (Surat al-A'raf [The Heights] 7:179)
  Hear this now, O foolish people, Without understanding, Who have eyes and see not, And
  who have ears and hear not. (Jer. 5:21)

• He is the First and the Last, and the Outward
  and the Inward; and He is the Knower of all
  things. (Surat al-Hadid [The Iron] 57:3)
  I am the First and I am the Last; Besides Me
  there is no God. (Isa. 44:6)

Other passages worthy of comparison are: Surat
Hud 11 and Psalm 14; Surat Yusuf 12 and Psalm 16;
Surat Ibrahim 14 and Psalm 35; Surat al-Hijr 15 and
Psalm 5; Surat al-Kahf 18 and Psalm 34.

Jewish Folklore

The II Targum of Esther, dating back to the second
century A.D., is consistently found to be the source of
Surat al-Naml (The Ant) 27:17–44. First, we will
look at the Quranic record:

And there were gathered together unto Solomon his armies of the jinn and humankind, and of the birds, and they were set in battle order; . . .

And he sought among the birds and said: How is it that I see not the hoopoe, or is he among the absent? I verily will punish him with hard punishment or I verily will slay him, or he verily shall bring me a plain excuse. But he was not long in coming, and he said: I have found out (a thing) that thou apprehendest not, and I come unto thee from Sheba with sure tidings. Lo! I found a woman ruling over them, and she hath been given (abundance) of all things, and hers is a mighty throne.

I found her and her people worshipping the sun instead of Allah; and Satan maketh their works fair-seeming unto them, and debarreth them from the way (of Truth), so that they go not aright . . .

(Solomon) said: We shall see whether thou speakest truth or whether thou art of the liars. Go with this my letter and throw it down unto them; then turn away and see what (answer) they return. (The Queen of Sheba) said (when she received the letter): O chieftains! Lo! there hath been thrown unto me a noble letter. . . .

They said: we are lords of might and lords of great prowess, but it is for thee to command; so consider what thou wilt command. She said: Lo! kings, when they enter a township, ruin it and make the honour of its people shame. Thus will they do. But lo! I am going to send a present unto them, and to see with what (answer) the messengers return. So when (the envoy) came unto Solomon, (the King) said: What! Would ye help me with wealth? But that which Allah hath given me is better than that which He hath given you. Nay it is ye (and not I) who exult in your gift. . . .

It was said unto her: Enter the hall. And when she saw it she deemed it a pool and bared her legs. (Solomon) said: Lo! it is a hall, made smooth, of glass.

She said: My Lord! Lo! I have wronged myself, and I surrender with Solomon unto Allah, the Lord of the Worlds.

◆ ◆

وَحُشِرَ لِسُلَيْمٰنَ جُنُوْدُهٗ مِنَ الْجِنِّ وَالْاِنْسِ وَ الطَّيْرِ فَهُمْ يُوزَعُوْنَ ۝

وَتَفَقَّدَ الطَّيْرَ فَقَالَ مَا لِيَ لَاۤ اَرَى الْهُدْهُدَ ۖ اَمْ كَانَ مِنَ الْغَآئِبِيْنَ ۝

لَاُعَذِّبَنَّهٗ عَذَابًا شَدِيْدًا اَوْ لَاَاذْبَحَنَّهٗ اَوْ لَيَأْتِيَنِّيْ بِسُلْطٰنٍ مُّبِيْنٍ ۝

فَمَكَثَ غَيْرَ بَعِيْدٍ فَقَالَ اَحَطْتُّ بِمَا لَمْ تُحِطْ بِهٖ وَ جِئْتُكَ مِنْ سَبَاٍ بِنَبَاٍ يَّقِيْنٍ ۝

اِنِّيْ وَجَدْتُّ امْرَاَةً تَمْلِكُهُمْ وَ اُوْتِيَتْ مِنْ كُلِّ شَيْءٍ وَّ لَهَا عَرْشٌ عَظِيْمٌ ۝

وَجَدْتُّهَا وَ قَوْمَهَا يَسْجُدُوْنَ لِلشَّمْسِ مِنْ دُوْنِ اللهِ وَ زَيَّنَ لَهُمُ الشَّيْطٰنُ اَعْمَالَهُمْ فَصَدَّهُمْ عَنِ السَّبِيْلِ فَهُمْ لَا يَهْتَدُوْنَ ۝

قَالَ سَنَنْظُرُ اَصَدَقْتَ اَمْ كُنْتَ مِنَ الْكٰذِبِيْنَ ۝

اِذْهَبْ بِكِتٰبِيْ هٰذَا فَاَلْقِهْ اِلَيْهِمْ ثُمَّ تَوَلَّ عَنْهُمْ فَانْظُرْ مَاذَا يَرْجِعُوْنَ ۝

قَالَتْ يٰۤاَيُّهَا الْمَلَؤُا اِنِّيْۤ اُلْقِيَ اِلَيَّ كِتٰبٌ كَرِيْمٌ ۝

اِنَّهٗ مِنْ سُلَيْمٰنَ وَ اِنَّهٗ بِسْمِ اللهِ الرَّحْمٰنِ الرَّحِيْمِ ۝

اَلَّا تَعْلُوْا عَلَىَّ وَأْتُوْنِىْ مُسْلِمِيْنَ ۩

قَالَتْ يَا أَيُّهَا الْمَلَؤُا أَفْتُوْنِىْ فِىْ أَمْرِىْ مَا كُنْتُ

قَاطِعَةً أَمْرًا حَتّى تَشْهَدُوْنِ ۝

قَالُوْا نَحْنُ أُولُوْا قُوَّةٍ وَّأُولُوْا بَأْسٍ شَدِيْدٍ ڌ وَّ

الْأَمْرُ إِلَيْكِ فَانْظُرِىْ مَاذَا تَأْمُرِيْنَ ۝

قَالَتْ إِنَّ الْمُلُوْكَ إِذَا دَخَلُوْا قَرْيَةً أَفْسَدُوْهَا وَ

جَعَلُوْا أَعِزَّةَ أَهْلِهَا أَذِلَّةً ۚ وَكَذَلِكَ يَفْعَلُوْنَ ۝

وَإِنِّىْ مُرْسِلَةٌ إِلَيْهِمْ بِهَدِيَّةٍ فَنَاظِرَةٌ بِمَ يَرْجِعُ

الْمُرْسَلُوْنَ ۝

فَلَمَّا جَاءَ سُلَيْمَنَ قَالَ أَتُمِدُّوْنَنِ بِمَالٍ فَمَآ

اتنى اللهُ خَيْرٌ مِّمَّآ اتكُمْ ۚ بَلْ أَنْتُمْ بِهَدِيَّتِكُمْ

تَفْرَحُوْنَ ۝

قِيْلَ لَهَا ادْخُلِى الصَّرْحَ ۚ فَلَمَّا رَأَتْهُ حَسِبَتْهُ لُجَّةً

وَّكَشَفَتْ عَنْ سَاقَيْهَا ۚ قَالَ إِنَّهُ صَرْحٌ مُّمَرَّدٌ مِّنْ

قَوَارِيْرَ ۗ قَالَتْ رَبِّ إِنِّىْ ظَلَمْتُ نَفْسِىْ وَأَسْلَمْتُ مَعَ

سُلَيْمَنَ لِلّهِ رَبِّ الْعَلَمِيْنَ ۩

From the II Targum of Esther, we read:

> Solomon . . . gave orders . . . I will send King and armies against thee . . . (of) Genii beasts of the land the birds of the air. Just then the Red-cock (a bird), enjoying itself, could not be found; King Solomon said that they should seize it and bring it by force, and indeed he sought to kill it.

But just then the cock appeared in the presence of the King and said, "I had seen the whole world (and) know the city and kingdom (of Sheba) which is not subject to thee, My Lord King. They are ruled by a woman called the Queen of Sheba. Then I found the fortified city in the Eastlands (Sheba) and around it are stones of gold and silver in the streets. By chance the Queen of Sheba was out in the morning worshipping the sea, the scribes prepared a letter, which was placed under the bird's wing and away it flew and (it) reached the Fort of Sheba. Seeing the letter under its wing (Sheba) opened it and read it.

"King Solomon sends to you his Salaams. Now if it please thee to come and ask after my welfare, I will set thee high above all. But if it please thee not, I will send kings and armies against thee."

The Queen of Sheba heard it, she tore her garments, and sending for her Nobles asked their advice. They knew not Solomon, but advised her to send vessels by the sea, full of beautiful ornaments and gems . . . also to send a letter to him.

When at last she came, Solomon sent a messenger . . . to meet her. . . . Solomon, hearing she had come, arose and sat down in the palace of glass. When the Queen of Sheba saw it, she thought the glass floor was water, and so in crossing over lifted up her garments. When Solomon seeing the hair about her legs, (He) cried out to her. . . .[11]

The New Testament

Surat al-Ma'idah (The Table Spread) 5, Surat Maryam (Mary) 19, Surat al-Imran (The Family of 'Imran) 3, and several other Surats are full of New Testament references. The Quran mentions Jesus ninety-seven times, plus Zachariah and his son, John, along with the disciples of Jesus. This indicates that Muhammad knew much more than the average Arab of his time about the New Testament

Scriptures. After all, his uncle, Waraqa, translated portions of the Gospels into Arabic, and Buhaira, a Nestorian monk, was his secret teacher. There are 131 passages in the Quran in which the Bible is referred to as the Law, Psalms, and the Gospel.[12]

Furthermore, numerous passages in the Quran so closely parallel passages in the New Testament, which is six hundred years older than the Quran, that one can safely conclude that Muhammad borrowed some of the content of his "revelations" from the truly inspired text of the New Testament Scriptures. Here are a few choice examples:

- Ah, woe unto worshipers who are heedless of their prayer; who would be seen (at worship). (Surat al-Ma'un [Small Kindnesses] 107)
  Therefore, when you do a charitable deed, do not sound a trumpet before you as the hypocrites do in the synagogues and in the streets, that they may have glory from men. (Matt. 6:2)

- They taste not death therein, save the first death. . . . (Surat al-Dukhan [the Smoke] 44:56)
  He who overcomes shall not be hurt by the second death. (Rev. 2:11)

- Lo! they who deny Our revelations and scorn them, for them the gates of Heaven will not be opened nor will they enter the Garden until the camel goeth through the needle's eye. (Surat al-A'raf [The Heights] 7:40)
  And again I say to you, it is easier for a camel to go through the eye of a needle than for a rich man to enter the kingdom of God. (Matt. 19:24)

- And the dwellers of the Fire cry out unto the dwellers of the Garden; Pour on us some water or

some of that wherewith Allah hath provided you.
(Surat al-A'raf [The Heights] 7:50)
Then he cried and said, "Father Abraham, have
mercy on me, and send Lazarus that he may dip
the tip of his finger in water and cool my tongue;
for I am tormented in this flame." (Matt. 16:24)

• And when Jesus son of Mary said: O Children of
Israel Lo! I am the messenger of Allah unto you,
confirming that which was (revealed) before me
in the Torah, and bringing good tidings of a mes-
senger who cometh after me, whose name is the
Praised One. (Surat al-Saff [The Ranks] 61:6)
. . . The word which you hear is not Mine but the
Father's who sent Me . . . But the Helper, the
Holy Spirit, whom the Father will send in My
name, He will teach you all things, and bring to
your remembrance all things that I said to you.
(John 14:24, 26)

• But Lo! a Day with Allah is as a thousand years
of what ye reckon. (Surat al-Hajj [The Pil-
grimage] 22:47)
But, beloved, do not forget this one thing, that
with the Lord one day is as a thousand years, and
a thousand years as one day. (2 Pet. 3:8)

Apocryphal Fables

Surat al-Imran (The Family of 'Imran) 3:35–37
closely follows a spurious gospel account, *The Prot-
evangelion's James the Lesser*. This second century
A.D. apocryphal Christian fable tells the story of
Zachariah, his wife, and John the Baptist. The
Quranic passage reads:

**(Remember) when the wife of 'Imrān said: My
Lord! I have vowed unto Thee that which is in my**

belly as a consecrated (offering). Accept it from me,
Lo! Thou, only Thou, art the Hearer, the Knower!
And when she was delivered she said: My Lord! Lo! I
am delivered of a female—Allah knew best of what
she was delivered—the male is not as the female;
and lo! I have named her Mary, and lo! I crave Thy
protection for her and for her offspring from Satan
the outcast. And her Lord accepted her with full acceptance and vouchsafed to her a goodly growth: and
made Zachariah her guardian. Whenever Zachariah
went into the sanctuary where she was, he found that
she had food. He said: O Mary! Whence cometh unto
thee this (food)? She answered: It is from Allah. Allah giveth without stint to whom He will.

◆ ◆

The Protevangelion's James the Lesser 4:2, 5:9, and 7:4 states:

> And Anna (wife of Joachim) answered, 'As the Lord my God liveth, whatever I bring forth, whether it be male or female, I will devote it to the Lord my God, and it shall minister to him in holy things, during its whole life' . . . and called her name Mary . . . And the high-priest received her, and blessed her, and said, 'Mary, the Lord God hath magnified thy name to all generations, and to the very end of time by thee will the Lord shew his redemption to the children of Israel.'[14]

Christian Heresies

It is intriguing and instructive to discover why Muhammad did not believe in the Trinity and the divinity or resurrection of Jesus Christ. To understand this, we must examine the prevalent deviant doctrines of Nestorius and his followers, sectarian Christians who migrated to Arabia 140 years before Muhammad's birth. Muhammad apparently drew his denials from their heresy.

Nestorius was patriarch of Constantinople from A.D. 428 to 431. Orthodox Christians believed, as per scriptural teaching, that Jesus had two natures, one divine and one human. Although the two were distinct, they were joined together in one person. Nestorius, however, insisted that in Christ Jesus both a divine and a human person acted in unity, but were not the one divine person with both a divine nature and a human nature.

In A.D. 431 the Council of Ephesus judged the Nestorian beliefs to be heretical. Nestorius was deposed as patriarch. He and his followers were driven out of the Roman Empire and took refuge in Persia,

Arabia, India, China, and Mongolia. Their followers are identified as Nestorians or Monophysites (the Greek word *monos* means single, and *physis* means nature.)[15]

Waraqa ibn Nofal, considered to be Muhammad's uncle, was also a Nestorian and is alleged to have translated portions of the Gospels into Arabic. He was very influential to Muhammad. Khadija, Muhammad's first wife, is rumored to have been a Nestorian Christian.

At least one branch of the Nestorians still exists in the Middle East. Called the East Syrian Church, its number as of 1980 was estimated at 300,000.

Most Christian scholars believe that Muhammad came in contact with Nestorians during his business travels to Damascus and Egypt with his uncle's caravans, then later with Khadija's caravans. The Nestorians established monasteries on the caravan routes and entertained travelers like Muhammad frequently. Buhaira, a Nestorian monk, is recognized as one of the most influential men in Muhammad's knowledge of the Scriptures. The descriptions of hell in the homilies of Ephraim, a Nestorian preacher of the sixth century, resemble Muhammad's descriptions of hell.[16]

What was Muhammad doing between the time he married Khadija and his prophetic call, a period of fifteen years? Could he have been learning from Buhaira and Waraqa and reading some available biblical scrolls?

Heathenism

The ancient Arabs reportedly had seven celebrated temples dedicated to the seven planets. The temple at Sana was built in honor of Venus, and the one at

Mecca was consecrated to Saturn. Could the Islamic idea of seven heavens have come from these temples?

Stone worship prevailed at an early period among the Arabs, as among many other nations. Stones, shaped like the famed Egyptian obelisks and ten feet high, are on top of Mt. Seir in Petra, South Jordan. The ancient Nabatean Arabs worshipped these stone-carved pillars.

Muslim writers say that Adam, the first man, built the Ka'bah on earth, exactly below the spot its perfect model occupies in heaven. Ka'bah refers to the building in which the stone is housed. Supposedly, one thousand angels have been appointed to guard the structure. Apparently, they were careless in their duties because Abraham and his son Ishmael are said to have rebuilt it after a flood destroyed it! Several centuries later, the Meccans had to reconstruct again after another flood.

The stone within the Ka'bah structure is shaped somewhat like an egg and is about seven inches long. Muslims believe that at first it was whiter than milk, but it has become black from the sin of those who touched it.[17]

Ka'bah is an Arabic word which means a cube. The structure is also called Baitu'llah, the "house of God." At first, the Ka'bah was open at the top and exposed to torrents of rain, which eventually destroyed it. However, when Kussai ibn Kilab reconstructed the Ka'bah, he added a roof.

Some idols of the ancient Arabs are mentioned by name in the Quran. Al-Lat, the chief idol at Ta'if, is supposed to mean "the goddess." Al'Uzza probably symbolized the planet Venus, although it was worshiped as the form of a babul tree. Manat was a large sacrificial stone. Suwa was a female deity, Yaghus

was in the form of a lion, Ya'uk in the shape of a
horse, and Nasr had the image of an eagle. In front of
the Ka'bah was the great image of Hobal, the guardian deity of Mecca. [18]

The Secrets of Enoch and the Testament of Abraham

We must further compare *The Secrets of Enoch*, a
second-century A.D. Egyptian work in Arabic, 1:4–10
and 2:1, and the Quranic record of Muhammad's
Mi'raj, which is recognized as the night in which he
went to heaven by way of Jerusalem. A'isha, surprisingly enough, declared emphatically, "the body
of the prophet of Allah did not disappear but Allah
took away his spirit by night."[19] Here is the passage
in Surat Bani Isra'il (The Children of Israel) 17:1:

**In the name of Allah, the Beneficent, the Mer-
ciful. Glorified be He Who carried His servant by
night from the Inviolable Place of Worship to the Far
Distant Place of Worship the neighbourhood whereof
We have blessed, that We might show him of Our
tokens! Lo! He, only He, is the Hearer, the Seer.**

◆ ◆

بِسْمِ اللهِ الرَّحْمٰنِ الرَّحِيْمِ ۝
سُبْحٰنَ الَّذِيْ اَسْرٰى بِعَبْدِهٖ لَيْلًا مِّنَ الْمَسْجِدِ
الْحَرَامِ اِلَى الْمَسْجِدِ الْاَقْصَا الَّذِيْ بٰرَكْنَا حَوْلَهٗ
لِنُرِيَهٗ مِنْ اٰيٰتِنَا ؕ اِنَّهٗ هُوَ السَّمِيْعُ الْبَصِيْرُ ۝

The elaborate story of this vision is expounded in
Mishkat al Masabih, composed in A.D. 620. Muham-

mad told how the angel Gabriel took him on the
winged animal, Al-Buraq, and showed him all the
seven levels of heaven in one night. Muhammad announced that he had seen Adam, Abraham, Moses,
Jesus, and others.

However, the night journey was not really so marvelous. The tale and its details appear originally in
The Secrets of Enoch, which predates Muhammad
by four centuries. Here is an excerpt from *Enoch*
1:4–10 and 2:1:

> **On the first day of the month I was in my house and
> was resting on my couch and slept and when I was
> asleep great distress came up into my heart and
> there appeared two men. They were standing at my
> couch and called me by name and I arose from my
> sleep. Have courage, Enoch, do not fear; The Eternal
> God sent us to thee. Thou shalt today ascend with us
> into heaven. The Angels took him on their wings and
> bore him up to the first heaven.[20]**

As to the description of what Muhammad saw in
the various levels of heaven, one can find an earlier
record of the very same details in *The Testament of
Abraham*.[21]

Although Muhammad claimed he went to Jerusalem and worshiped at the temple in his spirit, the
temple had been destroyed by Titus 570 years before
the vision! The "far distant place of worship" mentioned in Surat Bani Isra'il (The Children of Israel)
17:1 refers to the Aqsa Mosque, which was built as a
church in Jerusalem by the Crusaders during the
twelfth century. In 1187 Saladin made it a mosque
after he conquered the Holy Land. In other words,
no such place existed at the time of the so-called
heavenly journey. Even the Dome of the Rock
mosque was not built until A.D. 691.

In the Hindu version of the story, the Prophet is Arta, the angel is Azar, and Adam is Ormazd. The original Hindu source is *Arta Viraf Namak*.[22]

Sabeanism

Ancient historians like Abi Isa the Moroccan tell that Sabeans were the first religious people whose language was Syriac. Even Adam spoke that language. Seba was said to be the same Seba, son of Cush, son of Ham, son of Noah, mentioned in Genesis 10:6, 7. Their worship was monotheistic; they offered sacrifices and prayed seven times a day. Muhammad apparently borrowed their idea but reduced the number of prayer times to five a day. The Sabeans fasted thirty days a year, breaking the fast at sunset—two more practices Muhammad "Islamized" during Ramadan. Dr. Ahmad Shah *(Theology— Muslim and Christian)*, an elderly scholar and dear friend, told me when I visited him in India in 1978 that some writers mistook the Sabeans for followers of John the Baptist because they baptized new members into their group. He adds that along with God, they also worshiped stars and a hierarchy of angels.

QURANIC PROBLEMS

"The great merit of Muhammad," says Osborn, "is that among a people given up to idolatry, he rose to a vivid perception of the unity of God and preached this great doctrine with firmness and constancy amid ridicule and persecution." "Being also a master in eloquence," says Sir William Muir, "his language was cast in the purest and most persuasive style of Arabian oratory."

The sinfulness of man, the necessity of faith, the duty of prayer, and the judgment of all men at the last day, are other truths which Muhammad forcefully taught. The Fatiha is a prayer which can be adopted by all much like the Lord's Prayer or the Twenty-third Psalm.

Exaggeration in the Quran

The simple narratives of the Bible are distorted and magnified to an incredible degree in the Muslim Quran. In the Surat al-Baqarah (The Cow) 2:259, for example, the Quran says Ezra, or 'Uzair, and his ass died "for a hundred years" and were then raised to life.

> Or (bethink thee of) the like of him who, passing by a township which had fallen into utter ruin, exclaimed: How shall Allah give this township life after its death? And Allah made him die a hundred years, then brought him back to life. He said: How long hast thou tarried? (The man) said: I have tarried a day or part of a day. (He) said: Nay, but thou hast tarried for a hundred years. Just look at thy food and drink which have not rotted! Look at thine ass! And, that We may make thee a token unto mankind, look at the bones, how We adjust them and then cover them with flesh! And when (the matter) became clear unto him, he said: I know now that Allah is able to do all things.

◆ ◆

أَوْكَالَّذِى مَرَّعَلَى قَرْيَةٍ وَهِىَ خَاوِيَةٌ عَلَى عُرُوشِهَا

قَالَ أَنَّى يُحْيِى هٰذِهِ اللهُ بَعْدَ مَوْتِهَا فَأَمَاتَهُ اللهُ

مِائَةَ عَامٍ ثُمَّ بَعَثَهُ قَالَ كَمْ لَبِثْتَ قَالَ لَبِثْتُ

يَوْمًا أَوْبَعْضَ يَوْمٍ قَالَ بَل لَّبِثْتَ مِائَةَ عَـامٍ
فَانْظُرْ إِلَى طَعَامِكَ وَشَرَابِكَ لَمْ يَتَسَنَّهْ وَانْظُرْ
إِلَى حِمَارِكَ وَلِنَجْعَلَكَ آيَةً لِّلنَّاسِ وَانْظُرْ إِلَى الْعِظَامِ
كَيْفَ نُنشِزُهَا ثُمَّ نَكْسُوهَا لَحْمًا فَلَمَّا تَبَيَّنَ لَهُ
قَالَ أَعْلَمُ أَنَّ اللَّهَ عَلَى كُلِّ شَيْءٍ قَدِيرٌ

The Bible says that God gave the Ten Commandments on Mount Sinai. Abodah Sarah, a second century A.D. Jewish fable, states,

I raised (by shaking it from its roots) the Mountain (Sinai) to be a covering over you as it were, a lid.

In the Quran we read in Surat al-A'raf (The Heights) 7:171 and in Surat al-Ma'idah (The Table Spread) 5:60:

And when We shook the Mount above them as it were a covering, and they supposed that it was going to fall upon them (and We said): Hold fast that which We have given you, and remember that which is therein, that ye may ward off (evil). Shall I tell thee of a worse (case) than theirs for retribution with Allah? Worse (is the case of him) whom Allah hath cursed, him on whom His wrath hath fallen! Worse is he of whose sort Allah hath turned some to apes and swine, and who serveth idols. Such are in worse plight and further astray from the plain road.

وَإِذْ نَتَقْنَا الْجَبَلَ فَوْقَهُمْ كَأَنَّهُ ظُلَّةٌ وَظَنُّوا أَنَّهُ وَاقِعٌ
بِهِمْ خُذُوا مَا آتَيْنَاكُم بِقُوَّةٍ وَاذْكُرُوا مَا فِيهِ

لَعَلَّكُمْ تَتَّقُونَ ۞

قُلْ هَلْ أُنَبِّئُكُم بِشَرٍّ مِّن ذَٰلِكَ مَثُوبَةً عِندَ اللَّهِ ۚ
مَن لَّعَنَهُ اللَّهُ وَغَضِبَ عَلَيْهِ وَجَعَلَ مِنْهُمُ الْقِرَدَةَ
وَالْخَنَازِيرَ وَعَبَدَ الطَّاغُوتَ ۚ أُولَٰئِكَ شَرٌّ مَّكَانًا
وَأَضَلُّ عَن سَوَاءِ السَّبِيلِ ۞

Contradiction of Science

In Surat al-Kahf (The Cave) 18:86, it is said:

Till, when he reached the setting-place of the sun, he found it setting in a muddy spring, and found a people thereabout: We said: O Dhū'l-Qarneyn! Either punish or show them kindness.

◆ ◆

حَتَّىٰ إِذَا بَلَغَ مَغْرِبَ الشَّمْسِ وَجَدَهَا تَغْرُبُ
فِي عَيْنٍ حَمِئَةٍ وَوَجَدَ عِندَهَا قَوْمًا ۗ قُلْنَا يَا ذَا
الْقَرْنَيْنِ إِمَّا أَن تُعَذِّبَ وَإِمَّا أَن تَتَّخِذَ فِيهِمْ
حُسْنًا ۞

Only the superstitious in the age of Muhammad believed that the sun would ever set in a muddy spring!

Islamic Fatalism

Muslims believe that whatever has or shall come to pass in this world, whether it be good or bad, proceeds entirely from the divine will and has been irrevocably fixed and recorded on a preserved tablet.

It is true, as already stated, that some passages of the Quran seem to attribute freedom to man, while others teach a clear and distinct fatalism. The followers of Muhammad have no knowledge of God as a loving Father who has made us free moral beings. Surat al-Taubah (Repentance) 9:52 reads:

> **Say: Can ye await for us aught save one of two good things (death or victory in Allah's way)? while we await for you that Allah will afflict you with a doom from Him or at our hands. Await then! Lo! we are awaiting with you.**

◆ ◆

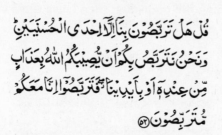

Abrogation of Quranic Verses

Muslims resolve some internal contradictions in the Quran by stating that certain passages of the Quran are *mansukh,* or annulled by verses revealed chronologically later than themselves, which are called *nasikh.* This is taught by Muhammad in Surat al-Baqarah (The Cow) 2:106:

> **Such of Our revelations as We abrogate or cause to be forgotten, We bring (in place) one better or the like thereof. Knowest thou not that Allah is Able to do all things?**

♦ ♦

مَا نَنسَخْ مِنْ ءَايَةٍ أَوْ نُنسِهَا نَأْتِ بِخَيْرٍ مِّنْهَا أَوْ
مِثْلِهَا أَلَمْ تَعْلَمْ أَنَّ اللَّهَ عَلَىٰ كُلِّ شَىْءٍ قَدِيرٌ ﴾

What is called "the sword verse" in Surat al-Tau-bah (Repentance) 9:5 annuls 124 verses which originally encourage tolerance.

Then, when the sacred months have passed, slay the idolaters wherever ye find them, and take them (captive), and besiege them, and prepare for them each ambush. But if they repent and establish worship and pay the poor-due, then leave their way free. Lo! Allah is Forgiving, Merciful.

♦ ♦

فَإِذَا انسَلَخَ الْأَشْهُرُ الْحُرُمُ فَاقْتُلُوا الْمُشْرِكِينَ
حَيْثُ وَجَدتُّمُوهُمْ وَخُذُوهُمْ وَاحْصُرُوهُمْ وَ
اقْعُدُوا لَهُمْ كُلَّ مَرْصَدٍ فَإِن تَابُوا وَأَقَامُوا الصَّلَوٰةَ وَ
ءَاتَوُا الزَّكَوٰةَ فَخَلُّوا سَبِيلَهُمْ إِنَّ اللَّهَ غَفُورٌ رَّحِيمٌ ﴾

One tradition has it that 'Ayisha declared emphatically that the Surat al-Saff (The Ranks) 61 had 200 verses during Muhammad's lifetime. But when Uthman standardized the Quran, the Surat had only 72 verses.[23]

This idea is certainly unacceptable and foreign to an all-wise God who, according to this Muslim doctrine, is presented as an ignorant Allah who dictates

wrong commands and later corrects them because
they do not work. Compare this belief of Muslim theology with what Christ Jesus announced according
to Matthew 5:17 and 19.

> **"Do not think that I came to destroy the Law or the
> Prophets. I did not come to destroy but to fulfill.
> Whoever therefore breaks one of the least of these
> commandments, and teaches men so, shall be called
> least in the kingdom of heaven; but whoever does
> and teaches them, he shall be called great in the
> kingdom of heaven."**

Another evidence of fickle faith concerns the direction of a Muslim's daily prayers. Muhammad communicated to his early followers in Mecca that the
Qiblah, the physical direction of their prayers,
should be toward Ka'bah. Once he migrated to Medina, he changed the direction toward Jerusalem, to
please the predominant Jewish population in Medina. Then seventeen months later, Allah changed
His mind the third time by commanding Muhammad to look toward Mecca and no longer toward
Jerusalem.

A man makes mistakes and needs to correct them,
but such is not the case with God. God has infinite
wisdom and cannot contradict Himself. Does God
have two Qurans if this system of abrogation is
valid? What does one do with this emphatic declaration in Surat al-An'am (Cattle) 6:34?

> **. . . there is none That can alter the Words (And
> Decrees) of Allah.**

◆ ◆

وَلَا مُبَدِّلَ لِكَلِمَتِ اللّهِ ²⁴

Muhammad professed to have a revelation, through Gabriel, whenever it suited his purpose. Many students of Muhammad's life say some "messages from heaven" were given to justify his political and moral conduct, as well as to match his religious precepts. Battles were fought, wholesale executions inflicted, wives added, and territories annexed, these students say, under pretext of the Almighty's sanction.

WOMEN'S INFERIORITY IN ISLAM

Polygamy and Unlimited Divorce

And if ye fear that ye will not deal fairly by the orphans, marry of the women, who seem good to you, two or three or four; and if ye fear that ye cannot do justice (to so many) then one (only) or (the captives) that your right hands possess. Thus it is more likely that ye will not do injustice.

◆ ◆

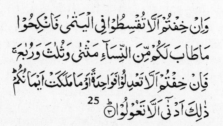

وَإِنْ خِفْتُمْ أَلَّا تُقْسِطُوا فِى الْيَتَمَى فَانكِحُوا
مَا طَابَ لَكُم مِّنَ النِّسَاءِ مَثْنَى وَثُلَثَ وَرُبَعَ
فَإِنْ خِفْتُمْ أَلَّا تَعْدِلُوا فَوَاحِدَةً أَوْ مَا مَلَكَتْ أَيْمَانُكُمْ
ذَلِكَ أَدْنَى أَلَّا تَعُولُوا ²⁵

When the leading Muslim men complained to 'Ali of the licentious practice of his son, Hasan, he told them the remedy lay in their own hands: they could refuse Hasan their daughters altogether. At that time, Hasan had married and divorced seventy times.[26]

One is bound to ask, if Muhammad brought us a greater and more perfect revelation, then why do we seem to regress instead of progress with the moral standards of the Quran? Jesus Christ enunciated, "He who made them at the beginning made them male and female" (Matthew 19:4). If God wanted man to have four wives, He would have made more than one Eve for Adam!

A Muslim husband may cast his wife adrift without giving a single reason or even notice. The husband possesses absolute, immediate, and unquestioned power of divorce. No privilege of a corresponding nature is reserved for the wife.

Here are two more verses from Surat al-Nisa (Women) (4:11, 176) in which the inferiority of women in Islam is most obvious.

> **And give unto the women, (whom ye marry) free gift of their marriage portions; but if they of their own accord remit unto you a part thereof, then ye are welcome to absorb it (in your wealth). They ask thee for a pronouncement. Say: Allah hath pronounced for you concerning distant kindred. If a man die childless and he have a sister, hers is half the heritage, and he would have inherited from her had she died childless. And if there be two sisters, then theirs are two-thirds of the heritage, and if they be brethren, men and women, unto the male is the equivalent of the share of two females. Allah expoundeth unto you, so that ye err not. Allah is Knower of all things.**

وَاٰتُوا النِّسَآءَ صَدُقٰتِهِنَّ نِحْلَةً فَاِنْ طِبْنَ
لَكُمْ عَنْ شَىْءٍ مِّنْهُ نَفْسًا فَكُلُوْهُ هَنِيْٓئًا
مَّرِيْٓئًا ۞

يَسْتَفْتُوْنَكَ قُلِ اللّٰهُ يُفْتِيْكُمْ فِى الْكَلٰلَةِ اِنِ امْرُؤٌا
هَلَكَ لَيْسَ لَهٗ وَلَدٌ وَّلَهٗٓ اُخْتٌ فَلَهَا نِصْفُ مَا تَرَكَ
وَهُوَ يَرِثُهَآ اِنْ لَّمْ يَكُنْ لَّهَا وَلَدٌ فَاِنْ كَانَتَا اثْنَتَيْنِ
فَلَهُمَا الثُّلُثٰنِ مِمَّا تَرَكَ وَاِنْ كَانُوْٓا اِخْوَةً رِّجَالًا
وَّنِسَآءً فَلِلذَّكَرِ مِثْلُ حَظِّ الْاُنْثَيَيْنِ يُبَيِّنُ اللّٰهُ
لَكُمْ اَنْ تَضِلُّوْا وَاللّٰهُ بِكُلِّ شَىْءٍ عَلِيْمٌ ۞

Wife Scourging

Men are in charge of women, because Allah hath
made the one of them to excel the other, and because
they spend of their property (for the support of
women). So good women are the obedient, guarding
in secret that which Allah hath guarded. As for those
from whom ye fear rebellion, admonish them and
banish them to beds apart, and scourge them. Then,
if they obey you, seek not a way against them. Lo!
Allah is ever High Exalted, Great.

◆ ◆

اَلرِّجَالُ قَوَّامُوْنَ عَلَى النِّسَآءِ بِمَا فَضَّلَ اللّٰهُ بَعْضَهُمْ
عَلٰى بَعْضٍ وَّبِمَآ اَنْفَقُوْا مِنْ اَمْوَالِهِمْ فَالصّٰلِحٰتُ
قٰنِتٰتٌ حٰفِظٰتٌ لِّلْغَيْبِ بِمَا حَفِظَ اللّٰهُ وَالّٰتِيْ تَخَافُوْنَ
نُشُوْزَهُنَّ فَعِظُوْهُنَّ وَاهْجُرُوْهُنَّ فِى الْمَضَاجِعِ

وَاضْرِبُوهُنَّ فَإِنْ أَطَعْنَكُمْ فَلَا تَبْغُوا عَلَيْهِنَّ
سَبِيلًا إِنَّ اللَّهَ كَانَ عَلِيًّا كَبِيرًا ۝ 27

Slave Girls Become Concubines

In addition to the four wives allowed by law, a
Muslim can have an unlimited number of slave girls
as concubines (sexual partners). This practice abro-
gates God's commands against fornication. Surat al-
Nisa (Women) 4:24 states,

> **And all married women are forbidden unto you
> save those (captives) whom your right hands possess.
> It is a decree of Allah for you. Lawful unto you are all
> beyond those mentioned, so that ye seek them with
> your wealth in honest wedlock, not debauchery. And
> those of whom ye seek content (by marrying them),
> give unto them their portions as a duty. And there is
> no sin for you in what ye do by mutual agreement
> after the duty (hath been done). Lo! Allah is ever
> Knower, Wise.**

◆ ◆

وَالْمُحْصَنَاتُ مِنَ النِّسَاءِ إِلَّا مَا مَلَكَتْ أَيْمَانُكُمْ
كِتَابَ اللَّهِ عَلَيْكُمْ وَأُحِلَّ لَكُمْ مَا وَرَاءَ ذَلِكُمْ أَنْ
تَبْتَغُوا بِأَمْوَالِكُمْ مُحْصِنِينَ غَيْرَ مُسَافِحِينَ فَمَا
اسْتَمْتَعْتُمْ بِهِ مِنْهُنَّ فَآتُوهُنَّ أُجُورَهُنَّ فَرِيضَةً
وَلَا جُنَاحَ عَلَيْكُمْ فِيمَا تَرَاضَيْتُمْ بِهِ مِنْ بَعْدِ
الْفَرِيضَةِ إِنَّ اللَّهَ كَانَ عَلِيمًا حَكِيمًا ۝

One wonders if the idea of sexual slavery is pro-
jected and perpetuated even into heaven itself once

we read in Surat al-Naba (The Tidings) 78:33, about the pleasures of Paradise including young women for concubines.

SWORD AND SLAVERY IN ISLAM

Intolerance and Religious Oppression

While at Mecca, Muhammad, realizing that he was surrounded by enemies, taught his followers toleration. He was simply a teacher commissioned to deliver a message. Even for a time at Medina, he was moderate. In Surat al-Baqarah (The Cow) 2, verse 256, it states,

> **There is no compulsion in religion. The right direction is henceforth distinct from error. And he who rejecteth false deities and believeth in Allah hath grasped a firm handhold which will never break. Allah is Hearer, Knower.**

◆ ◆

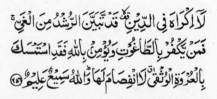

But it was very different after Muhammad's power was established. When the Muslim armies went forth to attack the surrounding tribes, or other nations, they offered them three options: accept Islam, pay tribute, or die by the sword (see the Repentance Surat, verse 29).

Let us put you in that position with these choices.

What would you and your family choose? Numerous Christians paid with their lives. Yet the numbers of those who took the easy way out were far greater. As a result, many church buildings were turned into mosques to please the conquering Muslims, and a shroud of spritual darkness covered huge areas of the Middle East, North Africa, and Spain. History informs us that the twelve months following Muhammad's death were spent in bitter, bloody battles to subdue the Arab tribes who became apostate.[28]

Around one million Armenian Christians were savagely slaughtered by the Turkish Muslims at the beginning of the twentieth century. Since then, an Armenian secret organization has assassinated a top Turkish leader or diplomat in some country in the world every year. This is the Armenian's method of impressing on the minds of the world the horror of that atrocity and their insistence on revenge.

According to a twenty-three-page report filed March 28, 1987, by Khartoum University professors Ushari Mahmud and Suleyman Ali Baldo, more than one thousand Dinka citizens, including women and children, were massacred in the western Sudan town of Diem in 1987. The *Baptist Record* newspaper of November 5, 1987, added that dozens of pastors have been killed and many churches destroyed since Islamic law was imposed in 1983, when Sudan was officially declared an Islamic republic.

Another report appeared in the *Baptist World Alliance* newsletter of September, 1987, indicating that 130 church buildings and pastor's homes of all Christian denominations in Kadona State in Nigeria were destroyed by Muslim rioters.

Surat al-Taubah (Repentance) 9:29 gives the following instructions for dealing with Jews and Christians:

Fight against such of those who have been given the Scripture as believe not in Allah nor the Last Day, and forbid not that which Allah hath forbidden by His messenger, and follow not the religion of truth, until they pay the tribute readily, being brought low.

◆ ◆

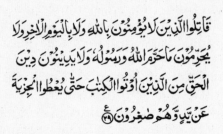

In Islamic countries, Christian missionaries are forbidden to preach to Muslims. Some governments even prohibit any Christian activity whatsoever in their particular countries (Libya, Afghanistan, and Saudi Arabia). In fact, a person has to be a Muslim in order to obtain citizenship in Saudi Arabia.

Religious liberty is unknown where Islam is the creed of the majority. Of course, Muslims are quick to take full advantage of the freedom of religion which is practiced throughout the Western world. This is demonstrated in the Muslim centers established in every major European and American city in the last fifteen years. France had but one mosque in 1974. Now there are fifteen hundred.

According to a tradition of Ibn 'Abbas and 'Ayisha, the prophet is said to have permitted the blood to be shed of him "who abandons his religion and separates himself from the community."[29] This practice continues in some Muslim countries. However, the backslider is to be given an opportunity to repent in the Western world, rather than have his blood shed. (See Surat al-Imran [The Family of 'Imran] 3:83–90.)

Slavery Sanctioned

Muhammad enjoined Muslims to treat slaves kindly, but Muslims are under no obligation to release them. Slaves, male or female, Muslim, heathen, Jew, or Christian, may be bought and sold like cattle. The female slaves are completely under the control of their masters. Surat al-Nisa (Women) 4:36 states:

And serve Allah. Ascribe nothing as partner unto Him. (Show) kindness unto parents, and unto near kindred, and orphans, and the needy, and unto the neighbour who is of kin (unto you) and the neighbour who is not of kin, and the fellow-traveller and the wayfarer and (the slaves) whom your right hands possess. Lo! Allah loveth not such as are proud and boastful . . . .

◆ ◆

وَاعْبُدُوا اللّٰهَ وَلَا تُشْرِكُوا بِهِ شَيْئًا وَبِالْوَالِدَيْنِ
اِحْسَانًا وَبِذِى الْقُرْبٰى وَالْيَتٰمٰى وَالْمَسٰكِيْنِ وَالْجَارِ
ذِى الْقُرْبٰى وَالْجَارِ الْجُنُبِ وَالصَّاحِبِ بِالْجَنْبِ وَ
ابْنِ السَّبِيْلِ وَمَا مَلَكَتْ اَيْمَانُكُمْ اِنَّ اللّٰهَ لَا يُحِبُّ
مَنْ كَانَ مُخْتَالًا فَخُوْرَانِ

When the Christian nations of Europe were trying to suppress slavery, Muslims were its greatest supporters and involved with slave trading. Up until a

few decades ago, Muslim Arabs converted a large
portion of Central Africa into a slave-hunting
ground. A gang would surround a peaceful village of
blacks, startle them by sudden gunshots, and shoot
any who attempted to defend themselves. They
would pinion the arms of the frightened male captives behind their backs, fasten their necks together
with cleft sticks, and then drive them, along with the
women and children, to the coast to be sold as
slaves.[30]

War Sanctioned

Surat al-Nisa (Women) 4:74 promises enormous
rewards to those who fight for Allah:

> **Let those fight in the way of Allah who sell the life
> of this world for the other. Whoso fighteth in the way
> of Allah, be he slain or be he victorious, on him We
> shall bestow a vast reward.**

◆ ◆

فَلْيُقَاتِلْ فِى سَبِيلِ اللهِ الَّذِينَ يَشْرُونَ الْحَيٰوةَ
الدُّنْيَا بِالْآخِرَةِ وَمَنْ يُقَاتِلْ فِى سَبِيلِ اللهِ فَيُقْتَلْ
اَوْ يَغْلِبْ فَسَوْفَ نُؤْتِيهِ اَجْرًا عَظِيمًا ۝

Muhammad gives himself a self-serving, so-called
divine order to fight. This is perhaps the basis for
calling Islam "the religion of the sword." Surat al-
Nisa (Women) 4:84 says:

> **So fight (O Muhammad) in the way of Allah—
> Thou art not taxed (with the responsibility for any-**

one) except for thyself—and urge on the believers.
Peradventure Allah will restrain the might of those
who disbelieve. Allah is stronger in might and
stronger in inflicting punishment.

◆ ◆

فَقَاتِلْ فِى سَبِيلِ اللهِ لَا تُكَلَّفُ إِلَّا نَفْسَكَ وَحَرِّضِ
الْمُؤْمِنِينَ عَسَى اللهُ أَنْ يَكُفَّ بَأْسَ الَّذِينَ
كَفَرُوا وَاللهُ أَشَدُّ بَأْسًا وَأَشَدُّ تَنْكِيلًا ۝

Finally, here is another gruesome order given by
Allah through Muhammad according to Surat al-
Ma'idah (Table Spread) 5:33:

The only reward of those who make war upon Allah and His messenger and strive after corruption in
the land will be that they will be killed or crucified,
or have their hands and feet on alternate sides cut
off, or will be expelled out of the land. Such will be
their degradation in the world, and in the Hereafter
theirs will be an awful doom.

◆ ◆

إِنَّمَا جَزَاءُ الَّذِينَ يُحَارِبُونَ اللهَ وَرَسُولَهُ وَيَسْعَوْنَ
فِى الْأَرْضِ فَسَادًا أَنْ يُقَتَّلُوا أَوْ يُصَلَّبُوا أَوْ تُقَطَّعَ
أَيْدِيهِمْ وَأَرْجُلُهُمْ مِنْ خِلَافٍ أَوْ يُنْفَوْا مِنَ الْأَرْضِ
ذَلِكَ لَهُمْ خِزْيٌ فِى الدُّنْيَا وَلَهُمْ فِى الْآخِرَةِ عَذَابٌ
عَظِيمٌ ۝

THE GOSPEL OF BARNABAS

One of the favorite sources used by Muslims to support their erroneous views of Christ and the Holy Bible is the spurious *Gospel of Barnabas*. Because of its importance as a Muslim apologetic tool, we must examine its veracity and claims.

HISTORY OF THE GOSPEL

The first mention of Barnabas is found in the New Testament book of Acts. He was a Cypriot Jew, a Levite by tribe, and the friend and sponsor of Saul of Tarsus.

The only known manuscript of the Gospel traditionally attributed to him in existence today is the eighteenth-century copy in Italian. No one has ever seen or mentioned an original copy in Arabic. Furthermore, there is no evidence to support such a claim that there is an authentic *Gospel of Barnabas*.[31]

Barnabas himself is mentioned in Acts 4:36, but with the name Joseph. He sold his field and gave the proceeds to the apostles to distribute among the needy. His kindness prompted them to call him Barnabas, which means "Son of Encouragement." In the so-called *Gospel*, the author makes a serious blunder by suggesting throughout his book that the name Barnabas was given him by Jesus and that he was one of the Twelve.

Later in Acts, we are told of the reluctance of the church in Jerusalem to accept Saul of Tarsus as a bonafide believer, since he had gained notoriety before his conversion as a persecutor of Christians:

But Barnabas took him and brought him (Saul) to the apostles. And he declared to them how he had seen the Lord on the road, and that He had spoken to him, and how he had preached boldly at Damascus in the name of Jesus.[32]

Here in Acts, Barnabas is the friend of Paul. However, in the *Gospel of Barnabas*, he is Paul's bitter enemy (see also Acts 11:26).

One of the most interesting events in the joint ministry of Barnabas and Paul is recounted in Acts 15:1–2. The author of the alleged *Gospel* declares emphatically that Paul's preaching of Jesus as the Son of God and his forcing of circumcision on the Gentiles was totally opposed by Barnabas; the account in Acts reveals the opposite:

And certain men came down from Judea and taught the brethren, "Unless you are circumcised according to the custom of Moses, you cannot be saved." Therefore, when Paul and Barnabas had no small dissension and dispute with them, they determined that Paul and Barnabas and certain others of them should go up to Jerusalem, to the apostles and elders, about this question.

The Gospel's Popularity Among Muslims

The current *Gospel of Barnabas* circulating among Muslims is popular because: (1) it counteracts "Pauline Christianity"; (2) its Jesus denies that He is the Messiah; and (3) its Jesus prophesies the coming of Muhammad. Yet, this eighteenth-century forgery is a false document from beginning to end. Christians and Muslims should reject it because it contradicts both the Bible and the Quran. The Bible states clearly in

Matthew 16:20, "Then He commanded His disciples that they should tell no one that He was Jesus the Christ." It was not time to reveal Himself yet.

The Quran declares emphatically in Surat al-Imran (The Family of 'Imran) 3:45:

> **O Mary! Lo! Allah giveth thee glad tidings of a word from Him, whose name is the Messiah, Jesus, son of Mary, illustrious in the world and the Hereafter, and one of those brought near (unto Allah).**

Pope Gelasius and the Gospel of Barnabas

Almost five centuries after Barnabas's death, the *Gospel of Barnabas* is mentioned by Pope Gelasius I (A.D. 492–496). Because of its heretical teaching, Pope Gelasius forbade Christians to read it. The book was Gnostic in origin and denied the deity of Christ as well as His incarnation. Such a book could have fallen into the hands of Muhammad, providing him with the glaring absurdities of the Quranic account of Christ.

Beyond the biblical account, there is nothing known of what happened to Barnabas except a tradition that states he ministered in his later years in Alexandria and Rome. One is surprised to learn that another apocryphal book, the *Epistle of Barnabas*, claimed Alexandria as its origin. This is not to be confused with the *Gospel of Barnabas* to which our Muslim friends attach so much import.

The Eighteenth-Century Copy is a Forgery

In the eighteenth century, an Italian copy of the *Gospel* surfaced. It is definitely a forgery because it quotes lines from the Quran, which, of course, dates to the seventh, not the first, century. The author seems to be familiar with the *Gospel* forbidden by Pope Gelasius and its heretical teachings. The author of this forgery also quotes Dante's *Divine Comedy*, which was written in the thirteenth century!

Although the *Gospel of Barnabas* was written as an ideal "Islamic Gospel," presenting the life of Christ as 'Isa of the Quran rather than the Lord Jesus Christ, no one with any intellectual integrity should ever accept it as anything but a forgery.

THE MYSTERY OF PBUH UNVEILED

Before we go on, we must deal with the term *pbuh*. This cryptic word is accepted by Muslims as an abbreviation for "peace be upon him." It is respectfully spoken as well as written after repeating the name of Muhammad. Although it is supposed to be the rendering of an Arabic phrase, it is actually not a true translation—only half of it is. The Arabic phrase is *Salla-llahu 'alayhi wassalam*. It occurs in the Quranic text and literally reads, "Lo! Allah and His angels pray upon the prophet. Oh yea who believe, pray on him and salute him with peace."

One is utterly confounded when the literal and real translation is understood. Why do our Muslim friends hide the true meaning of *pbuh?* Is it because the Arabic statement is embarrassing since it contradicts Muslim doctrine?

How is Allah supposed to pray to Muhammad and greet Him or anyone else for that matter? Does Allah pray? And if He does, to whom does He pray? Is this passage not contrary to Muslim theology, which teaches that Allah is prayed to but He never prays to anyone else? Or does Allah really pray to other human beings or only to Muhammad, Allah's own prophet? The confusion of this popular Islamic expression leaves one perplexed and hanging in the air.

THE EARLY ADVANCES OF ISLAM

Muslims sometimes cite the rapid spread of Islam as a proof of its divine origin, but other explanations may be given, some of which will be mentioned.

Suited for the Arabs

The predominant characteristics of the ancient Arab were an almost inconceivable vain-glory and self-conceit. He was never weary of contemplating and boasting of his own perfections. Muhammad was precisely the Prophet to win such a race. The Arab gloried in his language; Muhammad declared that it was a Divine language—the decrees of God had been written in it from all eternity. The Arab gloried in the traditional practices and customs of the desert—murder, predatory war, slavery, polygamy, concubinage. Muhammad impressed upon all these usages the seal of a Divine sanction. The Arab gloried in the holiness of Mecca. Muhammad affirmed it to be the single portal whereby men could enter into Paradise. In a word, he took the Arab people just as he found them, and declared all that they did to be very good and sacred from change. The fancied revelation gratified the vanity of the Arabs, but it pronounced on them a sentence of perpetual barbarism. Such as they were when the Prophet lived, such are the Arabs now. Their condition is proof that Islam is incapable of elevating a people to a higher level.[33]

It has been well said that "the Allah of Muhammad spares the sins the Arab loves." As an Arab, this writer will object strongly to such general characterization. Yet much truth is found in the above stated evaluation of my people.

Incentives of Plunder and Conquest

The Muslims' early raids were not aimed exclusively at conquest or conversion. Rather, they were simply part of the Bedouin skirmishing traditions and were carried out primarily for economic motivations—the booty and tribute that amounted to 50 percent of one's wealth were healthy incentives for impoverished desert warriors—thus the spread of Islam was more an economic phenomenon than a religious one. Barely a century after Muhammad's revelation claims began, Muslim soldiers and traders stood from Spain in the west, across North Africa and the Middle East, to the borders of China.

The Desert, the Camel, and the Horse Advantage

The Arab Bedouins were the masters of the desert. They trapped their enemies in sandstorms and dry riverbeds. Although they fought few battles, their victories were decisive. The Battle of Yarmuk, A.D. 631, led by by Khalid, was fought in a sandstorm, giving the Muslims the advantage, because they were more familiar than the Byzantines with desert warfare.

For mobility, the Bedouins used the swift, sure-footed Arabian horse, whose flaring nostrils can take in large quantities of air. The one-humped camel, which can drink twenty-five gallons of water in ten minutes and survive for days on a diet of thorny bushes and dried grass, was used for endurance. The camel has a double row of eyelashes and is able to close its nostrils for long periods of time as protection from sandstorms. Additionally, its soft, two-toed feet serve the same purpose as balloon tires on a dune buggy, and it can run faster than any other animal on the desert sands. The camel and the Arabian

horse gave the Arabs a definite advantage in warfare.

Expectation of Religious Merit
through Jihad (Holy War)

All who die "fighting in the ways of the Lord"
(Jihad) are richly rewarded, while those who draw
back are sorely punished, according to Surat al-Fath
(Victory) 48:16–17.

While attending a Foreign Missions Conference in
June 1986, in North Carolina, I sat in on the special
discussions on world religions. To my utter surprise,
the forty-minute slide presentation with its "expert"
narrator on world religions attempted to impress
the group of two hundred that Islam is *mistakenly*
called "the religion of the sword." I stood up and
challenged the speaker to explain how that was true
when the Quran commands Muhammad to fight and
Muhammad conducted twenty-seven battles and
planned thirty-nine others.

The Spiritual Vacuum Created by a
Lukewarm Christianity

Every human soul seeks the ultimate reality, the
truth. Whenever this goal eludes them, they find
substitutes in philosophy, materialism, religions,
cults, and various other substitutes. Even now we
live in a world of substitutes. We no longer want
sugar, therefore sweetener substitutes are offered.
"Coca-Cola" advertises that their product is "the real
thing!"

The majority of Christians of that time were neither living holy lives nor sharing their faith in order
to lead Muhammad and his contemporaries to
Christ Jesus, the ultimate reality. It is to our extreme

sorrow and eternal shame that the Arabs ended up following Muhammad instead of Christ. In fact, I am convinced, as an Arab, that Muhammad would have been one of the most powerful disciples of Jesus had he lived in Palestine during Jesus' earthly ministry.

However, Muhammad, instead, became a warrior, orator, and the uncrowned emperor of Arabia. He used religion as his literary theme and the sword to enforce his beliefs. The surats are titles of his poems and prose in an expressive language. Others before him had used prose and poetry effectively to win a place of honor by hanging them in the Ka'bah long before Muhammad's emergence on the horizon of Arabia.

The Bankruptcy of Heathenism

The Arab tribes were getting very restless. Their heathen practices never could satisfy the longing in their hearts. The 360 local idols increased their hunger for the truth. The idea of an Almighty Creator captured their imagination. This made Muhammad's teaching that much more attractive.

ISLAMIC GROWTH TODAY

Population Explosion in Muslim Countries

Our world's population grew to more than five billion in July 1986. The statistics provide evidence that the greatest increases in population have been occurring in Third World countries that are non-Christian, such as Hindu, Muslim, and Socialist countries. The belief, especially among the illiterate Muslims, is that Allah's favor upon a family is shown by its large size. Riches are also a sign of His favor;

thus, Arabs accept oil as evidence of His pleasure with them.

The children who are born in a Muslim home are automatically counted as Muslims, with no choice provided for anything else. One can deduce that this comprises the major reason for the increase in the number of Muslims in the world. Indonesia, with a population of 168 million, has more Muslims than the entire Arab world, then Bangladesh, Pakistan, and India in that order.

Oil Riches Used to Propagate Islam

The new resurgence of Islam is partially due to the billions of oil dollars reaped from the terrifying hikes in oil prices since 1973. Although the picture drastically changed in 1986, still petroleum dollars are being used to build Muslim centers in every major city in the world and every sizable city (over 500,000 population) in the United States. Literature, the Quran itself, and magazines proclaiming the praises of Islam are published and distributed daily throughout the world.

Accepting Islam for Economic Reasons

Many of the poorer countries of the Third World, particularly those in Africa, have denounced Israel, Christian missionaries, and the West in general in order to receive Muslim funds. With the influx of financial aid rushes in the Muslim religion and proselyting of citizens.

Non-Muslims Change Names for Employment

In Egypt alone there have been between 20,000 to 50,000 people every year for 25 years who changed their Christian names to Muslim names to gain employment in the Muslim-controlled economy. Prejudice in the predominantly Muslim countries has forced thousands of people to switch their names, if not their Christian allegiance.

A Fanatical Desire to Conquer the World

At the Battle of Tours, France, in A.D. 732, the Muslims were stopped in their tracks as their armies advanced to conquer the world. But now the cry is intensifying, as we heard in England in the summer of 1985: "If we can take London for Islam, we can take the world." Their effort is militant, represented by men like Ayatollah Khomeini of Iran, military regimes like Colonel Gadhafi of Libya, and the tragic civil war in Lebanon.

According to the United States State Department's Office of Counter-Terrorism, there were more than 800 international terrorist incidents in 1985, with 2,223 casualities in that bloody year. This was a 60 percent increase over the 1978 to 1983 yearly averages. Facts and figures indicate that the majority of these incidents were sponsored by fanatical Muslim groups.

Furthermore, it is believed that an extreme Muslim group, perhaps the Muslim Brotherhood, engineered the assassination of President Anwar Sadat of Egypt in 1983. Mr. Sadat, along with American President Carter and Israeli Prime Minister Begin of Israel, shared the 1978 Nobel Peace prize for their roles in the peace treaty between Egypt and Israel.

Nevertheless, something else must be recognized in connection with the Palestinian terrorists. I am a former Palestinian, but I cannot condone their atrocities carried out to force the world to take another

look at their desperate lot. Even as this book is being
prepared for the press, the whole world is sickened
at the six-month-long riots, demonstrations, and
bloodshed between Palestinian Arabs and Israelis
on the West Bank. Tragically, over two hundred Palestinian Arabs have been killed so far. But since we
have given the displaced Jews a homeland, why not
the Palestinians? After all, did they not live there for
centuries and know no other homeland except Palestine? Unless they are given the self-determination
to choose the West Bank as their Palestine or the
West Bank as a federation with Jordan, peace in the
Middle East will continue to be elusive. The Libyan
bombing by the United States in 1986 was merely a
treatment for the symptom of the illness. We must
still deal with the real problem—the Palestinian
homeland.

On February 4, 1987, I was one of numerous
speakers, greeters, and singers at the Annual National Prayer Breakfast held at the Washington Sher-
aton Hotel. Many dignitaries from the national and
international scene sat with me on the huge platform. The attendance was nearly two thousand. Ed-
win Meese, then Treasury Secretary of the United
States, spoke on terrorism. Reverend Stephen Olford
spoke on "A Biblical View of Israel." I was the only
Palestinian Arab on the program.

Before Meese delivered his address, Ed McAteer,
president of the Religious Roundtable, introduced
me as a member of a new P.L.O. He announced P.L.O.
stands for Palestinians Loving Others to a tu-
multuous round of applause. Greeting them first in
Arabic, then interpreting, "I greet you in the name of
Jesus, my Lord and Savior, and the man from my
hometown of Nazareth," I nearly brought the house
down.

In a brief, two-minute speech, I shared my testimony, and how God's love had changed my heart, attitude, and will, teaching me, through Christ, to forgive even those who were responsible for the deaths of my father, an uncle, and a cousin. Concluding, the Holy Spirit reminded me of an idea an Arab pastor from London was inspired to proclaim:

> **The Jews now have a place. But they have no peace. My Palestinian people someday will have a place. Yet that will not guarantee peace either. What we need is not just a place but a person, a person who declared, "If the son has made you free you are free indeed." And in the name of the Lord Jesus, the Prince of peace, I want to say to you I love you and God bless you.**

The response was electrifying, unbelievable, and very humbling. The audience and the speakers alike began to stand and applaud. Out of thirty or more participants on the program, mine was the only speech which received a standing ovation. To God be the glory! They did not stand for me but for Jesus Christ—the One who changed me.

Disaffection with Prejudiced Organized Religions

The prime example of this is none other than Cassius Clay of world boxing fame. When he became the world champion and discovered persistent prejudice against his color, he turned to the Black Muslims who welcomed him with open arms. The young boxer did not realize that prejudice—racial, sexual, national, and religious—permeated Islam. However, I have personal knowledge of a ten-hour visit between him and evangelist Billy Graham where

Mohammad Ali, now his Muslim name, admitted his dissatisfaction with Islam after embracing it for twenty years.

At least 6,000 Britons have sought Islam as a result of their disaffection with organized Christianity in England in the past five years. One such person is the famous singer Cat Stevens, a pop musician.

In other words, no matter what one's religion is, it does not provide the ultimate reality. A person needs a relationship with Christ Jesus because only He can satisfy our souls.

Immigration of Muslims into the West

The number of Muslims in the West has not increased because of conversion, but because of immigration of Muslims by the millions to the West. The recent changes in immigration laws and the leniency of the previously restricted quotas from Third World countries has brought this Muslim influx.

Marriages of Younger Muslim Men to non-Muslim Women

The thousands of Muslim students who travel to study in the numerous institutions of higher learning in Europe and the United States find the alluring and sophisticated girls here much more attractive than their docile counterparts at home. Of course, a further truth is obvious to any observing individual. Many young men would rather marry and live in the West with its freedoms and opportunities than return to the old-fashioned traditions and modern tragedies of the war-torn Muslim world and its instability.

Sign of the Early Return of Christ

We are to recognize that the anti-Christ is not only a mere man who appears shortly before the coming of the true Christ, but also a movement which denies that Jesus of Nazareth is the Son of God. I know of no more militant movement on earth equal to Islam (except communism) in its fulfillment of this role. The increase in the followers of such a religion indicates the end is not far away. The certain judgment by Christ of this ungodly world is getting nearer.

The recent famine calamities which occurred in Ethiopia fulfill the predictions of Christ. The death of two thousand in Bhopal, India, because of the poisonous gas, the terror in Mexico City due to the destructive earthquake, and the unexpected tragedy in the Cameroon with the underground volcanic gas have rocked millions into wondering if we are indeed approaching the end time. Jesus revealed these shocking events as stark realities ushering in the judgment of the world.

> "And you will hear of wars and rumors of wars. See that you are not troubled; for all these things must come to pass, but the end is not yet. For nation will rise against nation, and kingdom against kingdom. And there will be famines, pestilences, and earthquakes in various places. All these are the beginning of sorrows. Then many false prophets will rise up and deceive man."[34]

It is madness for a sensible person not to prepare himself for the coming of the end. Everybody seems to sense a syndrome of gloom and the coming of a cloud of doom. Yet we have the Good News: Jesus Christ came to save sinners. Are you ready to receive Him as your compassionate Redeemer? Because if

you do not, He will have to become your just Judge
and declare: "I tell you I do not know you, where you
are from. Depart from Me, all you workers of iniquity."[35] Jesus is still promising, "Come to Me, all you
who labor and are heavy laden, and I will give you
rest" (Matthew 11:28). Why wait any longer?

Let us therefore pray and labor with such love,
dedication, and understanding that Muslims may
come to the light of Christ. Pray with me that the veil
of Muhammad shall be removed from their groping
eyes to see the loving face of God, in the person of
His only Son, Jesus, who died to set them and all of
mankind free.

CHAPTER SIX

THE QURAN EXPOSED

❊ ❊ ❊

Thus We have revealed it as a Lecture in Arabic, and have displayed therein certain threats, that peradventure they may keep from evil or that it may cause them to take heed. . . .

◆ ◆

وَكَذَلِكَ أَنْزَلْنَهُ قُرْآنًا عَرَبِيًّا وَصَرَّفْنَا فِيهِ مِنَ الْوَعِيدِ لَعَلَّهُمْ يَتَّقُونَ أَوْ يُحْدِثُ لَهُمْ ذِكْرًا ۝ [1]

Say: Verily, though mankind and Jinn should assemble to produce the like of this Qur'ān, they could not produce the like thereof though they were helpers one of another.

◆ ◆

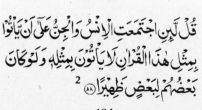

قُلْ لَّئِنِ اجْتَمَعَتِ الْإِنْسُ وَالْجِنُّ عَلَى أَن يَأْتُوا بِمِثْلِ هَذَا الْقُرْآنِ لَا يَأْتُونَ بِمِثْلِهِ وَلَوْ كَانَ بَعْضُهُمْ لِبَعْضٍ ظَهِيرًا ۝ [2]

IS THE QURAN A MIRACLE?

It is claimed by Arab scholars that the literary style of the Quran is superior to all other books in the Arabic language. Although this is not totally true, this no more proves its inspiration than a man's strength demonstrates his wisdom, or a woman's beauty her virtue. Only by its teachings, principles, and content can a book be judged rightly, not by its eloquence, elegance, or poetic strength. By reading the life of Muhammad and the history of the Quran, one could conclude that the Quran reflects the life and character of Muhammad. The following is the opinion of the famed Dr. Tisdall, who is one of the most capable twentieth-century studies of the Quran.

The Qur'an breathes the air of the desert, it enables us to hear the battle-cries of the Prophet's followers as they rushed to the onset, it reveals the working of Muhammad's own mind, and shows the gradual declension of his character as he passed from the earnest and sincere though visionary enthusiast into the conscious imposter and open sensualist.[3]

WAS MUHAMMAD REALLY ILLITERATE?

Modern-day scholars of the Quran have begun to accept the term "Gentile Prophet" as a more correct term for "Al Nabi Al Ummi," "The Illiterate Prophet" (Surat al-A'raf [The Heights] 7:158).

OTHER SIMILAR POEMS ARE AVAILABLE

The Quran is not a unique literary masterpiece. There are numerous examples of other beautifully

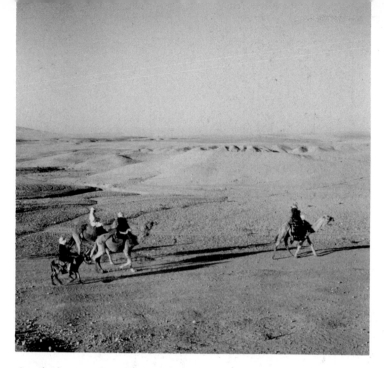

Camel riders near the Red Sea. The camel is the ship of the desert. It can go without water for weeks and survive intense heat and sandstorms. In Muhammad's day, camels gave Muslims a clear advantage in warfare.

Bedouin chieftains in traditional dress. In spite of the desert's heat, Bedouins commonly wear long, wool garments. Although the heavy wool makes them perspire profusely, it also retains their perspiration, thereby creating a cool environment for them.

TOP: A Bedouin family in Atur, Saudi Arabia

MIDDLE: Two Bedouin women dressed in garments dating back to medieval days in style

BOTTOM: A bustling outdoor market in Bethlehem, Israel

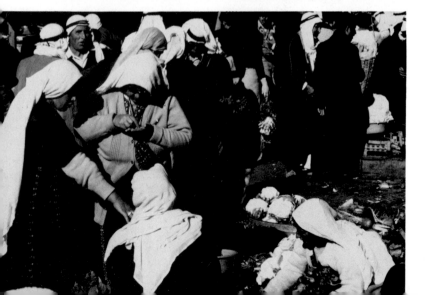

A camel rider outside of Jerusalem, on a hill overlooking the Dome of the Rock—one of the oldest and most beautiful mosques in the world. The Islamic shrine stands on Mount Moriah, a site revered by the three great monotheistic faiths—Judaism, Christianity, and Islam.

RIGHT: Muslims bowing in front of the Dome of the Rock with their bodies turned toward Mecca. The Dome of the Rock was first built in A.D. 691. The shrine's exterior is an octagon, with each side measuring 63 feet in width. The dome rises 108 feet from the ground and has a diameter of 78 feet.

The Dome of the Rock's interior. Although the mosque's architectural style is Byzantine, its elaborate decorations are oriental. Marble slabs up to 18 feet high, walls decorated with gleaming Persian tiles, and aluminum plates impregnated with gold make the mosque a striking sight.

Muslims arriving in Mecca, the goal of their pil-
grimmage. Every Muslim is expected to make
at least one trip to Mecca in his or her lifetime.
Since the journey can be especially arduous on
the elderly or infirm, they are allowed to send
someone in their place. This journey plays an
essential role in a Muslim's salvation.

Worshipers around the Ka'bah shrine in Mecca. One of the most holy sites to Muslims is the Ka'bah, a cubelike shrine 50 feet high and nearly 40 feet square in the courtyard of the Sacred Mosque—the place toward which Muslims face in daily prayer. Muslims believe that the Ka'bah is the first shrine erected by Abraham and Ishmael. Within its walls and around its perimeter, about 360 idols were eventually set up and left standing until Muhammad destroyed them and allegedly reestablished the Abrahamic religion in A.D. 632. The only object he left unharmed in the Ka'bah was a wall painting of the likeness of the baby Jesus resting in Mary's arms. During Islamic religious ceremonies in Mecca, worshipers are transformed into ghostlike figures as they circle the Ka'bah.

Arabesque depicting in Arabic John 1:14: "And the Word became flesh and dwelt among us, and we beheld His glory, the glory as of the only begotten of the Father, full of grace and truth."

Decorative cross with an Arabic translation of John 3:16: "'For God so loved the world that He gave His only begotten Son, that whoever believes in Him should not perish but have everlasting life.'"

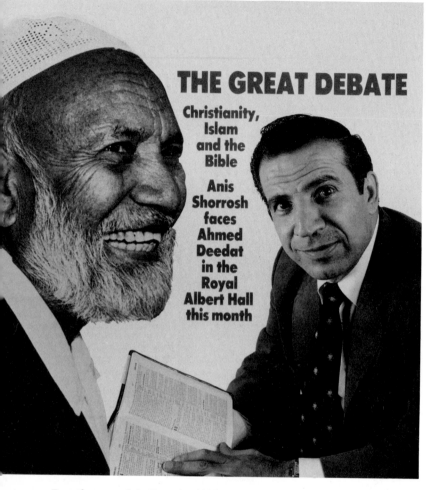

THE GREAT DEBATE

Christianity,
Islam
and the
Bible

Anis
Shorrosh
faces
Ahmed
Deedat
in the
Royal
Albert Hall
this month

From the cover of the December 1985 issue
of the *Today* magazine, London, England

crafted poems, epics, and scripture from the classical period, many much older than the Quran.

The Rig-Veda of the Aryans of India was composed in Sanskrit between 1000 and 1500 years B.C. It is larger than the Quran, similar in nature, and was written by several men. A blind poet by the name of Homer is responsible for the two most eloquent poems in the exquisite Greek language, *The Odyssey* and *Illiad*. What should we say of the *Gilgamesh Epic*, the *Code of Hammurabi*, the *Book of the Dead* from ancient Egypt, and other classical masterpieces? Just because these materials are unique or eloquent does not necessarily give them the status of divine inspiration.

Imraul Qais, some of whose poems were among the famed *Muallaqat* (Suspended Poems) at Ka'bah, was one of the most expressive of the ancient Arab poets before Muhammad. In one of his poems, which was not part of the *Muallaqat* collection, appear four verses which were "borrowed" and inserted by Muhammad into the Quran (Surat al-Qamar [The Moon] 54:1, 29, 31, and 46).

Imraul Qais's daughter once heard this Surat recited aloud. She immediately recognized her father's poem and demanded to know how her father's verses had become part of a divine revelation, supposedly preserved on stone tablets in heaven![4]

OLD OR NEW REVELATION?

Revelation is the process by which God imparts to man truths which cannot be known naturally. For example, since man was not created until the sixth day, God had to reveal to Moses details reflected in Genesis 1–5.

The uniqueness of the Quran is also claimed to be

due to the information it presents regarding the past and the future. However, these claims cannot be substantiated.

Quranic Teachings

The teachings of the Quran concerning God, creation, Adam and Eve, sin, the Fall, angels, heaven, hell, Abraham, Moses, the Hebrew race, and prophets had already been revealed and proclaimed in the Old Testament. Muhammad added nothing new. Perhaps some of this was new to his hearers, but Jews and Christians knew even more from their Bibles. Muhammad's revelations were in no way superior to the revelations given by earlier prophets; neither did they unquestionably provide evidence of a fresh divine revelation. All the above-mentioned truths and more had been revealed and taught for centuries before the birth of Muhammad.

One of the perplexing statements in the Quran can be construed as a revelation indeed, but not a divine one! It is the unequivocal Quranic declaration that General Alexander the Great of Macedonia was a prophet. How on earth or in heaven can a heathen general whose debauchery and drunkenness contributed to his death at thirty-three ever be considered a prophet of God Almighty? That is some revelation in the "Book whose tablets are preserved in heaven" (Surat al-Kahf [The Cave] 18:83–100).

Theological authorities demand that six conditions be fulfilled before any supposed revelation can be accepted as true revelation.

(1) It must satisfy the yearning of the human spirit to obtain eternal happiness.

(2) It must coincide with the conscience, which is the moral law written in man's mind.

(3) It must reveal God's true attributes.

(4) It must confirm man's reasoning that God is one.

(5) It must make very plain the way of salvation.

(6) It must reveal God Himself in books, through prophets, and in person.[5]

Neither Muhammad nor the Quran fulfills all of these six requirements. The Quran only fulfills the fourth criterion. The other five are missing.

Muhammad's Prophecies

As to the so-called prophecies of Muhammad, no one who diligently studies these verses can accept such a claim. Let us examine some of the twenty-one passages which are claimed as prophetic. The first group deals with promises of victory.

Such claims are made before a battle to infuse courage in the fighting forces. One of any two opposing generals who makes such a prediction will of necessity win. Yet that victory can by no means constitute a claim by the general that he is a prophet, or as Muhammad was declared to be, "the Seal of the Prophets" or a "Messenger of Allah."

There is no doubt that Augustus Caesar, Ghangiz Khan, Taimur Lang, and even the famed Arab warrior Salah Eddin promised their followers success in battle. Yet no one considers that the fulfillment of their promises makes them prophets or apostles of God! The fighting Arabs became almost invincible due to their belief in Muhammad's divine mission to wage war against the Quraish, the Jewish tribes, neighboring countries, and the world. What more weighty reason could any human being find to achieve than being told "Allah Almighty commands it and that is His Divine Desire"? In fact, one finds this clearly enunciated in the following story related in *Hayatul Qulub* (vol. 2, chap. 30):

> Muhammad informed his Companions that the caravan had passed and that the Quraish were advancing towards them, and that God Most High had commanded him to fight a Jihâd with them. On hearing this his Companions became very much afraid and very anxious . . . and cried out loud and wept. Therefore, to encourage them and enable them to fight manfully a battle upon which so much depended, Muhammad repeated Sûrat al-Qamar (The Moon) 54:44, 45.[6]

The promise of victory, Muhammad declared, came from God. The Muslims were encouraged tremendously and fought valiantly and won. Can these words be justly called prophetic?

One should never overlook that biblical standards of prophecy demanded 100 percent accuracy, according to Deuteronomy 18:20–22:

> But the prophet who presumes to speak a word in My name, which I have not commanded him to speak, or who speaks in the name of other gods, that prophet shall die. And if you say in your heart, "How shall we know the word which the Lord has not spoken?"—when a prophet speaks in the name of the Lord, if the thing does not happen or come to pass, that is the thing which the Lord has not spoken; the prophet has spoken it presumptuously; you shall not be afraid of him.

The following Quranic passage is supposed to validate the prophethood of Muhammad:

> The Romans have been defeated in the nearer land, and they, after their defeat, will be victorious within ten years—Allah's is the command in the former case and in the latter—and in that day believers will rejoice.

◆ ◆

الٓمّٓ ۚ

غُلِبَتِ الرُّوۡمُ ۙ

فِىۡۤ اَدۡنَى الۡاَرۡضِ وَهُمۡ مِّنۡۢ بَعۡدِ غَلَبِهِمۡ سَيَغۡلِبُوۡنَ ۙ

فِىۡ بِضۡعِ سِنِيۡنَ ۙ لِلّٰهِ الۡاَمۡرُ مِنۡ قَبۡلُ وَمِنۡۢ بَعۡدُ ؕ

وَيَوۡمَئِذٍ يَّفۡرَحُ الۡمُؤۡمِنُوۡنَ ۙ ⁷

But this alleged prophecy has several problems. First, there is no conclusive evidence of when the prophecy was first given, making it impossible to date the ten-year limit accurately. Second, the passage is ambiguous in several places since it is written in Cufik Arabic, which does not use vowels. Third, the Muslims' rising power was evident to everyone around, and it didn't take a prophet to predict their eventual triumph over the infidels. Fourth, the prophecy declared victory within ten years. In reality, it took Muhammad and his armies twelve years from the generally accepted date of the prophecy to subdue these enemies. Fifth, the Arabic word *bid'i*, which is translated as "ten years," signifies not ten years but no less than three years and no more than nine. In other words, Muhammad missed the prophecy's deadline by at least three years!

The Human Source of the Quran

Having studied the Quran, I think it was composed this way. Muhammad was collecting his prose and poems and trying to edit them before publishing them when he unexpectedly died. In my opinion, this is the reason the narratives are so disjointed

and even at times seem contradictory. Any Arabic
language expert with patience can eliminate this
problem by reorganizing the narratives into logical
sequence.

There is hardly a single complete narrative on any
given topic recorded in one Surat. Instead, bits and
pieces are recorded here and there. In fact, the entire
Quran, according to scholarly investigation, must be
read backwards to give the correct chronological
and logical perspective.

Surely, if God speaks only Arabic and sent down
the Quran from heaven in Arabic, he would certainly
have used more discretion, better organization, and
a glowing sequence of facts and events. The chaotic
condition of the English translation of the Quran is a
glaring example of the disorganization in the original Cufik dialect of Arabic.

How can the one God send two clashing revelations, the Bible and the Quran, to confuse men? It is
not the Bible which is contradictory and confusing.
No, it is definitely the Quran. If Muslims insist that
the Bible is corrupt, I will have to declare that the
evidence, much of which I have presented in this
book, vindicates the Bible and condemns the Quran.
No reasonable person presented with the evidence
can believe otherwise.

MISTAKES IN THE ARABIC
OF THE QURAN

Muslims believe Arabic is the language of Allah.
They believe that the Arabic Quran is the perfect, ex-
act representation of Allah's words. That is why only
the Arabic Quran is considered authoritative and
why so many Muslims who know no Arabic memorize portions of the Quran in Arabic. However,

Muhammad used a number of foreign words or phrases in the Quran, leaving questioners wondering if "God's language" is deficient enough to need help from other languages.

Foreign Words

(1) "Pharaoh" comes from the Egyptian language and means king or potentate. It is repeated eighty-four times in the Quran.

(2) "Adam" and "Eden," repeated twenty-four times, are Accadian words. A more correct term for "Adam" in Arabic would be *basharan* or *insan*, meaning mankind. "Eden" would be the Arabic *janna*, or garden.

(3) "Abraham" comes from the Assyrian language, and would be more accurately represented by the Arabic *Abu Raheem*.

(4) *Haroot* and *Maroot* are Persian, not Arabic, names of angels. Additionally, *Sirat* should have been *Altareeq*, which means "the path." *Hoor* is the Persian word whose Arabic counterpart is *Tilmeeth*, meaning "a disciple." *Jinn* normally refers to good spirits or evil demons, and the Arabic word is *ruh*. *Firdaus* is a Persian word which means *Jannah* in Arabic and refers to the highest, or seventh, heaven.

(5) *Taboot, taghouth, zakat, malakout* are Syriac words.

(6) *Heber, sakinah, maoon, turat,* and *jehannim* come from the Hebrew language.

(7) *Injil*, which means "gospel," comes from the Greek language, and the correct word in Arabic is *bisharah*.

Poor Grammar

(1) Surat al-Baqara (The Cow) 2:177.

The word *Sabireen* in Arabic, صَابِرِينَ , should

have been *Sabiroon,* صَابِرُونَ , because of its position in the sentence.

(2) Surat al-A'raf (The Heights) 7:160.

"And we divided them into twelves tribes"

اثْنَتَى عَشَرَةَ أَسْبَاطاً , should have been

أَثْنَى عَشَرَ سِبْطاً

(3) Surat al-Nisa (Women) 4:162.

The statement "especially the diligent in prayer,"

وَالْمُقِيمُونَ الصَّلاةَ , should have been

وَالْمُقِيمِينَ الصَّلاةَ

(4) Surat al-Ma'idah (The Table Spread) 5:69.

Al Sabieen, الصَّابِئِينَ , is the more correct

Arabic than *Sabioon* الصَّابِئُونَ

(5) Surat al-Munafiqun (The Hypocrites) 63:10.

The word أَكُنُ , "I shall be," must be أَكُونُ according to its position in a correct Arabic sentence.

(6) Surat al-Imran (The Family of 'Imran) 3:59.

The words كُنْ فَيَكُونُ are a gross error in Arabic. The grammatical structure demands

كُنْ فَكَانَ

THE QURAN MISQUOTES THE OLD TESTAMENT

Adam and Eve and Their Two Sons

But (the other's) mind imposed on him the killing of his brother, so he slew him and became one of the losers. Then Allah sent a raven scratching up the ground, to show him how to hide his brother's naked corpse. He said: Woe unto me! Am I not able to be as this raven and so hide my brother's naked corpse? And he became repentant. For that cause We decreed for the Children of Israel that whosoever killeth a human being for other than manslaughter or corruption in the earth, it shall be as if he had killed all mankind, and whoso saveth the life of one, it shall be as if he had saved the life of all mankind. Our messengers came unto them of old with clear proofs (of Allah's sovereignty) but afterwards, lo! many of them became prodigals in the earth.

◆ ◆

اِنِّیْۤ اُرِیْدُ اَنْ تَبُوۤأَ بِاِثْمِیْ وَاِثْمِكَ فَتَكُوْنَ مِنْ اَصْحَابِ النَّارِۚ وَذٰلِكَ جَزٰٓؤُا الظّٰلِمِیْنَ ۞

فَطَوَّعَتْ لَهٗ نَفْسُهٗ قَتْلَ اَخِیْهِ فَقَتَلَهٗ فَاَصْبَحَ مِنَ الْخٰسِرِیْنَ ۞

فَبَعَثَ اللّٰهُ غُرَابًا یَّبْحَثُ فِی الْاَرْضِ لِیُرِیَهٗ كَیْفَ یُوَارِیْ سَوْءَةَ اَخِیْهِ ۚ قَالَ یٰوَیْلَتٰۤی اَعَجَزْتُ اَنْ اَكُوْنَ مِثْلَ هٰذَا الْغُرَابِ فَاُوَارِیَ سَوْءَةَ اَخِیْ ۚ فَاَصْبَحَ مِنَ النّٰدِمِیْنَ ۞

مِنْ اَجْلِ ذٰلِكَ ۚ كَتَبْنَا عَلٰی بَنِیْۤ اِسْرَآءِیْلَ اَنَّهٗ مَنْ

قَتَلَ نَفْسًا بِغَيْرِ نَفْسٍ أَوْ فَسَادٍ فِي الْأَرْضِ فَكَأَنَّمَا
قَتَلَ النَّاسَ جَمِيعًا وَمَنْ أَحْيَاهَا فَكَأَنَّمَا أَحْيَا النَّاسَ
جَمِيعًا وَلَقَدْ جَاءَتْهُمْ رُسُلُنَا بِالْبَيِّنَاتِ ثُمَّ إِنَّ كَثِيرًا
مِنْهُمْ بَعْدَ ذَلِكَ فِي الْأَرْضِ لَمُسْرِفُونَ ⁸ ۝

The biblical record is quite different, omitting the raven and the burial method:

> **Now Adam knew Eve his wife, and she conceived and bore Cain, and said, "I have gotten a man from the LORD." Then she bore again, this time his brother Abel. Now Abel was a keeper of sheep, but Cain was a tiller of the ground.**
>
> **And in the process of time it came to pass that Cain brought an offering of the fruit of the ground to the LORD. Abel also brought of the firstlings of his flock and of their fat. And the LORD respected Abel and his offering, but He did not respect Cain and his offering. And Cain was very angry, and his countenance fell.**
>
> **So the LORD said to Cain, "Why are you angry? And why has your countenance fallen? If you do well, will you not be accepted? And if you do not do well, sin lies at the door. And its desire is for you, but you should rule over it."**
>
> **Now Cain talked with Abel his brother; and it came to pass, when they were in the field, that Cain rose against Abel his brother and killed him.⁹**

The difference in these passages between the Quran and the Bible is traced to Pirke Rabbi Eleazer, as we noted in chapter four.

> **Adam and Eve, sitting by the corpse (of Abel) wept not knowing what to do, for they had as yet no**

**knowledge of burial. A raven coming up, took the
dead body of its fellow (mate), and having scratched
up the earth, buried it thus before their eyes. Adam
said, Let us follow the example of the raven, and so
taking up Abel's body buried it at once.[10]**

Abraham is considered the patriarch of both the
Jews (through his son Isaac) and the Arabs (through
his son Ishmael). Abraham was called a Hebrew
(Genesis 14:13), and this term was used ever after to
refer to Isaac's children, the Jews.

Since the Muslims also call Abraham Father, there
are several Quranic passages referring to him. However, the Quran's Abraham is not at all like the Abraham of the Bible's earlier record.

Abraham in the Quran

**Then he reduced them to fragments, all save the
chief of them, that haply they might have recourse to
it.**

**They said: Who hath done this to our gods? Surely
it must be some evil-doer. They said: We heard a
youth make mention of them, who is called Abraham. They said: Then bring him (hither) before the
people's eyes that they may testify. They said: Is it
thou who hast done this to our gods, O Abraham?**

**He said: But this, their chief hath done it. So ques-
tion them, if they can speak. Then gathered they
apart and said: Lo! ye yourselves are the wrongdoers.
And they were utterly confounded, and they said:
Well thou knowest that these speak not. He said:
Worship ye then instead of Allah that which cannot
profit you at all nor harm you? Fie on you and all
that ye worship instead of Allah! Have ye then no
sense?**

**They cried: Burn him and stand by your gods, if ye
will be doing.**

We said: O fire, be coolness and peace for Abraham!

Then turned he to their gods and said: Will ye not eat? What aileth you that ye speak not?

Then he attacked them, striking with his right hand. And (his people) came toward him, hastening.

He said: Worship ye that which ye yourselves do carve when Allah hath created you and what ye make?

They said: Build for him a building and fling him in the red-hot fire.

◆ ◆

فَجَعَلَهُمْ جُذَاذًا إِلَّا كَبِيرًا لَّهُمْ لَعَلَّهُمْ إِلَيْهِ يَرْجِعُونَ ۝

قَالُوا مَنْ فَعَلَ هَذَا بِآلِهَتِنَا إِنَّهُ لَمِنَ الظَّالِمِينَ ۝

قَالُوا سَمِعْنَا فَتًى يَذْكُرُهُمْ يُقَالُ لَهُ إِبْرَاهِيمُ ۝

قَالُوا فَأْتُوا بِهِ عَلَى أَعْيُنِ النَّاسِ لَعَلَّهُمْ يَشْهَدُونَ ۝

قَالُوا أَأَنْتَ فَعَلْتَ هَذَا بِآلِهَتِنَا يَا إِبْرَاهِيمُ ۝

قَالَ بَلْ فَعَلَهُ كَبِيرُهُمْ هَذَا فَاسْأَلُوهُمْ إِنْ كَانُوا يَنْطِقُونَ ۝

فَرَجَعُوا إِلَى أَنْفُسِهِمْ فَقَالُوا إِنَّكُمْ أَنْتُمُ الظَّالِمُونَ ۝

ثُمَّ نُكِسُوا عَلَى رُؤُوسِهِمْ لَقَدْ عَلِمْتَ مَا هَؤُلَاءِ يَنْطِقُونَ ۝

قَالَ أَفَتَعْبُدُونَ مِنْ دُونِ اللهِ مَا لَا يَنْفَعُكُمْ شَيْئًا وَلَا يَضُرُّكُمْ ۝

أُفٍّ لَكُمْ وَلِمَا تَعْبُدُونَ مِنْ دُونِ اللهِ أَفَلَا

تَعْقِلُونَ ۝

قَالُوا حَرِّقُوهُ وَانْصُرُوا آلِهَتَكُمْ إِنْ كُنْتُمْ فَاعِلِينَ ۝

قُلْنَا يَا نَارُ كُونِي بَرْدًا وَسَلَامًا عَلَى إِبْرَاهِيمَ ۝ 11

فَرَاغَ إِلَى آلِهَتِهِمْ فَقَالَ أَلَا تَأْكُلُونَ ۝

مَا لَكُمْ لَا تَنْطِقُونَ ۝

فَرَاغَ عَلَيْهِمْ ضَرْبًا بِالْيَمِينِ ۝

فَأَقْبَلُوا إِلَيْهِ يَزِفُّونَ ۝

قَالَ أَتَعْبُدُونَ مَا تَنْحِتُونَ ۝

وَاللَّهُ خَلَقَكُمْ وَمَا تَعْمَلُونَ ۝

قَالُوا ابْنُوا لَهُ بُنْيَانًا فَأَلْقُوهُ فِي الْجَحِيمِ ۝ 12

No such record is found in the Bible. However, *Midrash Rabbah*, a second-century A.D. Jewish folktale, features the same story nearly four centuries before it found its way into the Quran.

> Terah (Abraham's father) used to make idols. A woman carrying in her hand a cup of wheat flour said (to Abraham), place this (food) before the idols . . . one said I will eat it first, then another said I'll eat it first. Abraham getting up took his staff in his hand, and having broken the idols with it . . . placed the staff in the hand of the largest (idol). His father coming up said: Who has done this?
>
> Abraham said . . . the largest one took the staff and broke them all to pieces. His father said, why do you tell such a foolish tale? Do these (idols) know anything? Nimrod said: If you argue with me about things which I am unable to worship other than fire, into it I will cast you. So let the god you worship

deliver you therefrom. So Abraham went down into
the flames and remained there safe and unhurt.[13]

Abraham in the Bible

Now Terah lived seventy years, and begot Abram,
Nahor, and Haran. This is the genealogy of Terah:
Terah begot Abram, Nahor, and Haran. Haran begot
Lot. And Haran died before his father Terah in his
native land, in Ur of the Chaldeans. Then Abram and
Nahor took wives: the name of Abram's wife was
Sarai, and the name of Nahor's wife, Milcah, the
daughter of Haran the father of Milcah and the fa-
ther of Iscah. But Sarai was barren; she had no child.
And Terah took his son Abraham and his grandson
Lot, the son of Haran, and his daughter-in-law Sarai,
his son Abram's wife, and they went out with them
from Ur of the Chaldeans to go to the land of Canaan; and they came to Haran and dwelt there.[14]

Abraham's father is wrongly called Azar in the
Quran (Surat al-An'am [Cattle] 6:74). The Bible,
however, which is much earlier than the Quran,
names him correctly as Terah (Genesis 11:26).[15]

Summary of Quranic Errors
Concerning Abraham

Abraham didn't have two sons, but eight. (Genesis
25:13–15); not two wives, but three. He did not raise
his descendants in the Valley of Mecca, but in
Hebron (Genesis 13:6–12), which is called by his
name in Arabic to this day, El Khaleel, The friend of
God (Isaiah 41:8). Genesis 11:28–31 tells us that his
hometown was Ur in Chaldea, not Mecca. He wan-
dered through Haran as Genesis 11:31 tells us, not
Arabia. He went to Canaan as God instructed him in

Genesis 12:4–6, not to Mecca's valley. There is no record that Abraham and Ishmael went to Arabia and built the Ka'bah in Mecca, although Abraham did spend several years in Egypt.

In Surat al-Saffat (Those Who Set the Ranks) 37:100–112, we read of Abraham's sacrifice of his son. But which son? The Bible states it was Isaac (see Genesis 22), yet the Quran intimates it was Ishmael.[16] When legends are told and retold, they do change. The common denominator of the original story was Abraham, and it was easier to get the story mixed up by oral tradition than by the written one.

We Arabs have considered Abraham as our earliest father through Hagar and Ishmael. Historically, however, the first father of the Arabs, according to Genesis 10:25–30, was Qahtan or Joktan. The names of some of his sons are reflected in geographical locations in contemporary Arabia, such as Sheba, Hazarmaveth, Ophir, and Havilah. A third strain came from Abraham's nephew, Lot, whose two daughters gave birth from incest to the Moabites and Ammonites (see Genesis 24). A fourth strain came from Jacob's twin brother, Esau, according to Genesis 36. Finally, and most people forget this strain, Keturah, Abraham's third wife, gave birth to six sons, who also became forefathers of more Arab tribes.

The struggle between Isaac's and Ishmael's descendants for the blessing of Abraham (see Genesis 22:17) continues till this very day. Yet it is neither Isaac nor Ishmael who were to bless the world, but Messiah Jesus, as Galatians 3:16 affirms:

Now to Abraham and his Seed were the promises made. He does not say, "And to seeds," as of many, but as of one, "And to your Seed," who is Christ.

God still promised to bless Ishmael, too. But his special covenant was established with Isaac, as Genesis 17:18–19 reveals:

> **And Abraham said to God, "Oh, that Ishmael might live before You!"**
> **Then God said: "No, Sarah your wife shall bear you a son, and you shall call his name Isaac; I will establish My covenant with him for an everlasting covenant, and with his descendants after him."**

The four promises made to the Arabs by God through Ishmael have been fulfilled precisely:

> **"And as for Ishmael, I have heard you. Behold, I have blessed him, and will make him fruitful and will multiply him exceedingly. He shall beget twelve princes, and I will make him a great nation. But My covenant I will establish with Isaac."[17]**

(1) With three-fourths of the free world's oil reserves, the Arabs believe they are definitely blessed.

(2) There are 167 million Arabs as of 1987, which fulfills "will multiply him exceedingly." Ten million Arabs claim Christianity.[18]

(3) "He shall beget twelve princes" is fulfilled in that there are almost twice that many countries claiming to be Arab.[19]

(4) "I will make him a great nation" was fulfilled when the Muslim Empire was a reality from the seventh to the twelfth centuries.

MOSES

Moses wrote the first five books of the Old Testament roughly two thousand years before Muhammad delivered the Quran. Parts of the Pentateuch (the first five books of the Bible) tell us about Moses' birth, childhood, young adulthood, exile from Egypt, call to lead God's people, leadership of the Hebrews, and finally his death just outside the Promised Land.

The Quran also mentions Moses in several places, but it contradicts the earlier historical record of the Pentateuch. The Quran says baby Moses was adopted by Pharaoh's wife; the Bible says Moses was adopted by Pharaoh's daughter (see Exodus 2:5–10). The Quran calls Haman a friend of Pharaoh; the Bible places Haman one thousand years later in the book of Esther. The Quran says God appeared to Moses in the fire in the valley of Tuwa; the Bible says it was on Mt. Horeb (see Exodus 3:1). The Quran says the golden calf worshiped by the Israelites in the wilderness was molded by a Samaritan; the Bible says Aaron made the golden calf (see Exodus 32:2–4). (In fact, the term *Samaritan* was not used until 722 B.C., several hundred years after the events recorded in Exodus.) The Quran says the cow sacrificed by Moses was yellow. The Bible says it was red (see Numbers 19:1, 2).

These are just a few of the contradictions between the Quran and the Old Testament.

THE QURAN MISQUOTES THE NEW TESTAMENT

The Story of Zacharias

The Quran

(Remember) when the wife of 'Imrān said: My Lord! I have vowed unto Thee that which is in my belly as a consecrated (offering). Accept it from me,

Lo! Thou, only Thou, art the Hearer, the Knower!

And when she was delivered she said: My Lord! Lo! I am delivered of a female—Allah knew best of what she was delivered—the male is not as the female; and lo! I have named her Mary, and lo! I crave Thy protection for her and for her offspring from Satan the outcast.

And her Lord accepted her with full acceptance and vouchsafed to her a goodly growth: and made Zachariah her guardian. Whenever Zachariah went into the sanctuary where she was, he found that she had food. He said: O Mary! Whence cometh unto thee this (food)? She answered: It is from Allah. Allah giveth without stint to whom He will.

Then Zachariah prayed unto his Lord and said: My Lord! Bestow upon me of Thy bounty goodly offspring. Lo! Thou art the Hearer of Prayer.

And the angels called to him as he stood praying in the sanctuary: Allah giveth thee glad tidings of (a son whose name is) John, (who cometh) to confirm a word from Allah, lordly, chaste, a Prophet of the righteous.

He said: My Lord! How can I have a son when age hath overtaken me already and my wife is barren? (The angel) answered: So (it will be). Allah doth what He will.

He said: My Lord! Appoint a token for me. (The angel) said: The token unto thee (shall be) that thou shalt not speak unto mankind three days except by signs. Remember thy Lord much, and praise (Him) in the early hours of night and morning.[20]

The Quranic story of Zacharias has its origins in *Protevangelion's James the Lesser*, a second-century A.D. apocryphal Christian fable, and from Luke 1:5–20. Here is the reconstruction of the Protevangelion story with the direct quotations found in the Quran italicized for emphasis.

And Anna (wife of Joachim) answered, "As the Lord my God liveth, *whatever I bring forth, whether it be male or female, I will devote it* to the Lord my God, and it shall minister to him in holy things, during its whole life . . . *and called her name Mary* . . . And the high-priest received her, and blessed her, and said, " *Mary, the Lord God hath magnified thy name* to all generations, and to the very end of time *by thee* will the Lord shew his redemption to the children of Is-rael."

But Mary *continued in the temple* as a dove edu-cated her there, *and received her food from the hand of an angel.* Then the high-priest *(Zacharias)* entered into the Holy of Holies, and taking away with him the breastplate of judgment *made prayers* concern-ing her.[21]

Muhammad's eighth wife, Maryam, was a Chris-tian slave girl from Ethiopia. Al-Moqawqas, the Gov-ernor of Egypt, sent her along with her sister and a white mule as gifts to Muhammad. It is very likely that Maryam either brought copies of the above doc-uments with her, or simply related the stories of Jesus, the son of Mary, to Muhammad. Upon closer scrutiny of the chronological order of the Surats, you will have to agree with me that the popular name for Jesus, "Son of Mary," began in the Quranic text after Maryam entered Muhammad's life.

The Bible

Luke's Gospel gives the accurate record in chapter one, verses 5–20:

There was in the days of Herod, the king of Judea, a certain priest named Zacharias, of the division of Abijah. His wife was of the daughters of Aaron, and her name was Elizabeth. And they were both righteous before God, walking in all the commandments and ordinances of the Lord blameless. But they had no child, because Elizabeth was barren, and they were both well advanced in years.

So it was, that while he was serving as priest before God in the order of his division, according to the custom of the priesthood, his lot fell to burn incense when he went into the temple of the Lord. And the whole multitude of the people was praying outside at the hour of incense.

Then an angel of the Lord appeared to him, standing on the right side of the altar of incense. And when Zacharias saw him, he was troubled, and fear fell upon him. But the angel said to him, "Do not be afraid, Zacharias, for your prayer is heard; your wife Elizabeth will bear you a son, and you shall call his name John. And you will have joy and gladness, and many will rejoice at his birth. For he will be great in the sight of the Lord, and shall drink neither wine nor strong drink. He will also be filled with the Holy Spirit, even from his mother's womb. And he will turn many of the children of Israel to the Lord their God. He will also go before Him in the spirit and power of Elijah, 'to turn the hearts of the fathers to the children,' and the disobedient to the wisdom of the just, to make ready a people prepared for the Lord."

And Zacharias said to the angel, "How shall I know this? For I am an old man, and my wife is well advanced in years."

And the angel answered and said to him, "I am Gabriel, who stands in the presence of God, and was sent to speak to you and bring you these glad tidings. But behold, you will be mute and not able to speak until the day these things take place, because you did not believe my words which will be fulfilled in their own time."

One of the obvious mistakes in the Quranic story is its claim that Zacharias was speechless for three days, whereas the Gospel states (verse 20) that it was actually nine months. There are other incompatible statements which become apparent upon reading the three above-mentioned records.

Mary, the Mother of Jesus

One of the most absurd mistakes in the Quran is the reference to Mary as the sister of Aaron. Her identity seems to be quite mixed up. Let us look at Surat Maryam (Mary) 19:28 first:

Oh sister of Aaron! Thy father was not a wicked man nor was thy mother a harlot.

◆ ◆

يَا أُخْتَ هَٰرُونَ مَا كَانَ أَبُوكِ امْرَأَ سَوْءٍ وَمَا
كَانَتْ أُمُّكِ بَغِيًّا ۝

The Mary of the Quran depicted as the mother of Jesus is 1,570 years removed from the real Mary, as indicated from Numbers 26:59: "The name of Amram's wife was Jochebed the daughter of Levi, who was born to Levi in Egypt; and to Amram she bore Aaron and Moses and their sister Miriam."

The valiant effort of Muslim theologians to explain that the Quran is simply stating her descendency from the priestly family of Aaron and Imran is totally unsatisfactory. This mistaken Quranic identity is obvious. Compare the much older historical record of the New Testament's Luke 1:26–35:

Now in the sixth month the angel Gabriel was sent by God to a city of Galilee named Nazareth, to a virgin betrothed to a man whose name was Joseph, of the house of David. The virgin's name was Mary.

And having come in, the angel said to her, "Rejoice, highly favored one, the Lord is with you; blessed are you among women!"

But when she saw him, she was troubled at his saying, and considered what manner of greeting this was.

Then the angel said to her, "Do not be afraid, Mary, for you have found favor with God. And behold, you will conceive in your womb and bring forth a Son, and shall call His name JESUS. He will be great, and will be called the Son of the Highest; and the Lord God will give Him the throne of His father David. And He will reign over the house of Jacob forever, and of His kingdom there will be no end."

Then Mary said to the angel, "How can this be, since I do not know a man?"

And the angel answered and said to her, "The Holy Spirit will come upon you, and the power of the Highest will overshadow you; therefore, also, that Holy One who is to be born will be called the Son of God."

Now, to solve the problem for our Muslim theologians, I direct their attention to a simple solution. First, Elizabeth was called the daughter of Aaron, which refers to the fact that she was from the lineage of Aaron. Mary, the mother of Jesus, came to visit her while Elizabeth was six months pregnant with John the Baptist. In Luke's Gospel the story is told in one and the same chapter, as indicated above. Apparently, because Muhammad heard numerous stories, he could not accurately remember the details from either the Apocrypha or the Gospels. The end result was the gross mistake of making Mary the daughter of Amram and the sister of Aaron.

The Birth of Jesus

We are told in the Quran that the miraculous birth of Jesus took place under a palm tree (Surat Maryam [Mary] 19:21–26). This story first appeared in an apocryphal fable of the second century A.D. The relevant portions of the story are italicized:

> *Now on the third day after Mary was wearied in the desert* by the heat, she asked Joseph to rest for a little *under the shade of a Palm Tree.* Then Mary looking up and seeing its branches laden with fruit (dates) said, "I desire if it were possible to have some fruit." Just *then the child Jesus looked up (from below)* with a cheerful smile, *and said* to *the Palm Tree,* "Send down some fruit. Immediately *the tree bent itself (toward her)* and *so they ate.* Then Jesus said, "O Palm Tree, arise; be one of my Father's trees in Paradise, but with thy roots open the fountain *(rivulet) beneath thee* and bring water flowing from that fount.[22]

After presenting the Quranic and the apocryphal references, let us now consider the accurate record of Matthew 1:25–2:6:

> [Joseph] did not know her till she had brought forth her firstborn Son. And he called His name JESUS.
>
> Now after Jesus was born in Bethlehem of Judea in the days of Herod the king, behold, wise men from the East came to Jerusalem, saying, "Where is He who has been born King of the Jews? For we have seen His star in the East and have come to worship Him."
>
> When Herod the king heard these things, he was troubled, and all Jerusalem with him. And when he had gathered all the chief priests and scribes of the people together, he inquired of them where the

Christ was to be born. So they said to him, "In Bethlehem of Judea, for thus it is written by the prophet:

'But you, Bethlehem, in the land of Judah,
Are not the least among the rulers of Judah;
For out of you shall come a Ruler
Who will shepherd My people Israel.'"

Fables about Jesus

Two of the most far-fetched and fantasy-filled fables ever attributed to Jesus are recorded in the
Quran.

Then she pointed to him. They said: How can we
talk to one who is in the cradle, a young boy?
He spake: Lo! I am the slave of Allah. He hath
given me the Scripture and hath appointed me a
Prophet . . . .

◆ ◆

فَأَشَارَتْ إِلَيْهِ قَالُوا كَيْفَ نُكَلِّمُ مَن كَانَ فِي

الْمَهْدِ صَبِيًّا ۝

قَالَ إِنِّي عَبْدُ اللَّهِ ۚ آتَانِيَ الْكِتَابَ وَجَعَلَنِي

نَبِيًّا ۝ 23

The *First Gospel of the Infancy of Jesus Christ,*
which is a second-century Arabic apocryphal fable
from Egypt, is the source for this Quranic fable:

. . . Jesus spake even when he was in the cradle, and
said to his mother: "Mary, I am Jesus the Son of God.
That word which thou didst bring forth according to
the declaration of the angel. . . ."

Next, we look into the tale that Jesus breathed life into birds of clay. According to Surat al-Imran (The Family of 'Imran) 3:49:

> **And will make him a messenger unto the children of Israel, (saying): Lo! I come unto you with a sign from your Lord. Lo! I fashion for you out of clay the likeness of a bird, and I breathe into it and it is a bird, by Allah's leave.**

◆ ◆

The source for this Quranic fiction is found in the earlier *Thomas' Gospel of the Infancy of Jesus Christ*, an apocryphal fable from the second century.

> **Then he took from the bank of the stream some soft clay, and formed out of it twelve sparrows . . . Then Jesus clapping together the palms of his hands, called to the sparrows, and said to them: "Go, fly away."[24]**

Neither of the above quotations from either source are recognized by biblical scholars, historians, or theologians as authentic events in the life of Christ.

Feeding the Disciples

The New Testament records several instances when Jesus supernaturally obtained or multiplied food for the needy. However, there is no biblical or historical evidence for the following Quranic story:

> **Jesus, son of Mary, said: O Allah, Lord of us! Send down for us a table spread with food from heaven, that it may be a feast for us, for the first of us and for the last of us, and a sign from Thee. Give us sustenance, for Thou art the Best of Sustainers.**

> **Allah said: Lo! I send it down for you. And whoso disbelieveth of you afterward, him surely will I punish with a punishment wherewith I have not punished any of (My) creatures.**

◆ ◆

Perhaps Muhammad was confusing his Bible stories again. Maybe he was misapplying and confusing the events of Acts 10:10–16:

> **Then [Peter] became very hungry and wanted to eat; but while they made ready, he fell into a trance and saw heaven opened and an object like a great sheet bound at the four corners, descending to him and let down to the earth. In it were all kinds of four-footed animals of the earth, wild beasts, creeping things, and birds of the air.**

> **And a voice came to him, "Rise, Peter; kill and eat."**

But Peter said, "Not so, Lord! For I have never eaten anything common or unclean."

And a voice spoke to him again the second time, "What God has cleansed you must not call common."

This was done three times. And the object was taken up into heaven again.

THE QURAN MISREPRESENTS
THE HOLY SPIRIT

The Quran also presents a very confused and often contradictory view of the Holy Spirit. According to different parts of the Quran, the Holy Spirit is God's own breath (Surat al-Hyjr [Al-Hijr] 15:29); the angel Gabriel (Surat Maryam [Mary] 19:17); and divine inspiration (Surat al-Nahl [The Bee] 16:2).

Muslim Interpreters

Muslim theologians are at a loss to explain what is meant by the Holy Spirit. Some declare it is the teaching of Jesus or Gabriel, as Baidawi believes. Others accept it to mean the name of Allah, by which Jesus raised the dead. Still others will tell you that it really means the gospel itself, which Jesus preached.

I will never forget one memorable encounter I had with a grand old Muslim in Multan, Pakistan, in 1975. A missionary took me to see this Muslim gentleman who had taught him and numerous others the Urdu language. Shortly after we arrived at this elder's house, the conversation gravitated from Urdu to Arabic to Muhammad. The teacher was totally unprepared for my explanation that *Paracleton* is not a prophetic reference by Jesus to Muhammad. I explained that it was instead a Greek word meaning helper or comforter, and referred specifically to the

Holy Spirit, who came on the apostles on the day of
Pentecost (see Acts 1 and 2). I challenged him to look
into the matter linguistically and textually, which
we did together. The wise teacher was very recep-
tive, and through that wonderful word *Paracleton*,
the Holy Spirit opened his heart and he received
Jesus Christ as his personal Savior and Lord. The
missionary was utterly overwhelmed and excitedly
told me as we left, "I have never known my teacher
to be open to the gospel before today." Hallelujah for
the miracle of the Holy Spirit!

The New Testament and the Holy Spirit

No one can receive satisfactory answers concerning the Holy Spirit from the Quran. The best information and the brightest light on this subject is
found in the New Testament. Here is how the Holy
Spirit is presented in the Bible:

- The Third Person of the Trinity (Matthew 28:19)
- The Inspirer of Scripture (2 Peter 1:21)
- The Companion of Christian believers (John
  16:7)
- The Convictor, Convincer, Converter of sinners
  (John 16:9–11)
- The heavenly Gift (Acts 10:45)
- The One who indwells the believer (1 Corin-
  thians 3:16)
- The Seal of God's approval in the believer (Ephe-
  sians 4:30)
- The Downpayment of the believer's inheritance
  (Ephesians 1:13–14)
- The Anointer of believers (2 Corinthians 1:
  21–22)
- The Baptizer of believers (1 Corinthians 12:13)
- The One who must fill believers (Ephesians 5:18)

- The One who calls individuals to God's service (Acts 13:2–3)
- The Giver of special gifts (1 Corinthians 12: 4–11)
- The Producer of spiritual fruits in believers (Galatians 5:22–23)

In fact, the entire book of Acts is a detailed account of the work of the Holy Spirit in the followers of Jesus of Nazareth during the early years of Christianity. Furthermore, that same Holy Spirit is at work throughout the world today. Yet never once does the Holy Spirit in any text of the Bible refer to Muhammad, the Quran, or Islam.

CHAPTER SEVEN

———————

THE BIBLE

❉ ❉ ❉

WHY ARE THERE SO MANY
BIBLE VERSIONS?

Muslims, by and large, accept Mr. Deedat's position that the real Torah of the Jews and the Injil of
the Christians were different books from the books
we have today. However, except for the so-called Gospel of Barnabas, there has never been a time in history when any Torah (law) or Injil (gospel), other
than the books of the Old and New Testaments, has
ever existed.

It is most unbelievable that Muslims declare that
God had the power to preserve the Quran from corruption for fourteen centuries yet was not capable to
do the same thing for the Torah and Injil! Mr. Deedat
and other Muslim leaders try to circumvent these
implications by ridiculing the multiple Bible versions. The King James, the New King James, the Revised Standard, the American Standard, are not
conflicting editions as Muslims are led to believe.
They are simply different English translations and
are compatible with the original Hebrew Old Testa-

ment and Greek New Testament, which have been preserved from even before the time of Muhammad.

There are more than fifty versions or translations of the Quran as well. Differences in these versions amount to nothing more than various translators' efforts to clearly express Arabic verses in the English language.

It is exciting to say that the average reader of the Bible in any language feels as if God is speaking in his own native language. Furthermore, the Bible is now translated into more than eighteen hundred languages and dialects, providing further evidence for the validity and need for its message.

WHY ARE THERE SO MANY DENOMINATIONS?

Christianity began as a relationship between God the loving Creator and man the crown of His creation through Christ the Savior. The earliest followers of Christ were called by three names: (1) followers of the Way, (2) sect of the Nazarene, and (3) Christians. During the following centuries, sadly enough, the clamor for honor, position, and personal glory led to a hierarchy of tremendous magnitude.

The first division of the Christian religion took place in the twelfth century when there was a split between the Eastern Church, with headquarters in Constantinople, and the Western Church, with headquarters in Rome. The second division took place under the leadership of Martin Luther during the sixteenth century and became known as the Protestant Reformation.

For the past three hundred years the evangelical group has emerged, particularly in America, within numerous denominations, such as Methodists, Baptists, Presbyterians, and Pentecostals. In the past three decades the charismatics have swept across denominational lines, claiming the loyalty of large numbers of people, some of whom have established their own churches, while others remain in the mainline of Christianity.

This writer believes wholeheartedly that the Christian faith is divided into two groups: the traditional, ritualistic, nominal Christians; and the converted, born-again, saved Christians. Members of both groups belong to various denominations. The followers of the Christian religion number more than 1.5 billion in a current total world population of 5 billion.

WAS THE BIBLE CHANGED BEFORE MUHAMMAD?

To those who claim corruption of our Holy Bible, we ask when did such corruption take place? If they say before the Quran, then the Quran places them in a dilemma. Allah commanded Muhammad to seek help from those who read the Bible in order to eliminate any doubts:

> And if thou (Muhammad) art in doubt concerning that which We reveal unto thee, then question those who read the Scripture (that was) before thee. Verily the Truth from thy Lord hath come unto thee. So be not thou of the waverers . . . .

فَإِن كُنتَ فِى شَكٍّ مِّمَّآ أَنزَلْنَآ إِلَيْكَ فَسْئَلِ الَّذِينَ
يَقْرَءُونَ الْكِتَـٰبَ مِن قَبْلِكَ لَقَدْ جَآءَكَ الْحَقُّ مِن
رَّبِّكَ فَلَا تَكُونَنَّ مِنَ الْمُمْتَرِينَ ۝ [1]

It is not in keeping with God's omniscience for Allah to refer Muhammad to those who read a corrupted book in order to eliminate any doubts. Furthermore, the Quran testifies to the authenticity of the Holy Bible with this verse:

And argue not with the People of the Scripture unless it be in (a way) that is better save with such of them as do wrong; and say: We believe in that which hath been revealed unto us and revealed unto you; our God and your God is One, and unto Him we surrender.

◆ ◆

وَلَا تُجَـٰدِلُوٓا۟ أَهْلَ الْكِتَـٰبِ إِلَّا بِالَّتِى هِىَ أَحْسَنُ إِلَّا
الَّذِينَ ظَلَمُوا۟ مِنْهُمْ وَقُولُوٓا۟ ءَامَنَّا بِالَّذِىٓ أُنزِلَ
إِلَيْنَا وَأُنزِلَ إِلَيْكُمْ وَإِلَـٰهُنَا وَإِلَـٰهُكُمْ وَٰحِدٌ وَّ
نَحْنُ لَهُۥ مُسْلِمُونَ ۝ [2]

WAS THE BIBLE CHANGED AFTER MUHAMMAD?

If corruption took place after the Quran, then anyone claiming corruption is saying that the Quran failed as a guard. In other words, if the Torah, the historical books, the psalms and the prophecies, the Gospels and the Epistles had been corrupted after the Quran, such a claim would indict the people of the Quran for neglecting the most important reason for which the Quran was given. If our Muslim friends insist that our book is not authentic, they should show us the authentic Old and New Testaments.

This the Christians have done. When they saw in the Torah prophecies about Christ their Lord, they made themselves guardians thereof and did their utmost to propagate them to the world. We ask why the Muslims have not done the same since they believe that the Torah and the Gospels contain prophecies and evidences about Muhammad? Muslims should consider verses in their Quran that testify to the authenticity of the Word of God—the Bible:

Lo! We, even We, reveal the Reminder, and lo! We verily are its Guardian. . . .

It is the law of Allah which hath taken course aforetime. Thou wilt not find for the law of Allah aught of power to change. . . .

And recite that which hath been revealed unto thee of the Scripture of thy Lord. There is none who can change His words, and thou wilt find no refuge beside Him.

◆ ◆

اِنَّا نَحْنُ نَزَّلْنَا الذِّكْرَ وَاِنَّا لَهُ لَحٰفِظُوْنَ ۞ [3]

سُنَّةَ اللّٰهِ الَّتِيْ قَدْ خَلَتْ مِنْ قَبْلُ وَلَنْ تَجِدَ
لِسُنَّةِ اللّٰهِ تَبْدِيْلًا ۞ [4]

وَاتْلُ مَآ أُوحِيَ إِلَيْكَ مِن كِتَابِ رَبِّكَ ۖ لَا مُبَدِّلَ
لِكَلِمَٰتِهِۦ وَلَن تَجِدَ مِن دُونِهِۦ مُلْتَحَدًا ۝ [5]

The word *Guardian* simply refers to God's guard as one who protects the books of God with its divine laws and truths.

A very serious question emerges: What attitude would the average Muslim take in the face of the following words of the Quran?

This is the Scripture wherein there is no doubt, a guidance unto those who ward off (evil):

Who believe in the unseen, and establish worship, and spend of that We have bestowed upon them;

And who believe in that which is revealed unto thee (Muhammad) and that which was revealed before thee, and are certain of the Hereafter. . . .

Say (O Muslims): We believe in Allah and that which is revealed unto us and that which was revealed unto Abraham, and Ishmael, and Isaac, and Jacob, and the tribes, and that which Moses and Jesus received, and that which the Prophets received from their Lord. We make no distinction between any of them, and unto Him we have surrendered.

الٓمٓ ۝ ذَٰلِكَ الْكِتَٰبُ لَا رَيْبَ ۛ فِيهِ ۛ هُدًى لِّلْمُتَّقِينَ ۝
الَّذِينَ يُؤْمِنُونَ بِالْغَيْبِ وَيُقِيمُونَ الصَّلَوٰةَ وَمِمَّا
رَزَقْنَٰهُمْ يُنفِقُونَ ۝
وَالَّذِينَ يُؤْمِنُونَ بِمَآ أُنزِلَ إِلَيْكَ وَمَآ أُنزِلَ مِن
قَبْلِكَ وَبِالْآخِرَةِ هُمْ يُوقِنُونَ ۝ [6]

قُولُوٓاءَامَنَّابِاللّٰهِ وَمَآأُنزِلَ إِلَيۡنَا وَمَآأُنزِلَ إِلَىٰٓ إِبۡرَٰهِـۧمَ
وَإِسۡمَٰعِيلَ وَإِسۡحَٰقَ وَيَعۡقُوبَ وَالۡأَسۡبَاطِ وَمَآ
أُوتِىَ مُوسَىٰ وَعِيسَىٰ وَمَآأُوتِىَ النَّبِيُّونَ مِن رَّبِّهِمۡ
لَا نُفَرِّقُ بَيۡنَ أَحَدٍ مِّنۡهُمۡ وَنَحۡنُ لَهُۥ مُسۡلِمُونَ ٧

We ask again how it is that the Quran commands those who believe in the Quran and what was revealed in it to make no distinction between their Quran and the biblical books which were before it if the books had been corrupted and changed? Would not such a claim of corruption be an indictment of the righteousness of God's truth and integrity?

Let's look at the truth from history. Christians from the beginning of the first century until now have suffered persecution and torture at the hands of the heathen and the Jews. Historians tell us that Christians faced martyrdom with joy. In obedience to His command to be "faithful unto death," they died rather than deny Christ. Many brought on themselves the worst forms of persecution because they refused to deny Christ or reject His gospel. They preferred any kind of death to temporary joy in life. One of the most thrilling books you can ever read is *By Their Blood: Christian Martyrs of the Twentieth Century* (published by Mott Media). The author, Dr. James Hefley, and his wife Marti, wrote this chronicle of modern martyrs, as well as this author's biography, *The Liberated Palestinian*. Even in our twentieth century, as the great church historian, Dr. Kenneth Latourette wrote, "The blood of the Christian martyrs is the foundation of the Christian church." The records of history tell of the masses of witnesses who were tortured and would not accept deliverance because they looked forward to their resurrection. Rather than deny Christ, they were willing to die for their conviction that He is the Son of God, the Savior of the world, and their personal Redeemer.

Can anyone possibly believe that Christians, who made such incredible sacrifices, would endure agony unto death for the teachings of a Bible, which had been deliberately mutilated to include falsehoods?

We ask a further question: Would the Christians have allowed anyone, no matter what his position, to change a single word of the gospel of God? Especially when they had the apostolic command, "But even if we, or an angel from heaven, preach any other gospel to you than what we have preached to you, let him be accursed" (Galatians 1:8).

Again, what could have been the incentive of the Christians to corrupt the Bible? Would such an incentive have been more preferable to them than their eternal life? Their Lord and Redeemer, whom they worshiped with their spirit and blood and with everything they held precious, had sealed His covenant with them by warning through His faithful apostle John:

> For I testify to everyone who hears the words of the prophecy of this book: If anyone adds to these things, God will add to him the plagues that are written in this book; and if anyone takes away from the words of the book of this prophecy, God shall take away his part from the Book of Life, from the holy city, and from the things which are written in this book.[8]

Let us emphasize and re-emphasize that the world has never lacked honest historians to preserve chronicled world events. Is there anyone, therefore, who can provide a historian, be he Jew, Muslim, devotee of any other religion, or devotee of none, who states or even suggests that there has ever been a conference between Jews and Christians with their differing beliefs and languages, to change the Word of God? Even if we presume such a conference did take place, shouldn't there have been preserved copies of the original deliberations to witness the collusion of the Jews and the Christians in changing the Bible? If, indeed, such had taken place, it would have meant that the controversy between the Jews and the Christians had to come to an end at the cost of preserving the law of God.

For anyone to claim that the biblical text has been changed or that the true text is not available, they must also contradict the plain contents of the Quran. The Quran testifies that the Bible is authentic and is beyond falsehood. Certainly, no Muslim who believes in God, His books, and His messengers is bold enough to assert that God sent the Quran to authenticate a forged, distorted, and changed book as far as the doctrines contained in it are concerned!

Let us remember the words of our Lord Jesus Christ, "Heaven and earth will pass away, but My words will by no means pass away" (Matthew 24:35).

Yes, the Word of God is like a seed which has life in it (Luke 8:11). It is like a lamp that shows us the way (Psalm 119:105).

Voltaire, the French atheist, predicted that the Bible would become a forgotten book as a result of his own writings against it. Ingersoll, the American scoffer, announced that within ten years the Bible

would no longer be read by anybody and in twenty
years totally forgotten. But the Holy Bible is still
alive and still the best seller around the globe. In fact,
Voltaire's own home has become a Bible book store!

CONCLUSION

Now that this book is being completed after la-
borious research, numerous changes, revisions, and
editing, I am very eager for something else. Indeed,
my earnest prayer and desire is to see more openness
among our peoples throughout the world. Islam has
for too long put up a formidable wall around itself
and its adherents. This is practically the twenty-first
century, a period in human history of enlighten-
ment, communication, and worldwide interest in
every field of endeavor. Everybody wants to know
the truth about everything.

The adherents to these two great faiths, which
claim the allegiance of almost half of the world's
population, are eager to know if Islam or Christianity or both present the ultimate truth of God's
revelation. I am hoping for more lively debates on
radio and television, more magazine and newspaper
articles and books, and more large meetings on college and university campuses in the Arab world, as
well as wherever the two religions meet.

After all, if both religions claim to be revealed
from God Almighty and they are in conflict with
each other, one must immediately conclude that
both cannot be right. Furthermore, God Himself will
not, by any stretch of the imagination, be the source
and inspiration of such confusion. In order to determine whether it is God or man that has gotten us

confused, let us, investigate the Quran, in particular, and Islam, in general, and the Bible, in particular, and Christianity, in general. Then we must untangle the confusion and get to the heart of the matter by trusting God's Holy Spirit. Christ promised that the Holy Spirit will lead us to a clear understanding of God's will.

> "But when the Helper comes, whom I shall send to you from the Father, the Spirit of truth who proceeds from the Father, He will testify of Me."[9]

> "However, when He, the Spirit of truth, has come, He will guide you into all truth; for He will not speak on His own authority, but whatever He hears He will speak; and He will tell you things to come."[10]

> Then Jesus said to those Jews who believed Him, "If you abide in My word, you are My disciples indeed. And you shall know the truth, and the truth shall make you free."[11]

PART TWO

THE GREAT DEBATE*

CHAPTER EIGHT

IS JESUS GOD?
PART ONE: Anis Shorrosh

◆ ◆ ◆

God, who at various times and in different ways spoke in time past to the fathers by the prophets, has in these last days spoken to us by His Son, whom He has appointed heir of all things, through whom also He made the worlds; who being the brightness of His glory and the express image of His person, and upholding all things by the word of His power, when He had by Himself purged our sins, sat down at the right hand of the Majesty on high, having become so much better than the angels, as He has by inheritance obtained a more excellent name than they. For to which of the angels did He ever say:

"You are My Son,
Today I have begotten You"?

And again:

"I will be to Him a Father,
And He shall be to Me a Son"?

But when He again brings the firstborn into the world, He says:

---

*Chapters 8–10 are edited from the transcript of the original debate which was held at Prince Albert Hall, in London, England, on December 15, 1985. Material in brackets is added for clarity.

235

"Let all the angels
   of God worship Him."

And of the angels He says:

"Who makes His angels spirits
And His ministers a flame of fire."

But to the Son He says:

"Your throne, O God, is forever and ever;
A scepter of righteousness is the scepter of Your
   Kingdom."[1]

Introduction

The distinguished governor of ancient Palestine,
Pontius Pilate, stood on a balcony overlooking a
crowd gathered in the courtyard of the Antonia Fortress in Jerusalem. He asked the restless crowd a
very serious question: "What then shall I do with
Jesus who is called Christ?" (Matthew 27:22).

Ever since that historic event over nineteen hundred years ago, the eternal destiny of every human
soul has depended on how one answers that question. The answer of the crowd on that early Friday
morning in Jerusalem was "Crucify Him!" The reason they gave to Pilate was, "According to our law He
ought to die because He made Himself the Son of
God" (John 19:7, 15).

Dreading a serious uprising, facing the jealous religious leaders, and seeking to please the demanding
crowd, the governor succumbed to public pressure
in spite of his forthright declaration three times, "I
find no fault in Him." Six hundred years later the

ذَكِيًّا

Quran also calls Him "Faultless"
[Surat Maryam (Mary) 19:19].

God's Existence

Creation, conscience, and history substantiate the
existence of God. Religion is man's serious effort at
finding God—so the sociologists and philosophers
tell us. But wait a minute! Is God lost for us to find
Him? Certainly not. He is the one who is looking for
us lost sinners.

Once again, to impress on you the importance of
this subject, I read from the Bible in English and
Arabic from 2 Corinthians 4:3–4:

> **But even if our gospel is veiled, it is veiled to those
> who are perishing, whose minds the god of this age
> has blinded, who do not believe, lest the light of the
> gospel of the glory of Christ, who is the image of
> God, should shine on them.**

Inspiration of the Bible

The Bible is the most extraordinary book in the
world. It has sixty-six books, written during a period
of fifteen hundred years by more than forty persons.
The authors were shepherds, kings, philosophers,
and fishermen. Some were rich, some were poor,
some even young. Yet the Bible shows itself an inspired book because the author is one—the Holy
Spirit. Second Peter 1:20–21 announces,

Knowing this first, that no prophecy of Scripture is of any private interpretation, for prophecy never came by the will of man, but holy men of God spoke as they were moved by the Holy Spirit.

One reason we know the Bible is inspired is because of the fulfillment of prophecies uttered centuries before the events took place. The Bible has influenced the uplifting of human society whenever it has been believed and practiced. Furthermore, the Bible's accuracy has been substantiated by historical documents, archaeological finds, and ancient manuscripts. There are nearly 25,000 old copies of parts or all of Old and New Testament Scriptures in museums around the world.

How many available copies of the Quran do we have and how old are they? Why did Othman order the burning of all other copies except Hafsa's, fifty-three years after the so-called revelations began? Codex Alexandrinus dates to around A.D. 325. The Codex Vaticanus dates back to the same time. The Dead Sea Scrolls, ancient copies of Old Testament books, can be traced to around 250 B.C.

Jesus, our Lord and Savior, proclaimed, "Heaven and earth shall pass away, but my word shall stand forever" (Matthew 24:35). Proverbs 30:5, 6 remind us that anyone who dares to add to God's Word will be exposed as a liar.

The One Triune God

The God the Bible reveals to us is one God. There is only one God. Yet, unfathomable as it is, mysterious as it is, this One True God, despite every unbeliever's rejection, is also a Triune God. It is not my discovery, but His own revelation of Himself in the

Bible. Remember, to say that the one *God* is three *persons* is not contradictory.

From the very first chapter of the Bible, the Trinity is assumed. God says in Genesis 1:26, "Let Us make man in Our image according to Our likeness." Was God discussing the making of the crown of His creation with Himself? In other words, was He talking to Himself or was He talking to someone else with His same standing and essence, those two later revealed clearly as the other two persons of the Trinity?

Genesis 3:22 gives another allusion to the Trinity: "Then the Lord God said, 'Behold, the man has become like one of Us, to know good and evil.'" This pattern is repeated in Genesis 11:7, when God determined to halt construction of the tower of Babel: "Come let Us go down and there confuse their language."

Many of you know Arabic, my "mother tongue." Our Arabic verbs and pronouns are very different from many other languages. The Old Testament, written in Hebrew, has similar verbs and pronouns. Arabic has a singular, a dual, and then a plural verb. "He ate" would be *Akal*. "They (two) ate" would be *Akalaa'*. And "they (three or more) ate" would be *Akalou*. In the Semitic language, the verb frequently identifies the number of persons involved in the action. "You" in Engish can refer to one, two, or a million, but not so in Arabic or Hebrew. Even the word *Elohim* is a plural word, which is the name for "God" in Hebrew.

In the New Testament

The Trinity is depicted powerfully during the baptism of Jesus:

> **And immediately coming up from the water, He saw the heavens parting and the Spirit descending upon Him like a dove. Then a voice came from heaven. "You are My beloved Son, in whom I am well pleased." (Mark 1:10, 11)**

The Trinity is also alluded to in the Great Commission, given by the risen Christ in Matthew 28:19: "Go therefore and make disciples of all the nations, baptizing them in the name of the Father and of the Son and of the Holy Spirit."

In addition to these allusions to the Trinity, there are a number of verses which clearly affirm the essentials of trinitarianism.

[By the doctrine of the Trinity, Christians mean that the one nature of God subsists eternally in three distinct persons. Note that I am not contradictorily asserting one God and three gods, or one person and three persons. It is true that one God cannot at the same time be three gods, and that one person cannot at the same time be three persons. But the biblical doctrine of the Trinity teaches that one God is three persons. Let us examine each part of our definition to see if the Bible supports it.

There Is Only One God

Like Islam, Christianity and the Bible affirm the supremacy of the one true God (1 Corinthians 8: 4–6). Isaiah 43:10 declares that there is only one true God and that no other gods have been formed before or after him. Galatians 4:8 says that false gods are not gods by nature. First Timothy 2:4 also asserts that there is only one God.]

JESUS CHRIST IS GOD

The question before us is a very serious one, "Is Jesus God?" Let me emphasize that if Jesus was not supernaturally born but rather born in the same manner as ordinary men, lived only as ordinary men do, died as we all do, and did not rise and go to heaven, then we have no case for the jury. He would be thrown out as an impostor.

Man can never become God, but God did become man. His name is Jesus the Christ, our Savior, Lord, and King! Let me interject a question. If Jesus is not the overwhelming figure of all history, why then does the Quran mention Him ninety-seven times and Muhammad only twenty-five times?

God's Visit with Abraham

For those of you who know the story of Abraham, let me refresh your memory. God came to Abraham as a man fifteen hundred years before God came into Bethlehem as a babe. Let us look at Genesis 18:1–3, 13, 14:

> Then the Lord appeared to him by the terebinth trees of Mamre, as he was sitting in the tent door in the heat of the day. So he lifted his eyes and looked, and behold, three men were standing by him; and when he saw them, he ran from the tent door to meet them, and bowed himself to the ground, and said, "My Lord, if I have now found favor in Your sight, do not pass on by Your servant. . . ."
> And the Lord said to Abraham, "Why did Sarah laugh, saying, 'Shall I surely bear a child, since I am old?' Is anything too hard for the Lord? At the ap-

pointed time I will return to you, according to the
time of life, and Sarah shall have a son."

Later on, as Abraham interceded for Sodom, we
notice that he spoke to the Lord as to one of the three
men (verses 23–25):

And Abraham came near and said, "Would You
also destroy the righteous with the wicked? Suppose
there were fifty righteous within the city; would You
also destroy the place and not spare it for the fifty
righteous that were in it? Far be it from You to do
such a thing as this, to slay the righteous with the
wicked, so that the righteous should be as the
wicked; far be it from You! Shall not the Judge of all
the earth do right?"

The last verse in Genesis 18 tells of this human
appearance of the great God of the universe: "So the
Lord went His way as soon as He had finished speaking with Abraham; and Abraham returned to his
place."

God Is Eternal: So Is Jesus

Before His birth in Bethlehem, Jesus existed. Look
at John 17:5:

"And now, O Father, glorify Me together with Yourself, with the glory which I had with You before the
world was."

Mr. Deedat told an audience in Birmingham, England, "I believe every word of Jesus that is written
in the Gospels." What does he think of these words
from the Gospel of John, affirming that God's name
belongs to Jesus?

"Your father Abraham rejoiced to see My day, and he saw it and was glad." Then the Jews said to Him, "You are not yet fifty years old, and have You seen Abraham?" Jesus said to them, "Most assuredly, I say to you, before Abraham was, I AM."[2]

Why "I AM"? If we read Exodus 3:13, 14, we understand that it is God's revelation of Himself in a name:

Then Moses said to God, "Indeed, when I come to the children of Israel and say to them, 'The God of your fathers has sent me to you,' and they say to me, 'What is His name?' what shall I say to them?"

And God said to Moses, "I AM WHO I AM." And He said, "Thus you shall say to the children of Israel, 'I AM has sent me to you.'"

The prophecy of Micah 5:2 told that Bethlehem would be the birthplace of the King, the Messiah. The passage concluded, saying, His "goings forth have been from of old from the days of eternity." Is this a description of a mere man, or indeed of God, who condescended to become a man?

Hebrews 13:8 states, "Jesus Christ is the same yesterday, today, and forever." The ringing prophecy of Isaiah 9:6 is awesome:

For unto us a Child is born, unto us a Son is given; and the government will be upon His shoulder. And His name will be called Wonderful, Counselor, Mighty God, Everlasting Father, Prince of Peace.

This is the God-man whose name is Jesus. To confirm this truth, listen to Proverbs 30:4:

Who has ascended into heaven, or descended? Who has gathered the wind in His fists? Who has bound the waters in a garment? Who has established all the ends of the earth? What is His name, and what is His Son's name, if you know?

What are the answers? Jesus our Lord, ten centuries later, gave us the answer in John 3:13, "No one has ascended to heaven but He who came down from heaven, that is the Son of Man who is in heaven."

Revelation 1:8 clearly referred to God Almighty: "'I am the Alpha and the Omega, the Beginning and the End,' says the Lord, 'who is and who was and who is to come, the Almighty.'"

But this Lord Almighty is revealed in verses seventeen and eighteen of the same chapter as Jesus Christ:

And when I saw Him, I fell at His feet as dead. But He laid His right hand on me, saying to me, "Do not be afraid; I am the First and the Last. I am He who lives, and was dead, and behold, I am alive forevermore. Amen. And I have the keys of Hades and of Death."

Do these incredible pronouncements, prophecies, and proclamations sound as if this supernaturally born Jesus is just a man, or truly the Incarnate Deity?

God Is Worshiped—So Is Jesus

In Matthew's Gospel we are told that the wise men of the East came to Bethlehem, seeking "Him who was born King." Note that they called the child "King" instead of the normal title, "Prince." We then

discover in Matthew 2:11, "They saw the young child
with Mary, His mother and fell down and worshiped
Him." May I encourage you to recognize that wise
men still worship Him!

Even demons recognized and worshiped Jesus.
Mark 5:6–7 tells us part of the story of a demon-pos-
sessed person: "But when he saw Jesus from afar, he
ran and worshiped Him. And he cried out with a
loud voice and said, "What have I to do with You,
Jesus, Son of the Most High God?'"

According to the ninth chapter of John, Jesus
healed a young man born blind. Then we read in
verses 35–38 the exciting end of the story:

> **Jesus heard that they had cast him out; and when
> He had found him, He said to him, "Do you believe in
> the Son of God?" He answered and said, "Who is He,
> Lord, that I may believe in Him?" And Jesus said to
> him, "You have both seen Him and it is He who is
> talking with you." Then he said, "Lord, I believe!"
> And he worshiped Him.**

Let me present your inquisitive minds and seeking
hearts with a glimpse of who Jesus is according to
Colossians 1:13–18:

> **He has delivered us from the power of darkness
> and translated us into the kingdom of the Son of His
> love, in whom we have redemption through His
> blood, the forgiveness of sins. He is the image of the
> invisible God, the firstborn over all creation. For by
> Him all things were created that are in heaven and
> that are on earth, visible and invisible, whether
> thrones or dominions or principalities or powers. All
> things were created through Him and for Him. And
> He is before all things, and in Him all things consist.**

**And He is the head of the body, the church, who is
the beginning, the firstborn from the dead, that in all
things He may have the preeminence.**

Who has all power over nature and the elements?
You say, of course, God. Then tell me who Jesus was
when He stilled the storm over Galilee (see Luke
8:22–25). And when He walked on the water (see
Mark 6:45–52)? And when He rose up to heaven at
the conclusion of His earthly ministry of redemption
(see Acts 1:4–11)? Elijah was taken up in a chariot of
fire. Jesus went up on His own.

God Has Power over Death—So Has Jesus

The familiar story of Jesus' raising Lazarus is
found in John 11. Lazarus's body had been in the
grave four days. Yet Jesus called him back to life.
Jesus also raised a twelve-year-old girl (Mark
5:21–43) and a teenage boy (Luke 7:11–17). Is it any
wonder that he declared, "I am the resurrection and
the life" (John 11:25)?

Jesus even had resurrection power over His own
life. He declared in John 2:19–21 that He would
raise Himself from the dead.

Only God Forgives Sin—So Does Jesus

The Bible clearly teaches that only God can forgive sin (see, for example, the Lord's Prayer). First
John 1:8–10 promises believers that if they confess
their sins to God, He will forgive them.

But Jesus also forgives sin. This is another proof
that He is God:

**Then they came to Him, bringing a paralytic who
was carried by four men. And when they could not**

come near Him because of the crowd, they un-
covered the roof where He was. And when they had
broken through, they let down the bed on which the
paralytic was lying.

When Jesus saw their faith, He said to the paralytic, "Son, your sins are forgiven you."

But some of the scribes were sitting there and reasoning in their hearts, "Why does this Man speak
blasphemies like this? Who can forgive sins but God
alone?"

And immediately, when Jesus perceived in His
spirit that they reasoned thus within themselves, He
said to them, "Why do you reason about these things
in your hearts? Which is easier, to say to the paralytic, 'Your sins are forgiven you,' or to say, 'Arise,
take up your bed and walk'? But that you may know
that the Son of Man has power on earth to forgive
sins"—He said to the paralytic, "I say to you, arise,
take up your bed, and go your way to your house."

And immediately he arose, took up the bed, and
went out in the presence of them all, so that all were
amazed and glorified God, saying, "We never saw
anything like this!"[3]

God Creates: So Does Jesus

[Only God can create from nothing. In Isaiah
44:24, the Lord God Himself stated that He created
everything by Himself. Hebrews 3:4 states that just
as every house has a builder, so the universe was
made by God.]

This prerogative of God is recognized in Jesus
when He fed five thousand (see Luke 9:10–17) from
five loaves and two fishes. On another occasion he
fed four thousand (see Mark 8:1–9) from seven
loaves and a few fishes.

[John 1:1–3 clearly declares that Jesus (called the

Word before his Incarnation, verse 14) is God and that everything which has ever been created has been created by Him. Colossians 1:15–17 affirms that everything was created by and for Jesus Christ. Truly He is one with the Father (John 10:30).]

A SUMMARY

Can we honestly deny the revealed truth? The credentials of Jesus of Nazareth are authentic and overwhelming. The prophets of old predicted His coming, predictions He faithfully fulfilled. Our Heavenly Father confirmed His relationship to Him as His unique Son. His miraculous works affirm His power. The Holy Spirit clarifies this truth to which the apostles and the New Testament testify powerfully.

Let me emphasize that Jesus is in reality God. The recordings of man-gods have been numerous throughout history. But this is the only true God-man.

Yet some still ask a very serious question. Why did Christ Jesus come if He were a mere prophet? The world did not need more prophets, priests, books, or miracle workers.

The God of heaven gives us the answer, "You shall call His name Jesus, because He will save His people from their sins" (Matthew 1:21). Jesus Christ came to save you and me from eternal death in hell—to give us eternal life in heaven. He came to save us from darkness and bring us to light, and from hate to love. He promised, "I have come that they may have life, and that they may have it more abundantly (John 10:10). Hear this declaration, "For the Son of man

has come to seek and to save that which was lost"
(Luke 19:10). The word *lost* is the same as *sinner*.
Since God's word (Romans 3:12) states, "All have
sinned," all of us become the object of God's concern.
All means everyone, including the prophets. The
Quran verifies,

Adam sinned (Surat 2:36; 7:22–23)
Abraham sinned (Surat 26:82)
Moses sinned (Surat 28:15–16)
David sinned (Surat 38:24–25)
Jonah sinned (Surat 37:142)
**Muhammad sinned (Surat 47:19; 48:1–2; 33:
36–38).**

The worst news is that the payment for sin is
death, but the good news is that "The gift of God is
eternal life through Jesus Christ our Lord" (Romans
6:23). A secret is revealed when we hear John the
Baptist's evaluation of Jesus: "Behold! The Lamb of
God who takes away the sin of the world!" (John
1:29).

How does He do this, you ask? By substitution. He
took our place. The first Adam fought the battle and
lost; thus, all of us are sinners. Jesus fought and won
so that we can become free children of God (see especially Romans 5). The tragedy of the cross becomes the triumph of the crucified. He who knew no
sin became sin for us that we may experience the
forgiveness of God made available to us through repentance and faith.

Why did the ancient Jews bring blood sacrifices to
the temple? Why does the Quran encourage them?
Because "without shedding of blood there is no remission" (Hebrews 9:22). Yet all the animal sacri-

fices were pointing to the ultimate sacrifice, Jesus the Lamb of God, whose blood covers our sins and even removes them. "For by grace you have been saved through faith, and that not of yourselves; it is the gift of God, not of works, lest anyone should boast" (Ephesians 2:8–9).

Isn't this fantastic! God demands good works as a result of salvation—not to obtain it. You don't have to go to Jerusalem, Mecca, Rome, or any other "holy" city. They are too small to contain the majesty of God. Ceremonial cleansing can wash the stain but never a heart full of sin. God is not impressed with our fastings or prayers. These promote self-righteousnss. God loves you and wants to save you by His grace through your faith in the Savior, Jesus Christ.

Finally, here is the whole truth in a nutshell. One is filled with awe, gratitude, and a sense of unworthiness once he reads the following words:

> **Let this mind be in you which was also in Christ Jesus, who, being in the form of God, did not consider it robbery to be equal with God, but made Himself of no reputation, taking the form of a servant, and coming in the likeness of men. And being found in appearance as a man, He humbled Himself and became obedient to the point of death, even the death of the cross. Therefore God also has highly exalted Him and given Him the name which is above every name, that at the name of Jesus every knee should bow, of those in heaven, and of those on earth, and of those under the earth, and that every tongue should confess that Jesus Christ is Lord, to the glory of God the Father.[4]**

CHAPTER NINE

IS JESUS GOD?
PART TWO: Ahmed Deedat

◆ ◆ ◆

Introduction

The subject, "Is Jesus God?" can very easily be solved by asking a counterquestion. Did Jesus claim to be God? Did He say, "I am God?" Did He say, "Worship Me?" And believe me, there is not a single and unequivocal statement in any of the 66 books of the Bible or the 73 of the Roman Catholic Bible where Jesus said, "I am God," or where He said, "Worship Me." There isn't. I would have been very happy to hear from the lips of Jesus this simple, straightforward, and explicit statement, "I am God" or "Worship Me," because I am a Muslim and we Muslims as a whole believe that Jesus Christ was one of the mightiest messengers of God. We believe in His miraculous birth, we believe that He was the Messiah, and we believe that He gave life to the dead by God's permission. He healed the lepers by God's permission.

MUSLIMS AND CHRISTIANS

This is the only real difference between the Muslim and the Christian—the divinity of Christ. And for that I say that our brother has not used a single statement from the lips of Jesus saying, "I am God" or "Worship Me." While He walked this earth, He never made such a statement. The nearest He came was a statement recorded in the book of Revelation, where Jesus supposedly says, "I am Alpha and Omega," meaning, "I am the first and the last."

Now, this book of Revelation was a dream. In the dream, John saw animals with eyes inside and outside and horns with eyes on it. This is a man who, if he eats too much, he has that type of experience. But while Jesus walked this earth, we will analyze what He actually said and what He did.

The Trinity

In the Christian catechism of the churches they say, "The Father is God, the Son is God, and the Holy Ghost is God, but they are not three Gods, but one God. The Father is Almighty, the Son is Almighty, and the Holy Ghost is Almighty. But there are not three Almighties, but one Almighty." It continues, "the Father is a person, the Son is a person, and the Holy Ghost is a person, but they are not three persons, but one person." I am asking, What language is that? Is that English? It sounds English, but that is not English. Person—person—person, but not three persons, but one person.

I say, what language is that? What is a person in the English language? Tell me. You Americanized Englishmen, tell me. What is a person in your language? If you and your two other brothers are identical triplets, we can't make out the difference between the three of you. If one of you commits a murder, can we hang the other? You say no. I say why not? You look alike. So he tells me, "No, he is a different person." What makes him a different person is his personality. If his personality is different, he is different, and when the Christian says, "In the name of the Father, and of the Son, and of the Holy Ghost," I say you have three distinct mental pictures in your mind. If you say you are of the Father, you are not of the Son and you are nothing of the Holy Ghost. Are you? These three pictures can never be superimposed into one. They will forever be three in your mind, unless the mind is diseased. You say these three are one, but the three will ever remain three.

Can Any Human Being Become God?

Now, as far as the Muslim is concerned, one's believing that any human being is God or is imitating God is an act of treason against God. Whether it is a Hindu idea of a God incarnate, or whether it is a Christian idea regarding God incarnate (God becoming man), the Holy Quran says, "That whosoever says that Jesus Christ, the son of Mary, is God is an act of blasphemy. It is treason against God." But Christ said, "Worship Allah, who is my Lord and your Lord. Whoever will associate anyone with Allah, in the fire of hell will be their dwelling place. And for the wrongdoers, they will be going to hell." And Jesus Christ, He is speaking about the Father in heaven. "He is your Father, and my Father." Again and again in the gospel of St. Matthew—you can start taking stock from chapter one, verse one—you will come across this phrase, "Your Father, thy Father, your Father, thy Father," thirteen times before the first time He used My Father.

Jesus Was a Man

It is an amazing situation that thirteen times the man is telling you that God Almighty is the Father of everybody. He is the Creator, Sustainer, Cherisher of

everybody, but physically, He does not beget because
begetting is an animal act. It belongs to the lower
animal act of sex. We do not attribute such an act of
God.

Christians keep on [talking about Jesus] repeating
the words, "Son of God." So we say, What about
Adam? Christendom will tell you. I say you are not
reading your Bible properly. You know God has got
sons by the tons in the Bible. Genesis 6:3 says, "And
the sons of God saw the daughters of men that they
were fair and took them to wife as they chose. And
when the sons of God came in to the daughters of
men and bore children to them, they became all men
of renown."

In the book of Exodus God says, "Israel is my son,
even my firstborn." Jeremiah says, "Ephraim is my
son, even my firstborn." In the New Testament we
are told, "As many as are led by the Spirit of God are
the sons of God." Every Tom, Dick, and Harry, if he
follows the will and plan of God, is a godly person.
In the language of the Jew—in the idiom of the
Jew—one says "Son of God," meaning righteous person.

The Meaning of Begotten

The Christian says, "No, Jesus is not like that." He
is begotten, not made. So I am asking, please explain
to me what you are trying to emphasize. What are
you really trying to tell me? Believe me, no Christian
in forty years has been able to open his mouth to tell
me what "begotten" means, [until I met] an American. He said it meant *sired* by God. I said, "What!
God sired a son?" So this is Jesus Christ? To the Muslim, this is a blasphemy, to say that Jesus is God.

But there is another blasphemy from the Christian
point of view. You see, the Christians, the Orthodox

Christians, the Anglican Christians, the Methodists, and all the Roman Catholics believe in the Holy Trinity, and they say that Jesus is the Second Person of the Trinity. You will never hear the words, "In the name of the Father, and of the Son, and of the Holy Ghost" as "In the name of the Son, the Holy Ghost, and the Father." It must ever be "In the name of the Father, and of the Son, and of the Holy Ghost." He is always the Second Person of the Trinity. If anybody in Christendom says that Jesus is the Father, it is a heresy. From the Muslim point of view, attributing divinity to any created human being is blasphemy. But from the Christian point of view—from the Church's point of view—if anybody attempts to say that Jesus is the Father, it is ancient heresy, which was condemned by the Roman Catholic church over a thousand years ago.

TRINITARIAN TITLES

Father and Son

I don't know why my Brother Shorrosh actually hit that fact, that he believes that Jesus is the Father. In his book, *The Liberated Christian* . . . he says on page 80, "My most loving Heavenly Father, I thank you for the miracles you have done in my life. The greatest miracle of all is the miracle that you loved me enough to die for me." Who? The Father died for him! And this is in church history an ancient heresy. It had been taken out one thousand years ago. But Jesus contradicts this statement, "Call no man your father on earth, for there is only one who is your Father which art in heaven" (Matthew 23:9).

Jesus is a man, walking this earth, which Peter testifies to in Acts 2:22. He says, "Ye men of Israel, hear these words, Jesus of Nazareth—a man—by miracles and signs which God did by Him." He was using Jesus in their midst. So He is not the Father. He says to the Jews, "Ye have neither heard His voice, the voice of God at any time nor seen His shape or form." The Jews were seeing Jesus. They did not harken to the message. But they were listening to Him; they were not deaf. They were seeing and they wanted to stone Him. He used to disappear and hide away, according to the Bible. So Jesus could not be the Father, and He could not be the God.

What is God Like?

The Bible gives us a test: What God is not! In the Quran, we are also given what God is not. But God is not like any thing you can think or imagine. Anything you think or imagine is not Him. In Islam we are given some ninety-nine attributes of God: He is kind, He is merciful, He is holy, and on and on. But there are certain things that He is not. The Bible also gives us what God is not. It says in the book of Job 25:4–6, "How then can man be justified with God?" How can you compare any human being with God? How can one be clean that is born of a woman? Anyone that is born of a woman is not good enough to compare with God. Whether it is Moses or Jesus or Muhammad or a Rama or a Krishna: anyone that a woman carried for nine months cannot be God. That is nonsense.

"When the moon is not bright enough nor the stars are impure enough in your sight, how much less is man?" (Job 25:5). Christians admit the truth that Jesus was born of a woman. They object: "No, no!" He was born miraculously. We agree. So that makes Him something supernatural! God Almighty, in this book, the Christian Bible, says, "How much less is man, if the sun, moon, and stars are nothing in His sight, what is man?" Who are we? Who are you? How much is a man who is a maggot? You know what is a maggot? Those worms that go on manure, human dung. You and I, according to this book of God, you are nothing more than a maggot. And the Son of Man—who?—is Jesus Christ. Explicit statement. In case you have in the back of your mind that Jesus is an exception, God Almighty goes out of His way to tell you, "Look, this Jesus of mine is no exception."

The Son of Man

Ask any Christian, Who is the Son of Man? Eighty-three times in the New Testament Jesus Christ is described as the Son of Man. "The foxes have holes, but the Son of Man has no place to lay his head." As Jonah was three days and three nights in the belly of the earth, so shall the Son of Man be. Ask any Christian missionary who is the Son of Man and they will say Jesus.

So Jesus is a worm. We are maggots. In other words, don't make a mistake, anyone who is born of a woman, and the Bible tells us in the Gospel of Luke 2:21, "When He was eight days old He was circumcised, and named Jesus, as told by the angel when He was in His mother's womb." How did He come out from there? Like you and me! I am asking, if you were a nurse and you went into the stable to deliver the child [Jesus] could you for one moment think that the helpless little creature with all the filth and the mud could be your God, your Jehovah, your Allah? No, the human mind repulses from the idea that his puny little creature—which made his mother impure for forty days—was God. She was impure for forty days and what made her impure?

The birth of an unholy God? No, he was a human child, like you and me.

The Bishops' Survey

The Anglicans in England today are a bit more reasonable. There was a short survey of Anglican bishops in June last year [1984], here in the United Kingdom. Half of the bishops say that Christians do not have to believe that Jesus Christ was virgin-born. No more, you do not have to believe it. If your salvation and mine depends on His virgin birth [meaning Jesus is, in fact, God]—if we are Christians— then Jesus must also die as a God, because one man can't carry the sins of the world. We say they didn't kill Him and they didn't crucify Him. But the Christian has to believe that Jesus must die as a God.

Do you believe that God died? Do you say that He is eternally immortal? So He dies—what happens with creation? You know about the electric power. Where does it come from, and how does it come into this station—through the substation or the head-station? If God Almighty's light is extinguished, who runs His universe? For three days and three nights He was away in the tomb, as our Christians say. For three days and three nights, who was controlling the universe?

The Father Is Greater Than Jesus

Jesus Christ never said at any time, "I am God" or "Worship Me." On the contrary, He said, "My Father is greater than I" (John 14:28). He said, "I can of myself do nothing" (John 5:30). God can do everything. God can do everything and anything! Except become a man, as my Brother Shorrosh says God can. Am I limiting God? I say no. I challenge people to prove to me that God can create another God, that He can create another uncreated. From the beginning, which has no beginning, as soon as He creates somebody, he is created. This is common sense. He can't create another God. A father cannot create two fathers, then a dozen fathers.

So my Hindu cousins are more consistent. They believe in millions of gods: anything is god; everything is god. Why are you so unreasonable that you make only one exception? Why shouldn't we have more gods, more sons?

Jesus says further, "[God] can't throw me out of His kingdom." Can He throw you out of His kingdom, out of His dominion? He can't. He can obliterate you, but He can't throw you out. Now, that doesn't mean He is limited? God Almighty can do anything, but what He does are godly things.

JESUS' MIRACLES

God Almighty Does Godly Things

Jesus says further, "If I cast out demons by the Spirit of God. . ." (Matthew 12:28). He had power to do this and to do that. He says, "All power is given unto me." Therefore, [He is saying] it is not His but is given to Him. By whom? By the Father in heaven. He gave Him the power to heal the blind and the lame and to raise the dead. According to the Bible, Jesus dried up the fig tree from its very roots. Where did He get the power?

When He performed these miracles in the New Testament, He said, "Glory to God for giving such power unto men." The glory is not to men but to God.

Jesus Does Not Know the Hour of His Return

My brother says that in the Quran it says that
Jesus knows the hour of judgment. I would like to
know where it says that. The Bible contradicts that.
It says, "But of that day and that hour knoweth no
man. No, not the angels, neither the Son." In other
words, in my knowledge, I am not like God. In my
power, I am not like God (see Mark 13:32). The big
question remains: Where does it say I am like God or
I am God?

Are God and Jesus the Same?

Is there a single Christian who can give me a verse
that says Jesus and God are the same thing? [Some-
one in the audience called out John 14:9, "He who
has seen me has seen the Father."]

In John 10:30, Jesus said, "I and my Father are
one." Now the context. I have been talking to people
for forty years, and when this verse is quoted—the
verse is there, you can't contradict that—I have not
come across one learned man of Christendom who
could give me the context.

The context starts with verse 23 of John 10 and
goes through verse 29. Jesus was walking on Solomon's porch in the Temple of Jerusalem. The Jews
surrounded Him and demanded, "How long do you
keep us in doubt? If You are the Christ, tell us
plainly." He was not [making His] claim clearly—
that was the charge by the Jews. But, in fact, He
didn't speak ambiguously: He put forth His claim
that He was the Son of God, the Christ, the Messiah.

The Jews put up a fight; they didn't like His
preaching. He called them a new generation of
vipers, whited sepulchres, you fools, you snakes, you
wicked and adulterous generation. Would you like to

hear people addressing you like that? You don't forget such denunciations in a hurry.

So they found Jesus alone, surrounded Him menacingly, and demanded, "You tell us." They wanted to pick a fight with Him. So Jesus said:

I told you and you believed me not. My sheep hear my voice and obey me and I give unto them eternal life and they shall never perish. And my Father which gave them to me is greater than all and no man is able to pluck them out of my Father's hand. I and my Father are one. [Free translation by the speaker.]

In this passage one can be assured that once a person accepts the faith, he remains in the faith. I, as a teacher, see to that, as well as God Almighty sees to that.

The Meaning of Oneness

"We are one." Jesus meant He and God were *one in purpose*. The Jews were looking for trouble. And if you are looking for trouble you don't have to go very far. You find it on the corner.

Then the Jews took up stones again to stone Him. Jesus answered them, "Many good works I have showed you from my Father. For which of those works do you stone me?" And they said, "For a good work we do not stone you but for blasphemy and because You being a man make of Yourself God" (John 19:31–33).

In other words, He was claiming to be God. That was another false charge. The first charge was that He was talking ambiguously. Another false charge leveled against him was, "You are claiming to be

God." The Christians agree with the Jews that Jesus did make such a declaration, but He was entitled to it.

Let us hear what Jesus Himself said. The Jews said He blasphemed; the Christians said He did not because He was entitled to the claim. What did Jesus say?

Jesus answered them, "Is it not written in your law, 'I said, Ye are gods?' If he called them gods, unto whom the word of God came. . ." (John 10:34,35).

Others Were Called Gods

God Almighty spoke to Moses and said, "Behold, I have made you a god to Pharaoh and out of him shall be thy prophet." Furthermore, in Psalm 82:6 we find, "Ye are gods and all of you are the children of the Most High." We are overwhelmed at the genius of the Jewish language, because when a person is called "god," he is not actually God.

Similarly, one finds in 2 Corinthians 2:4 that the devil is called "the god of this world." Is he, the devil, God? No! This is your language. It means he is in control, so you say he is god. Moses is god to Pharaoh, and the Jews are called gods. That is the genius of the Jewish language.

Now let us see once again what Jesus meant in John 10:34, 35. In essence, He said: "Is it not in your law I said ye are gods? Was that blasphemous because I said I am the Son of God? In other words, I said nothing, because God has got sons by the tons in every language. Why are you trying to find fault with me, when I only said, I am the Son of God, when others are called gods?

THE HUMANITY OF JESUS AND MARY

Listen, God Almighty says in Surat al-Ma'idah (The Table Spread) 5:75:

> The Messiah, son of Mary, was no other than a messenger, messengers (the like of whom) has passed away before him. And his mother was a saintly woman. And they both used to eat (earthly) food. See how we make the revelations clear for them, and see how they are turned away!

◆ ◆

مَا الْمَسِيحُ ابْنُ مَرْيَمَ إِلَّا رَسُولٌ قَدْ خَلَتْ مِن
قَبْلِهِ الرُّسُلُ وَأُمُّهُ صِدِّيقَةٌ كَانَا يَأْكُلَانِ الطَّعَامَ
انْظُرْ كَيْفَ نُبَيِّنُ لَهُمُ الْآيَاتِ ثُمَّ انْظُرْ أَنَّىٰ يُؤْفَكُونَ ۝

They Both Ate Food

So what is exceptional about "They ate food"? We all eat food, don't we? No, this refers to the idea that Jesus and Mary are supernatural gods. The Roman Catholics call Mary the "Mother of God." Jesus is the "Son of God." And Brother Shorrosh and many Christians believe that He is God in human form—He is God incarnate. So if they were such great gods, then why did they both eat food? If they ate food, they had the call of nature. If you eat, you must go to the toilet sooner or later—or to a bush or to the rocks. It can't be helped.

What God Does Not Say

God Almighty doesn't tell you those words. Listen to what He says: "See how we make all the revelations clear for them"—that they both ate food. The implications of eating food, "See how we make the revelations for them." Have another look. "How they are turned away!" Gone away from the true path, attributing to God an animal nature that He is like a man.

What is Meant by "God's Image"?

"We are made in His image." What image? [Our] image? This is a monkey image. We are all qualified monkeys. Some look like chimpanzees, some like baboons, some like something else. We are all glorified monkeys. Is that the image God is talking about? And the Christian says yes.

I said earlier that God testifies in the book of Genesis, quoted by Dr. Shorrosh, "And God said, 'Let there be light.'" I ask, Did God say the words with His mouth? The Christian answers affirmatively. Did He utter the words? Of course, He did. So God has got a mouth, certainly. So if He has a mouth, He has got teeth as well. Can you imagine a toothless God going "blah-blah-blah!" Can you imagine a God like that? What else?

He has got a tongue. Then He must have a larynx and lungs. Yes, sir. So when He is creating the sun, stars, and moon, He is talking and talking. God's mouth goes dry, and He has to lubricate it. Once that lubrication goes in, there must be an outlet as well. No? So what are you bringing God down to? An anthropomorphic conception, that is to say, God is like a man.

GOD'S NAME ELOHIM

Elohim Is a Plural of Respect

God's name is *Elohim,* "The God" (Genesis 1:3). Yes, it is a plural. My Arab brother says, "Of course." There are plurals and duals in Hebrew and Arabic. Singular, plural, and dual. The word is *Elohim*— Gods? I haven't seen a single Bible yet which said, "Gods said let there be light." The word should be *God.* What is this "im"? Ask the Jew, ask the Arab.

"Im" is a plural of respect. Allah says in the Quran, "It is we who have sent down the revelation and it is for us to protect it." Ask any Muslim. The most simple of us say it is one. Then who is this "us"? Ask the Arab.

No Arab for fourteen hundred years has pointed a finger at the Muslims telling them that they are worshiping more than one God. There is a plural of respect in every language. I should like Dr. Shorrosh to question me—to say see if there is supposed to be more than one God in the Quran. I say there are two types of plurals—the plural of respect and the plural of numbers—that exist both in Hebrew and in Arabic.

Jesus Was Like Adam

So Jesus ate and His mother ate. The Bible says, "The Son of Man [Jesus] came eating and drinking and they said, 'Behold, a gluttonous man and a winebibber'" (Matthew 11:19 and Luke 7:34). What then makes Jesus God? His birth? He was born without a human father, but He must have had a father. So His father was God? The Quran answers that very simply,

> Lo! the likeness of Jesus with Allah is as the like-
> ness of Adam. He created him of dust, then He said
> unto him: Be! and he is.

◆ ◆

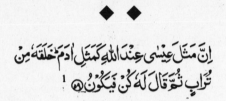

If Jesus is God, and the very Son of God because
He has no earthly father, then Adam is a greater God,
because he had no father and no mother! Simple,
basic common sense demands this deduction. It
stands to reason that if Jesus had no father, which
makes Him God, then Adam is a greater God because
he had no father *and* no mother.

JESUS' PRAYER

Why Does Jesus Pray?

This man, Jesus, He cried to God while He was on
the cross (Matthew 27:46), "My God, my God, why
hast thou forsaken me?" Whom is He crying to? Himself? Or is He putting up an act, dramatizing Himself by crying, "My God, my God, why do you let me
down?" If He is God how can He let Himself down?
Again, in Mark 15:34, He is crying to Allah. I am asking the Jehovah's Witnesses—they are among the
Christians; they go and harass people—when Jesus
said, "My God, why hast thou forsaken me," is this
something like "Jehovah, why hast thou forsaken
me?" The Witness says *no*.

In the book of Revelation 19:1, we read about

John's vision. He heard the angels in heaven singing, "Hallelujah! Hallelujah!" When Christians go into ecstasy, they shout, "Allelujah! Allelujah!" I am asking you what is Allelujah? "Jah" is an expression in Arabic, as "Oh, mother." Allelujah means "Yah is Allah," there is no other God. But God was not a child born in a stable by a virgin birth. What makes Him God? His miracles?

Before calling out Lazarus, Jesus prayed.

And Jesus lifted up his eyes, and said, Father, I thank thee that thou hast heard me. And I knew that thou hearest me always: but because of the people which stand by I said it, that they may believe that thou hast sent me. And when he thus had spoken, he cried with a loud voice, Lazarus, come forth.[2]

Jesus supposedly meant the people that stood by were superstitious and ridiculous people, knowing that they could say that He gave life to the dead and that He was God. For that reason He spoke to God loudly. Jesus was groaning in the spirit. He was pouring out His heart to God, saying something like this: "My friend Lazarus is dead. Oh Lord, bring him back from the dead." And God Almighty said, "Go ahead and ask what you want and you will get it." But after He called Lazarus out, He said, "Oh Lord, I know that thou has heard me and I know that thou hearest me always, but because of the people who stood by, I said it loudly so that they will believe that thou hast sent me." And He said, "He that is sent is not greater than the One who sent him. The words are not mine, but those of the Father that sent me. He has given me a commandment, what I should say and what I should speak, even as the Father has said unto me, so I speak." There is not a single or une-

quivocal statement in any version of the Bible where
Jesus says, "I am God" or where He says, "Worship
Me." If there is, we Muslims would have no hesita-
tion in accepting it.

SUMMARY

Simply because we know that Jesus Christ, as one
of the mightiest messengers of God, would never lie,
the question's being asked whether He was a liar or a
lunatic or God, doesn't make sense.

Why should you make such a proposition? Why
cannot the man be a mighty messenger of God? Why
should He be a liar or a lunatic? Again and again, in
Christian literature, evangelists say He was either a
liar or an impostor. Is the opposite of a liar, an impostor? Is the opposite of God, an impostor? Is the
opposite of God, a lunatic? No.

Jesus is dead. Why can't He be what He claimed to
be? He is the messenger of God and as such follows
him. Did He not announce, "He is not of me, whoever
does not take his cross and follow me?" And again,
"Take up your cross and follow me. If you follow me
you will have eternal life."

Listen to Him, harken to Him, obey what He
says—that is salvation. The proof of that, "Verily, verily, I say unto you unless your righteousness exceed
that of the scribes and the Pharisees, you shall by no
means enter the Kingdom of heaven." There is no
heaven for you, unless you are better than the Jew.
And you cannot be better than the Jew by not keeping the laws and the commandments. Listen to Him,
follow Him, and if you follow Him, you can't help
being a Muslim.

CHAPTER TEN

REBUTTAL, QUESTIONS AND ANSWERS FROM THE LONDON DEBATE

❋ ❋ ❋

CHRISTIAN REBUTTAL

Jesus Did Say He Was Lord

What a joy it is to make replies to my friend, Mr. Deedat.

Concerning the statement about Jesus saying He is God, I first call your attention to John 13:13, "You call Me Teacher and Lord, and you say well, for so I am." Remember, please, if the Queen of England walked in here, she would not have to tell you she was the queen. Jesus did not have to tell us every time He did something that He was God. When He answered Philip, He said, "You say show us the Father; it is sufficient. I have been with you so long and you don't know? He who has seen Me has seen the Father" (John 14:9). Our brother quoted another verse (John 10:30) which has the same idea.

The Book of the Revelation Is Not a Dream

As to Mr. Deedat's remarks about the book of the Revelation, we ask, did not the prophet of Arabia and the prophets of the Old Testament also have dreams? Did not God reveal Himself to them in dreams and visions? What do you do with the Miraj, which was a dream or a vision? According to Ibn Hisham, "The apostle of God used to say, 'In what reached me my eye was asleep, but my heart was awake.'"

God speaks through visions and dreams. And they do not come because your stomach is full or empty (as alleged by Mr. Deedat), but God chooses to use this method. And if He chooses dreams or visions for His revelation, so be it.

Questions on the Trinity

I think the problem with our Muslim friends is that they don't realize we are just as much against the Trinity of the days of the ancient Arab world as they are. You see, there was a group of heretics, called the Miriamites, who were converted from paganism to Christianity. They thought of Mary as the Queen of heaven, whom God married, and who gave birth to Jesus as a result of this union.

For God's sake, get this through your mind and heart. Jesus was not the Son of God as a man who was born through a sexual experience. His is a spiritual relationship. He came because He loves you. The Miriamites were just as wrong as they could be. Biblical Christianity asserts a Trinity of God as Father, Son, and Holy Spirit.

Does it not amaze you that in the ninety-nine excellent names of God in the Quran, not one is Love? Not one is Father? In the Bible you are not introduced to a God who is a dictator, who demands that you become His slave. God, instead, is presented as a loving Father who wants you and me and the whole world to *become His Sons.*

Mary Conceived by the Holy Spirit?

Who is the Holy Spirit? Is He an angel called Gabriel? No! Let me challenge you! Seventy-five percent of the glorious Quran in my expressive language of Arabic is from the Holy Bible. I would urge you with all my might to look into the Bible and find the main sources of the Quran.

The incarnation of God, who loves you and me, is [for us as it would be as if you were watching] ants trying to go from one point to another by a roundabout route instead of by a straight line. You would observe the wasted time and energy, so you would decide to show them a straighter and shorter path.

You would announce to them, "I will help you." But they would not understand your language. You would try to show them the way by pushing the nose of one and the tail of another. Alas, they would keep going back to their old ways.

So you would determine that the only way would be either for you to become an ant, or for them to become human. Now, bear in mind that they cannot become human because they do not have such creative powers. But let us suppose that you had the creative power to become incarnated as an ant. Now tell me, could you show them the better way? You say yes. Not on your life. Sorry, you are wrong. Because once you became an ant, you would end up thinking and moving just as the ants think and move. In order to fulfill your sacred mission, you must keep your human intelligence to be able to show them the right path.

Therefore, Jesus, God of the ages became incarnate. He came in human flesh; He never ceased being God. He ate as a man, slept as a man, and was tired as a man. He also used the title "Son of Man" to

identify Himself with humanity—you and me. But
He was also the Son of God; he held the universe
together as God (Colossians 1:17), even as His
human body lay in the grave. [In other words, Jesus
was the Son of God before He was born in Bethlehem. "Son of God" is one of His 365 titles.]

Mr. Deedat quoted Job, and he misquoted the
verse. The verse states very clearly, "How can a man
be justified?" which means, how can a man be made
right in the sight of God? Nobody can become right
in the sight of God without paying for his sin! Therefore, God made the provision in that Jesus takes our
place by shedding His blood as full payment for our
sins. Listen to this declaration. "I have come that you
may have life." Then again, "The blood of Jesus
Christ His Son cleanses us from all sin" (1 John 1:9).

The Angel Announced the Title of Jesus

Please remember that the angel announced to
Mary, "He will be great, and will be called the Son of
the Highest" (Luke 1:32). Are you telling me that the
angel was lying? The Lord was making a mistake
in making such an announcement? Jesus loves Mr.
Deedat. He loves you, and He pleads with you and
says, "Come unto me and I will give you rest. Come
unto me all the ends of the earth and be saved." Salvation is not exclusively for the Christians, neither
just for the Muslims, nor for only the Jews. Salvation
is offered to all of us. God loves us. He became the
Son of Man in order that men could become the
adopted sons of God. Because He cares!

As for the meaning of "My Father," His self-im-
posed limitation caused Him to say that. Yet let us
not forget that He said, "I and the Father are One."
He demonstrated this fact so eminently inasmuch as
He was always God the Son.

The Anglican Bishops' Problem

Jesus is God, whether the Anglican bishops agree or not. Let God be true and every man a liar. The bishops need to repent of their sins and trust the inerrant Word of God instead of their own logic. We need revival across this nation to stop doubts, wickedness, vileness, apostasy, and backsliding by turning away from our waywardness to following this loving, living Lord. Jesus must reign until the Father puts all His enemies under the feet of Jesus.

THE APPEAL OF THE GOSPEL

I invite you one and all to discover the truth, which is God in Christ, reconciling the world unto Himself. For a true Muslim will become a true Muslim and a true Christian can become a true Christian, when he accepts the gift of God, Jesus Christ, the Son of the living God, as Savior and Lord.

MUSLIM REBUTTAL

Jesus and the Father

Beginning with John 14:9, as quoted by my brother Shorrosh where Jesus, in answering Philip, said, "If you have seen Me, you have seen the Father": . . . If we look at it in its context again, there are a series of misunderstandings. Chapter 14 begins with a misunderstanding, and with this misunderstanding, the disciples continue.

In Chapter 14, Jesus told His disciples, "And whither I go, ye know and the way ye know"—that is, "You know where I am going and how to get there." So the disciples say, "Master, we know not whither thou goest and how can we know the way?"

They misunderstood. Jesus was speaking about a spiritual journey; they were thinking about a geographical location—Newcastle or Southhampton. But He was talking about God and how to go to God. So Jesus said, "I am the Way, the Truth, and the Life. No man cometh unto the Father but by Me." This was too heavy for them. They couldn't follow what He was talking about. One disciple asked, "Lord, show us the Father and it suffices us. It will be enough if you will just show us God. We want to see God with our physical eyes and that will be satisfaction enough for us."

In answer to that, Jesus replied, "Philip, you have been with me for so long. You are a Jew. As a Jew, you ought to know better than that. No man can see God and live. God has never been seen at any time, and you, being with me for three years, you still haven't understood my mission. If you want to see God with your physical eyes, you can look at the Son. If you have seen Me you have seen the Father. If you have understood Me, you would understand what God is." This was the language He was speaking when He said, "Seeing they see not; hearing, they hear not, neither do they understand." This seeing is not physical seeing. Jesus meant, "If you understood what I am, you would have understood what God is. You wouldn't make such a silly request." Jesus, therefore, was not claiming to be the Father.

The Trinity in 1 John 5:7

I would like to know who has heard this verse: "For there are three that bear record in heaven, the Father, the Word, and the Holy Ghost, and these three are One." Have you heard that before, Mr. Massabni? Do you read this in your Bible? First John 5:7 says, "For there are three that bear record in heaven, the Father, the Word (meaning Jesus), and the Holy Ghost, and these three are One." It is there in your Bible.

Here is the Holy Bible. You see, this verse I quoted you just now is to be found in the Roman Catholic version of the Bible. It is to be found in the Authorized King James Version of the Bible. It is there. But it has been thrown out of the Revised Standard Version of the Bible as a fabrication. All modern translations of the Bible do not have that verse any more. This has been thrown out, not by Muslim scholars, Jewish scholars, or Hindu scholars, but by thirty-two scholars of the highest eminence, backed by fifty cooperating denominations. They found that this was a fabrication and they threw it out!

The Ascension of Christ

Similarly, the ascension. In the Gospels of Matthew, Mark, Luke, and John, you find ascension twice, that Jesus ascended into heaven. Mark 16:19 says, "And Jesus was taken up into heaven." Luke 24:51 says, "And Jesus was taken up into heaven." Only two places in the Gospels mention the ascension. My brother quoted from the Acts. [In] the gospels [of] Matthew, Mark, Luke, and John, the ascension is mentioned in two places and those two places in the Revised Standard Version of the Bible have also been thrown out as fabrications.

Muslims Don't Call God Father

The fact that the word *Father* does not appear in the Holy Quran becomes a major point of criticism of Islam. You know, we are given ninety-nine attributes of God Almighty, but "Father" is not one of them. And *Father* in Arabic is easier than the word *Rub* (Lord). *Ab* in Arabic means "father." Why is "father" not given?

There are millions of people on earth who [have the misconception that God is a physical father]— that this Father in heaven begot a Son. Begetting is an animal act; it belongs to the lower animal acts of sex. So this word, *Father*, is eschewed, is taken out and never used, simply because there are people like my brother's [Shorrosh's] son at age four.

His [Dr. Shorrosh's] son, Salam, in *The Liberated Palestinian*, after he came out of the bath, pulled the plug, and the water ran out. He exclaimed, "I know now how rain falls." Dr. Shorrosh asked him how. The little boy said, "When Jesus has a bath in heaven, then pulls the plug, we have rain!" And for that, the little boy was given a hug and a kiss.

You see, that concept carries on. You are having an idea that God Almighty also is there somewhere in the heavens doing something similar. So because of this anthropomorphic concept, the Father idea has not been conveyed in Islam. These are not befitting the majesty of God: that God begets a son or that He is the Father in heaven, the loving Father, who goes and kills His own son for the sins of mankind. He can rectify you. But it is your mistake. Why should He kill his own son? I am asking—is that love? Somebody attacks and murders your wife or child or rapes your daughter, and now you can do nothing— you are utterly helpless. So what do you do? You go and kill your own son! And you call that love!

You say, this is a wrong concept of justice and ethics. You see, if you have the right concept, your behavior will become right.

QUESTION FOR THE CHRISTIAN

How Is a Person Saved?

Once again, I remind you, Jesus never told a lie. In John 3:14–16, He said:

> **"And as Moses lifted up the serpent in the wilderness, even so must the Son of Man be lifted up, that whoever believes in Him should not perish but have eternal life. For God so loved the world that He gave His only begotten Son, that whoever believes in Him should not perish but have everlasting life."**

When Abraham tried to provide his son as a sacrifice, God said, "No, I will provide the offering." Praise God that tonight we can say for a truth that God is Father, Son, and Holy Spirit—One in three, three in One, a mystery neither you nor I can understand fully, but not a contradiction.

Salvation is obtained by confessing and repenting from one's sins, then believing that Christ paid in full for our sins by His atoning death. Since the payment for sin is death, Jesus died in our place. By faith in His finished work on the cross we are saved from the punishment of sin. By living holy lives, we are being saved from the power of sin. When we get to heaven, we shall be saved from the presence of sin forever.

QUESTION FOR THE MUSLIM

Why Did Jesus Allow Thomas to Kneel at His Feet and Say to Him, "My Lord And My God"?

Jesus allowed this because Thomas was not present when Jesus went to the Upper Room for the very first time. And Jesus Christ demonstrated to His disciples that He was the same person, eating food—broiled fish and honeycomb (Luke 24:40–43). So the disciples testified to Thomas when he came along and met them (John 20:24–29). They told him, "The Master was here and ate food with us." Thomas said, "Except I put my finger into the print of the nails and put my hand into his side, I will not believe that Jesus was physically with us."

If they had told him that [Jesus] was a spirit, a ghost, a spook, [Thomas] would have believed because people believed in ghosts and spooks in those days far more readily than in anything else. So when Jesus came along the second time to the Upper Room, Thomas was there.

Jesus told Thomas, "Reach hither thy hand, reach hither thy finger and behold my hands, and put your hand into my side and don't be faithless."

So Thomas realized what a doubter, what a heel he had been. All the disciples were testifying that the Master was there, that He was alive and that He was eating broiled fish and honeycomb, and he couldn't believe. Thomas wanted proof, so Jesus told him to come and see. As Thomas realized that he had been a fool, he said, "My Lord, my God."

What? He was calling Jesus his Lord and his God? No. This is an exclamation people call out. Was Thomas calling Jesus his Lord and his God? If I said to Anis, "my God," would I mean Anis is my God? No. This is a particular expression.

WRITTEN QUESTION FOR THE MUSLIM

Please Explain How God Could Save the World Except by God Coming in the Flesh.

A law-abiding Jew came to Jesus seeking eternal life or salvation. In the words of Matthew 19:16–17: "Now behold, one came and said to Him, 'Good Teacher, what good thing shall I do that I may have eternal life?' So He said to him, 'Why do you call Me good? No one is good but One, that is, God. But if you want to enter into life, keep the commandments.'"

You will agree that if you or I were that Jew, we would infer from these words that salvation was guaranteed provided we kept the commandments without the shedding of any innocent blood. Unless, of course, Jesus was speaking with tongue in cheek, knowing full well that His own "forthcoming redemptive sacrifice," His "vicarious atonement" for the sins of mankind, was not many days hence.

Why would Jesus give him the "impossible" solution of keeping the law (as the Christian alleges) when an easier way was in the offing? Or did He not know what was going to happen—that He was to be crucified? Was there not a contract between Father and "Son" before the worlds began for His redeeming blood to be shed. Had He lost His memory? *No!* There was no such fairy-tale agreement as far as Jesus was concerned. He knew that there was only one way to God, and that was, as Jesus said, *Keep the commandments!*

WRITTEN QUESTIONS FOR THE CHRISTIAN

Please quote which Surat mentions that Jesus knows the day of judgment.

Here is what the Quran states Jesus said in Surat Zukhruf (Ornaments of Gold) 43:61:

And lo! verily there is knowledge of the Hour. So doubt ye not concerning it, but follow Me. This is the right path.

◆ ◆

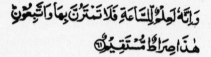

If Jesus was the Son of God, what has happened to him now?

We are told in the Bible that Jesus is now
1. at the right hand of the Father (Acts 6).
2. our high priest interceding for us (Hebrews 5:5).
3. our Lamb sitting on the throne (Revelation 22:3).
4. King of kings and Lord of lords (Revelation 19:6–10).

CHAPTER ELEVEN

CONCLUSION

❋ ❋ ❋

I have emphasized in this book the distinctives of and the differences between Christianity and Islam. This great debate will continue. Others, both Muslim and Christian, will continue to write and speak. This is the way it should be. Let us continue to reason together with our minds and hearts and turn away from violence.

Sadly, in my native Middle East today, some Muslims, Christians, and Jews live as warring neighbors. Note that I say "some." Most Muslims, Christians, and Jews deplore violence and desire to live in peace. They want to live in freedom from fear. They want only the opportunity to share their beliefs with fellow believers in one God.

My purpose here is not to discuss Middle Eastern politics. Jews say that where you find two Jews you find three opinions. That is also true of Muslims, who are divided into more than 150 sects, and Christians, who are separated into numerous denominations. The Bible lands where Abraham, Moses, and Christ Jesus walked are wracked with division, bitterness, and warfare because some professing Jews, Muslims, and Christians seek to enforce their beliefs by violence. This is not God's will, but it is the way things are. Let me, however, touch briefly on three major issues still fanning the flames of strife.

First, our Jewish friends point to Christian persecution of Jews through the centuries since Christ. Alas, this is true, but I would also ask them to remember that the persecution has been more political than religious. In the past and today, journalists and historians glibly refer to certain nations as "Christian" nations. There has never been a truly Christian nation though there have been and are today nations with Christians among their citizens.

Jews should not blame Christians, in whose hearts the Messiah of love dwells, for the evil deeds dictators and other political leaders have done in the name of Christ. I can testify that I am a Palestinian who loves the Jews because of Jesus. By the grace of God, I would not persecute Jews, even if I had the power to do so. The Christ who lives in me will not permit me to inflict evil upon anyone, including the children of Abraham, whether Jews or Arabs.

The persecution of Jews by political Christians has largely ceased. Indeed, Christians are the greatest support for Jewish rights in the world today. Christians, for example, call upon the Soviet Union to stop persecuting Jews and allow them to emigrate to Israel or anywhere else they so desire. Here and there, small pockets of animosity do remain between Christians and Jews. But the contention is not generated solely by the Christian. Some fanatical Jews in Israel would like to drive all Christians out of that land and even expel the minority of their fellow Jews who accept Jesus as their Messiah. But my Jewish friends assure me that these fanatics are not the majority in Israel, and I believe them.

The real warfare and terrorism in the Middle East is being waged among Muslims, Jews, and some who profess to be Christians. Note that I use the phrase "profess to be Christians." These so-called Christians who deal in terrorism and war are only Christians by culture. Their ancestors converted to Christianity many years ago, and their Christian identity has come down through families. They are Christians in the same sense that some Americans are called "Southerners" because they live in a certain part of the country and practice certain "Southern" customs.

Our Muslim friends continue to bring up the subject of the Crusades. Between the eleventh and thirteenth centuries, Europeans, who were called Christians because they lived in "Christian" countries, waged the Crusades to take the Holy Land from Muslims who had conquered this land by force in previous years. In other words, the Crusades were wars in response to previous wars. Many Crusaders were religiously motivated (wrongly so, I think), but many others had worldly aims and hoped to capture land and loot and open new trading opportunities in the Middle East.

Muslims rightly see the Crusades as a black page in Christian history. I and all true Christians agree. These barbarous acts by "Christian" armies cast shame upon the gospel of peace that Jesus brought.

Islamic history, however, is hardly innocent of the same wrongs. Following the command of Muhammad to fight all non-Muslims, his followers conquered the Holy Land by the sword and forbade Christian pilgrims access to holy sites in Jerusalem or demanded exorbitant fees for safe conduct to the sites. Thus the Crusades were not an all-out war against Islam. Originally, they were launched to force Muslims to let Christians visit and worship at sacred sites associated with Christ.

The Muslims were wrong to deny or take advantage of Christians wanting to visit sacred sites. The

Christians were also wrong to take up the sword against the Muslims who controlled these sites. It is wrong on both counts today.

Today, to the credit of Israel, the sacred sites are open to all. Muslims can visit the Dome of the Rock without fear and without charge. Christians can walk where Jesus walked and see traditional sites of His birth, crucifixion, resurrection, and ascension. Jews can come to the western wall of the old temple and offer their prayers, something denied them when they were not in control of East Jerusalem. Only fear keeps Muslim, Christian, and Jewish worshipers back—fear of Islamic terrorists. Indeed, Muslim fanatics have succeeded in their crusades of terror so well that the number of pilgrims who usually come to Jerusalem has shrunk by as many as 75 percent.

We shouldn't be surprised. When Muslims controlled the Holy Land before the Crusades, no one could question their decisions of right and wrong. They made themselves judge and jury, and they ruled by the sword. They declared might to be right, and they made Jews and Christians second-class citizens.

Since the bloody early centuries of Islam, many Muslims have come to reject the sword. These "moderate" Muslims want to live in peace. But the warlike Muslims intimidate their fellow peace-loving Muslims by terrorism. They hijack planes, kidnap innocents, murder and maim travelers—even little children—in airports, to accomplish their rule-or-ruin purposes. All while the atheistic Soviet Union, which is no friend of Islam or any other religion, provides the terrorists with arms.

Revenge for Israeli bombings and exploitation motivates many terrorist acts. As a Palestinian who lost his home and his father to Israel in 1948, I can understand this passion for revenge because I once burned with it too. I wanted to get a gun and explosives and cross the Jordan into Israel and kill every Jew in sight. Thank God, terrorist weapons were not as easily available then as today. I might have eventually obtained a weapon and set off on a mission of death and destruction, but Christ the Messiah "intercepted" me instead. Only when I surrendered to the King of Kings and the Prince of Peace did the hatred for Jews begin to drain from my heart. Thanks to God's grace, I reached the point in November 1973 where I was able to say on a television and radio interview in Israel, "I love you because of Jesus." Jesus of Nazareth solved my hate problem. He kept me from becoming a terrorist.

God Almighty had promised the land of ancient Canaan or modern Palestine to Abraham first:

And the LORD said to Abram, after Lot had separated from him, "Now lift up your eyes and look from the place where you are, northward and southward and eastward and westward; for all the land which you see, I will give it to you and to your descendants forever. And I will make your descendants as the dust of the earth; so that if anyone can number the dust of the earth, then your descendants can also be numbered."[1]

God confirmed this covenant to Isaac, according to Genesis 26:3, 4:

"Sojourn in this land and I will be with you and bless you, for to you and to your descendants I will give all these lands, and I will establish the oath which I swore to your father Abraham. And I will multiply your descendants as the stars of heaven, and will give your descendants all these lands; and by your

descendants all the nations of the earth shall be blessed."

The prophet Ezekiel, a thousand years later, asserted that the people called the children of Israel in the Bible would be brought back after being scattered (it happened in 586 B.C.), and their very hearts and natures would miraculously be changed:

"For I will take you from the nations, gather you from all the lands, and bring you into your own land. Then I will sprinkle clean water on you, and you will be clean; I will cleanse you from all your filthiness and from all your idols. Moreover, I will give you a new heart and put a new spirit within you; and I will remove the heart of stone from your flesh and give you a heart of flesh."[2]

The Arabs have been blessed with twenty-three countries and three million square miles of territory, yet many wonder why they covet the only place and space their half-brothers possess by God's promise. If the Arab nations would have more love and forgiveness instead of warfare and animosity, I am sure that my fellow Palestinians could find a more welcome attitude in Israel and eventually have a government of their own in cooperation or federation with Israel. Love and peace are much better than bitterness and bloodshed.

Today, in this last hour of human history, it seems the people in the Bible lands and in much of the rest of the world, as well, are being forced to side with Islam or Israel. Militant, warring Muslims are saying to their brothers, "If you do not fight with us, you are for Israel."

Why can't we—Jews, Christians, and Muslims—see God as more than a judge? He is righteous and holy, yes, but He is also merciful, loving, and forgiving. Saul of Tarsus, the great persecutor of the followers of the Messiah Jesus in the first century, discovered this. He wrote, "However, for this reason I obtained mercy, that in me first Jesus Christ might show all longsuffering, as a pattern to those who are going to believe on Him for everlasting life."[3]

Recently I heard astronomer Carl Sagan on "Good Morning America" tell about the radio telescope erected at Harvard University for the sole purpose of listening for a message from deep space. Dr. Sagan thinks that other civilizations may exist and that they may have gone through problems similar to the people on earth and somehow survived. Therefore, if we can pick up their message with the radio telescope, we can learn how not to self-destruct.

Dr. Sagan may be a brilliant astronomer, but he has missed the contact that has already been made from beyond earth. God has already come in Jesus, the Prince of Peace, to reconcile us to Himself and to one another. The almost two-thousand-year-old Christmas story far surpasses any hope that Dr. Sagan or anyone else may have for picking up a message from outer space.

Jesus paid our sin debt. He became our ransom. He gave Himself as a sacrifice for our sins that we might have life and life more abundantly. None of the great human prophets and leaders could do this. Islam's Muhammad did not even claim to die for our sins. Only Jesus could do this, because Jesus was God Incarnate, God's only begotten Son in human flesh, yet without sin. He was the Word who became flesh!

For God so loved the world that He gave His only begotten Son, that whoever believes in Him should not perish but have everlasting life.[4]

I have come that they may have life, and that they may have it more abundantly.[5]

Jesus said to him, "I am the way, the truth, and the life. No one comes to the Father except through Me."[6]

Only Jesus, not Muhammad, taught us to live in peace and survive by walking in love.

A new commandment I give to you, that you love one another; as I have loved you, that you also love one another. By this all will know that you are My disciples, if you have love for one another.[7]

Jesus the Messiah became both the Message and the Messenger from outer space. He was more than a prophet. We don't need a radio telescope at Harvard to tell us that. We don't need a Dr. Sagan to interpret this gospel or Injil. We can read it for ourselves in the Holy Scripture. We can experience salvation and redemption in our lives by inviting the Messenger to forgive our sins.

If you have not already done so, I pray that you will receive this Message and Messenger today so that you may be prepared to meet Him when He returns for His people.

For the Lord Himself will descend from heaven with a shout, with the voice of an archangel, and with the trumpet of God. And the dead in Christ will rise first.[8]

And God will wipe away every tear from their eyes; there shall be no more death, nor sorrow, nor crying; and there shall be no more pain, for the former things have passed away. Then He who sat on the throne said, "Behold, I make all things new." And He said to me, "Write, for these words are true and

faithful." And He said to me, "It is done! I am the Alpha and the Omega, the Beginning and the End. I will give of the fountain of the water of life freely to him who thirsts. He who overcomes shall inherit all things, and I will be his God and he shall be My son. But the cowardly, unbelieving, abominable, murderers, sexually immoral, sorcerers, idolaters, and all liars shall have their part in the lake which burns with fire and brimstone, which is the second death.[9]

NOTES

❋ ❋ ❋

Chapter 1: The Religion of Islam

1. J. Murdoch, *Arabia and Its Prophet* (Madras, India: The Christian Literature Society for India, 1922), 29.

2. Ghulam Sarwar, *Islam: Beliefs and Teachings* (London: The Muslim Educational Trust, 1984), 163.

3. Murdoch, 29.

4. Ibid., 26.

5. Ibid.

6. Ibid., 27.

7. Arthur Jeffrey, *Islam: Muhammad and His Religion* (Indianapolis, Ind: Bobbs-Merrill, 1958), 85.

8. Abd Al Masih, *Who Is Allah in Islam?* (Vallich, Austria: Light of Life, n.d.), 84–87.

9. C. George Fry and James R. King. *Islam: A Survey of the Muslim Faith* (Grand Rapids, Mich: Baker Book House, 1982), 48.

10. Ibid., 50.

11. Sarwar, 74, 75.

12. Norman Anderson, *The World's Religions* (Grand

Rapids, Mich: William B. Eerdmans Publishing Company, 1976), 121.

13. W. St. Clair-Tisdall, *The Sources of Islam* (New Delhi, India: Amarko Book Agency, 1973), 71–73.

14. David Lamb, *The Arabs* (New York: Random House, 1987), 287.

15. G. H. Jansen, "The Ayatollah Takes on Mohammed," *San Francisco Chronicle*, February 4, 1988, 22.

16. T. V. Thomas, *A Christian Apologetic toward Islam* (unpublished thesis, 1978), 31.

17. Josh McDowell and Don Stewart, *Handbook of Today's Religions* (San Bernardino, Cal: Here's Life Publishers, 1983), 383.

18. *The World Book Encyclopedia*, vol. 2 (Chicago: Field Enterprises, 1972), 24.

19. Ibid., 25, 26.

20. McDowell and Stewart, 397.

21. Don McCurry, ed., *Muslim Awareness* (Altadena, Cal: Samuel Zwemer Institute, 1984), 9.

22. Ibid., 6.

23. Jimmy Carter, *The Blood of Abraham* (Boston: Houghton Mifflin, 1985), 9, 12.

Chapter 2: The Life of Muhammad

1. Martin Lings, *Muhammad* (London: George Allen and Unwin Ltd., 1983), p. 22.

2. William Goldsack, *Muhammad in Islam: Sketches of Muhammad from Islamic Sources* (Madras, India: The Christian Literature Society for India, 1916), 12.

3. Ibid., 13.

4. Murdoch, 15.

5. Ibid.

6. Lings, 40, 41.

7. Murdoch, 16.

8. John Glubb, *The Life and Times of Muhammad* (New York: Stein and Day, 1971), 271.

9. Goldsack, 112—114.

10. Ibid., 18–22.

11. Ibid., 16.

12. *Surat al-Najm* (The Star) 53:19, 20.

13. Goldsack, 17.

14. *Surat al-Najm* (The Star) 53:21–23.

15. Lings, 96–100.

16. Ibid., 118–122.

17. Goldsack, 18.

18. Murdoch, 19.

19. Ibid., 20.

20. Ibid.

21. Lings, 172–188.

22. Murdoch, 20.

23. Ibid., 21, 22.

24. *Surat al-Ahzab* (The Clans) 33:35.

25. Lings, 237–242.

26. Ibid., 233.

27. *Surat al-Tahrim* (Banning) 66:51.

28. Aisha Abd El Rahman, *The Wives of the Prophet* (Morocco: Dar El Hilal, 1971), 165–170.

29. Ibid., 178–191.

30. Ibid., 208–214.

31. Lings, 229–39.

32. Ibid., 267, 268.

33. Murdoch, 23.

34. *Surat al-Ma'idah* (The Table Spread) 5:3.

35. Lings, 332–336.

36. Ibid., 337–339.

37. Ibid., 340, 341.

38. Lamb, 55, 56.

39. Murdoch, 25.

40. Lings, 345.

41. C. G. Pfander, *Balance of Truth* (London: the Religious Tracts Society, 1910), 227.

42. Ibid., 228.

Chapter 3: Jesus Christ According to Islam

1. H. A. R. Gibb and J. H. Kramers, *Shorter Encyclopedia of Islam* (Ithaca, N.Y.: Cornell University Press, 1953), 173.

2. Abd Al-Fadi, *The Person of Christ* (Rikon, Switzerland: The Good Way, n.d.), 8.

3. Ibid., 9.

4. Ibid., 10.

5. *Surat Maryam* (Mary) 19:29, 30.

6. Abd Al-Fadi, 18.

7. Ibid., 20, 21.

8. Ibid., 15.

9. *Surat al-Baqarah* (The Cow) 2:253.

10. *Surat al-Nisa* (Women) 4:171.

11. Abd Al-Fadi, 11, 12.

12. Ibid., 8.

13. Gibb and Kramers, 173.

14. Geoffrey Parrinder, *Jesus in the Quran* (Toronto, Canada: Fellowship of Faith, 1982), 53.

15. Abd Al-Fadi, 43.

16. Ibid., 39, 40.

17. Parrinder, 85.

18. Iskander Jadeed, *The Cross in the Gospel and Quran* (Rikon, Switzerland: The Good Way, n.d.), 5.

19. Parrinder, 109.

20. Abd Al-Fadi, 6.

21. James Robson, *Mishkat Al Masabih*, vol. II (Lahore, Pakistan: Ashraf Press, 1975), 1143.

22. M. Thomas Starkes, *Islam and Eastern Religions* (Nashville, Tenn: Convention Press, 1981), 37.

23. Ibid., 21.

Chapter 4: The Crucifixion: Fact or Fiction?

1. 1 Corinthians 15:1–4.

2. Jadeed, 10.

3. Ibid., 12.

4. Ibid., 13.

5. Ibid., 14.

6. Ibid., 14, 15.

7. Patrick Johnstone, *Operation World* (Bucks, England: Send the Light, 1978), 33.

8. Matthew Poole, *A Commentary on the Bible*, vol. 1 (London: Banner of Truth Trust, 1962), 10.

9. Anis Shorrosh, *Jesus, Prophecy and the Middle East* (Nashville, Tenn: Thomas Nelson, 1983), 17, 18.

10. Ibid., 22, 23.

11. William Whiston, *Josephus: Complete Works* (Grand Rapids, Mich: Kregel Publications, 1978), 18:3:3.

12. Jadeed, 33.

13. Galatians 3:28, 29.

Chapter 5: Islam Unveiled

1. *Surat al-Furqan* (The Criterion) 25:5.

2. John 8:32.

3. E. Stanley Jones, *The Word Became Flesh* (Nashville, Tenn.: Abingdon Press, 1963).

4. John 1:1, 14.

5. *Surat al-Waqi'ah* (The Event) 56:77–81.

6. *Surat Ta-Ha* (Ta-Ha) 20:133.

7. *Surat al-Ankabut* (The Spider) 29:48.

8. E. J. Elder, *Biblical Approach to the Muslim* (Houston, Tex: Leadership International, n.d.), 52–56.

9. St. Clair-Tisdall, 15.

10. W. St. Clair-Tisdall, *The Original Sources of the Qu'ran* (London: Society for Promoting Christian Knowledge, 1905), 65.

11. Ibid., 80–88.

12. Ibid., 115.

13. *Surat al-Imran* (The Family of 'Imran) 3:35–37.

14. *The Lost Books of the Bible* (New York: Bell Publishing Company, 1979), 26–28.

15. Glubb, 36.

16. Ibid., 96.

17. Lings, 3.

18. Murdoch, 14.

19. Goldsack, 36–39.

20. *The Secrets of Enoch (Idris)*, an Egyptian work in Arabic, second century A.D.

21. *The Testament of Abraham*, an Egyptian work in Arabic, second century A.D.

22. *Arta Viraf Namak*, a Hindu source, second century A.D.

23. *Al Nasikh Wal Mansukh*, 14.

24. See the English interpretation of the Quran, by A. Yusuf Ali.

25. *Surat al-Nisa* (Women) 4:34.

26. Glubb, 368.

27. *Surat al-Nisa* (Women) 4:34.

28. Gibb and Kramers, 413, 414.

29. Murdoch, 43.

30. Josh McDowell and John Gilchrist, *The Islam Debate* (San Bernardino, Cal: Here's Life Publishers, 1983), 94.

31. Ibid., 94–102.

32. Murdoch, 45.

33. Osborn, *Life of Mahomet*, 4:318.

34. Matthew 24:6–11.

35. Luke 13:27.

Chapter 6: The Quran Exposed

1. *Surat Ta-Ha* (Ta-Ha) 20:113.

2. *Surat al-Isra* (The Children of Israel) 17:88.

3. St. Clair-Tisdall, *The Original Sources*, 27.

4. Ibid., 44–49.

5. Pfander, 25. See also Norman Geisler and William Nix, *A General Introduction to the Bible* (Chicago, Ill: Moody, 1969), 133–147.

6. Pfander, 275, 276.

7. *Surat al-Rum* (The Romans) 30:1–4.

8. *Surat al-Ma'idah* (The Table Spread) 5:30–32.

9. Genesis 4:1–8.

10. St. Clair-Tisdall, *Sources*, 14, 15.

11. *Surat al-Anbiya'* (The Prophets) 21:58–69.

12. *Surat al-Saffat* (Those Who Set the Ranks) 37:91–97.

13. St. Clair-Tisdall, *Sources*, 14, 15.

14. Genesis 11:26–31.

15. Gibb and Kramers, 154.

16. Ibid., 178, 179.

17. Genesis 17:20, 21.

18. Lamb, 13.

19. Shorrosh, 57.

20. *Surat al-Imran* (The Family of 'Imran) 3:35–41.

21. *The Lost Books*, 26–28.

22. Ibid., 38.

23. *Surat Maryam* (Mary) 19:29, 30.

24. *The Lost Books,* 69.

25. *Surat al-Ma'idah* (The Table Spread) 5:112–115.

Chapter 7: The Bible

1. *Surat Yonus* (Jonah) 10:94.

2. *Surat al-Ankabut* (The Spider) 29:46.

3. *Surat al-Hijr* (Al-Hijr) 15:9.

4. *Surat al-Fath* (Victory) 48:23.

5. *Surat al-Kahf* (The Cave) 18:27.

6. *Surat al-Baqarah* (The Cow) 2:2–4.

7. Ibid., 2:136.

8. Revelation 22:18, 19.

9. John 15:26.

10. John 16:13.

11. John 8:31, 32.

Chapter 8: Is Jesus God? Part One

1. Hebrews 1:1–8.

2. John 8:56–58.

3. Mark 2:3–12.

4. Philippians 2:5–11.

Chapter 9: Is Jesus God? Part Two

1. *Surat al-Imran* (The Family of 'Imran) 3:59.

2. John 11:41–43.

Chapter 11: Conclusion

1. Genesis 13:14–16.

2. Ezekiel 36:24–26. See *Jesus, Prophecy and the Middle East*, particularly chapter 4, "Signs of the Return— Being Fulfilled," and chapter 5, "The Arabs in Prophecy," for greater detail on these matters.

3. 1 Timothy 1:16.

4. John 3:16.

5. John 10:10b.

6. John 14:6.

7. John 13:34, 35.

8. 1 Thessalonians 4:16.

9. Revelation 21:4–8.

BIBLIOGRAPHY

❉ ❉ ❉

ISLAM EXPLAINED

Abd El Rahman, Aisha. *The Wives of the Prophet*. Morocco: Dar El Hilal, 1971.

ABDO. *The Life of the Messiah in a Classical Arabic Tongue*. Larnaca, Cyprus: Izdihar Ltd., 1987.

Abdul-Haqq, Abdiyah Akbar. *Sharing Your Faith with a Muslim*. Minneapolis, Minn: Bethany House Publishers, 1980.

Al-Masih, Abd. *Why Is It Difficult for a Muslim to Become a Christian?* Villach, Austria: Light of Life, n.d.

Anderson, Sir Norman, ed. *The World's Religions*. Grand Rapids, Mich: William B. Eerdmans Publishers, 1976.

Azzam, Leila and Aisha Gouverneur. *The Life of the Prophet Muhammad*. London: The Islamic Tests Society, 1985.

Carter, Jimmy. *The Blood of Abraham*. Boston: Houghton Mifflin, 1985.

Cragg, Kenneth. *Sandals at the Mosque*. New York: Oxford University Press, 1959.

El Mu'alam, Muhammad. *Quran Kareem*. The Sunrise Press, 1983.

Elder, E. J. *Biblical Approach to the Muslim*. Houston, Tex: Leadership International, n.d.

Fry, C. George and James R. King. *Islam: A Survey of the Muslim Faith*. Grand Rapids, Mich: Baker Book House, 1982.

Gibb, H. A. R. and J. H. Kramers. *Shorter Encyclopedia of Islam*. Ithaca, N.Y.: Cornell University Press, 1953.

Glubb, John. *The Life and Times of Muhammad*. New York: Stein and Day, 1971.

Goldsack, William. *Muhammad in Islam: Sketches of Muhammad from Islamic Sources*. Madras, India: The Christian Literature Society for India, 1916.

Guillaume, A. *The Life of Muhammad*. London: Oxford University Press, 1955.

Hahn, Ernest. *Jesus in Islam: A Christian View*. Hyderabad, India: Henry Martyn Institute of Islamic Studies, 1984.

_____ *Muhammad the Prophet of Islam*. Hyderabad, India: The Henry Martyn Institute of Islamic Studies, 1981.

Hefley, James and Marti. *Arabs, Christians and Jews*. Plainfield, N.J.: Logos International, 1978.

_____ *By Their Blood: Christian Martyrs of the Twentieth Century*. Milford, Mich: Mott Media, 1979.

_____ *The Liberated Palestinian*. Wheaton, Ill: Victor Books, 1986.

Hughes, Thomas Patrick. *Dictionary of Islam*. New Delhi, India: Cosmo Publications, 1978.

Jadeed, Iskandar. *Did God Appear in the Flesh?* Rikon, Switzerland: The Good Way, n.d. (Arabic and English).

_____ *God and Christ*. Basel, Switzerland: Markaz Al-Shabiba, n.d. (Arabic and English).

────── *The Cross in the Gospel and the Quran.* Rikon, Switzerland: The Good Way, n.d. (Arabic and English).

────── *The Infallibility of the Torah and the Gospel.* Rikon, Switzerland: The Good Way, n.d. (Arabic and English).

────── *What Must I Do to Be Saved?* Rikon: Switzerland: The Good Way, n.d. (Arabic and English).

McDowell, Josh. *Evidence That Demands a Verdict,* vol. I. San Bernardino, Cal: Here's Life Publishers, 1986.

────── *Evidence That Demands a Verdict,* vol. II. San Bernardino, Cal: Here's Life Publishers, 1986.

McDowell, Josh and John Gilchrist. *The Islam Debate.* San Bernardino, Cal: Here's Life Publishers, 1983.

McDowell, Josh and Don Stewart. *Answers to Tough Questions.* San Bernardino, Cal: Here's Life Publishers, 1983.

────── *Handbook of Today's Religions.* San Bernardino, Cal: Here's Life Publishers, 1983.

Murdoch, J., ed. *Arabia and Its Prophet.* Madras, India: The Christian Literature Society for India, 1922.

Nehls, Gerhard. *Christians Answer Muslims.* South Africa: Life Challenge, 1980.

Parrinder, Geoffrey. *Jesus in the Qur'an.* Toronto, Canada: Fellowship of Faith, 1982.

Pfander, C. G. *Balance of Truth.* London: The Religious Tract Society, 1910.

────── *The Mizanu'l Haqq (Balance of Truth).* London: The Religious Tract Society, 1910 (Arabic edition).

Pfeiffer, Charles. *The Dead Sea Scrolls and the Bible.* Grand Rapids, Mich: Baker Book House, 1969.

Pickthall, Muhammad Marmaduke. *The Glorious Qur'an.* Grand Central Station, N.Y: Muslim World League, 1977.

Register, Ray G. *Dialogue and Interfaith Witness with Muslims*. Spanish Fort, Ala: Nall Printing Company, 1984.

Richards, Lawrence O. *The World Bible Handbook*. Waco, Tex: Word, 1982.

Robson, James. *Mishkat al-Masabih*, vols. I and II. Lahore, Pakistan: Ashraf Press, 1975.

Rudin, James and Marcia. *Prison or Paradise: The New Religious Cults*. Philadelphia, Penn: Fortress Press, 1980.

Sal, Jerjus and Hashem Al-Irabeh. *Secrets about the Quran*. Villach, Austria: Light of Life, n.d.

_____ *The Crucible of the Rise of Islam*. Villach, Austria: Light of Life, n.d.

Shah, E. Ahmad. *Theology: Muslim and Christian*. Lucknow: Lucknow Publishing House, 1970.

Sheikh, Bilquis. *I Dared to Call Him Father*. Trenton, N.J.: Chosen Books, 1978.

Shorrosh, Anis A. *Jesus, Prophecy and the Middle East*. Nashville, Tenn: Thomas Nelson, 1983.

Soper, Edmund David. *The Religions of Mankind*. New York: Abingdon Press, 1951.

Starkes, M. Thomas. *Islam and Eastern Religions*. Nashville, Tenn: Convention Press, 1981.

St. Clair-Tisdall, W. *Christian Reply to Muslim Objections*. Villach, Austria: Light of Life, 1980.

_____ *The Original Sources of the Qur'an*. London: Society for Promoting Christian Knowledge, 1905.

_____ *The Sources of Islam*. New Delhi, India: Amarko Book Agency, 1973.

Von Denffer, Ahmad. *'Ulum Al-Qur'an*. Leicester, UK: The Islamic Foundation, 1983.

Weller, Sam, ed. *The World's Great Religions*. New York: Time, Inc., 1957.

Whiston, William. *Josephus: Complete Works*. Grand Rapids, Mich: Kregel Publications, 1978.

Zwemer, Samuel M. *The Moslem World*, vol. XXII. Princeton, N.J.: Missionary Review Publishing Company, 1932.

The Glorious Quran. Jerusalem: The Islamic Orphanage Press, 1373 (Hijrah).

The Lost Books of the Bible. New York: Bell Publishing Company, 1979.

ISLAM EVALUATED

Al-Fadi, Abd. *The Person of Christ*. Rikon, Switzerland: The Good Way, n.d.

Al Khoury, Bishara Abdullah. *The Poetry of Al Akhtal the Younger*. Beirut, Lebanon: The Arabic Book House, 1972.

Al-Masih, Abd. *What Do You Think about Christ?* Rikon, Switzerland: The Good Way, n.d.

———— *Who Is Allah in Islam?* (trans. from German). Villach, Austria: Light of Life, n.d.

Alavi, K. K. *In Search of Assurance*. Rikon, Switzerland: The Good Way, n.d.

Ali, Maulana Muhammad. *A Manual of Hadith*. London and Dublin: Curzon Press Ltd., 1944.

Austin-Sparks, T. *The School of Christ*. London: David Wilkerson Ministries, 1964.

Baar, Marius. *The Unholy War*. Nashville, Tenn: Thomas Nelson, 1980.

Ben El Hasein, Abdu Abdullah. *The Commentary on the Ten Hanging Poems*. Beirut, Lebanon: Library of Life, 1979.

Blackwood, Andres W., Jr. *The Holy Spirit in Your Life.* Grand Rapids, Mich: Baker Book House, 1957.

Bright, Bill. *The Holy Spirit: The Key to Supernatural Living.* San Bernardino, Cal: Here's Life Publishers, 1980.

Butrus, Zachariah. *God Is One in the Holy Trinity.* Basel, Switzerland: Center for Young Adults, n.d.

Collins, Larry and Dominique Lapierre. *O Jerusalem!* New York: Pocket Books, 1972.

Deedat, Ahmed. *Al-Qur'an: The Ultimate Miracle.* Durban, South Africa: Islamic Propagation Center, 1983.

_____ *Christ (Peace Be Upon Him) in Islam.* Durban, South Africa: Islamic Propagation Center, 1983.

_____ *Crucifixion or Crucifiction.* Durban, South Africa: Islamic Propagation Center, 1984.

_____ *Is the Bible God's Word?* Durban, South Africa: Islamic Propagation Center, 1980.

_____ *Resurrection or Resuscitation.* Durban, South Africa: Islamic Propagation Center, 1978.

_____ *The God That Never Was.* Durban, South Africa: Islamic Propagation Center, 1985.

_____ *What Is His Name?* Durban, South Africa: Islamic Propagation Center, 1981.

_____ *What the Bible Says About Muhammad (PBUH).* Durban, South Africa: Islamic Propagation Center, 1976.

_____ *What Was the Sign of Jonah?* Durban, South Africa: Islamic Propagation Center, 1976.

_____ *Who Moved the Stone?* Durban, South Africa: Islamic Propagation Center, 1977.

Emmaus Bible School Staff. *What Christians Believe.* Chicago, Ill: Emmaus Bible School, 1951.

Ford, George. *Light of the World*. Rikon, Switzerland: The Good Way, n.d.

Freed, Ralph. *Reaching Arabs for Christ*. Chatham, N.J.: TransWorld Radio, 1972.

Hahn, Ernest. *Understanding Some Muslims' Misunderstandings*. Toronto, Canada: Fellowship of Faith, 1983.

Hamada, Louis Bahjat. *God Loves the Arabs, Too*. Nashville, Tenn: Winston-Derek Publishers, 1986.

Hatem, M. Abdel-Kader. *Land of the Arabs*. London and New York: Longman Group Ltd., 1977.

Hobohm, Mohummed Aman. *Islam's Answer to the Racial Problem*. Durban, South Africa: Islamic Propagation Center, 1983.

Hutchinson, John A. *Paths of Faith*. New York: McGraw Hill, 1969.

Ibraham, Ishak. *Black Gold and Holy War*. Nashville, Tenn: Thomas Nelson, 1983.

Jadeed, Iskandar. *Did God Appear in the Flesh?* Rikon, Switzerland: The Good Way, n.d. (Arabic and English).

―――― *God and Christ*. Basel, Switzerland: Markaz Al-Shabiba, n.d. (Arabic and English).

―――― *The Cross in the Gospel and the Quran*. Rikon, Switzerland: The Good Way, n.d. (Arabic and English).

―――― *The Infallibility of the Torah and the Gospel*. Rikon, Switzerland: The Good Way, n.d. (Arabic and English).

―――― *What Must I Do to Be Saved?* Rikon, Switzerland: The Good Way, n.d. (Arabic and English).

Jesus to the Muslims. *Outreach to Islam*. Republic of South Africa: Industrial Press, 1985 and 1986.

Jones, E. Stanley. *The Word Became Flesh*. Nashville, Tenn.: Abingdon Press, 1963.

Kusta, Yousif. *Is God One or Three?* Colorado Springs, Col: Al Nour, 1985.

Lahiz, 'Imad ud-Din. *The Life of the Rev. Mawlawi.* Lahore, Pakistan: n.d., 1957.

McGee, J. Vernon. *So.* Glendale, Cal: Griffin Printing and Lithograph Company, 1983.

Memmi, Albert. *Jews and Arabs* (trans. from French). Chicago, Ill: J. Philip O'Hara, Inc., 1975.

Parshall, Phil. *Beyond the Mosque.* Grand Rapids, Mich: Baker Book House, 1985.

_____ *Bridges to Islam.* Grand Rapids, Mich: Baker Book House, 1985.

_____ *New Paths in Muslim Evangelism.* Grand Rapids, Mich: Baker Book House, 1986.

Poole, Matthew. *A Commentary on the Bible.* London: Banner of Truth Trust, 1962.

Pudaite, Rochunga. *My Billion Bible Dream.* Nashville, Tenn: Thomas Nelson, 1982.

Rao, K. S. Ramakrishna. *Muhammad.* Durban, South Africa: Islamic Propagation Center, n.d.

_____ *Muhammad the Prophet of Islam.* Durban, South Africa: Islamic Propagation Center, 1985.

Ryan, Wendy, ed. *The Evangelical Round Table.* Princeton, N.J.: Princeton University Press, 1986.

Saideh, Khaleel. *Injil Barnaba.* Cairo, Egypt: Al Manar Press, 1908.

Saifi, Naseem. *Presenting Islam to the Christians.* Rabwah, Pakistan: A Tabshir Publication, 1961, 1973.

Sarwar, Ghulam. *Islam Beliefs and Teachings.* London: The Muslim Educational Trust, 1984.

Thanvi, Maulana Ashraf Ali. *Bahishti Zewar (Virtues to*

Earn Allah's Pleasure) (English version by Muhammad Masroor Khan Saroha). Lahore, Pakistan: Islamic Publications Ltd., 1982.

Thomas, T. V. *A Christian Apologetic toward Islam, Hinduism, and Buddhism* (unpublished thesis). Jacksonville, Fla: Luther Rice Seminary, 1978.

United Christian Council. *Let Jews and Arabs Hear His Voice.* Jerusalem: United Christian Council, n.d.

Witty, Robert G. *Holy Spirit Power.* Jacksonville, Fla: Pioneer Press, 1966.

Christian Witness among Muslims. Villach, Austria: Light of Life, 1971.

The Thailand Report on Muslims. Wheaton, Ill: Lausanne Committee for World Evangelization, 1980.

GLOSSARY

✳ ✳ ✳

'Abd Allah: 'Abd al-Muttalib's youngest son. Father of the Prophet.

Abu Bakr: A rich and much respected merchant of Mecca. The first man to believe in the Prophet and embrace Islam. He was the Prophet's closest friend and companion. He was the first Muslim Kaliph, according to Sunni Muslims.

'Ayisha: Muhammad's third wife and daughter of Abu Bakr.

'Ali: Son of Abu Talib. First cousin of the Prophet. 'Ali later married Fatimah, the youngest daughter of the Prophet.

Allahu Akbar: Phrase meaning "God alone is Great."

Aminah: The mother of the Prophet.

Ansar: The inhabitants of Medina who became Muslims and asked the Prophet to come and live with them.

Assalamu Aleikum Wa Rahmatullah Wa Barakatuhu: Phrase used by the Muslims in greeting, meaning: "May the peace, mercy, and grace of Allah be upon you."

Bahira: A Nestorian monk who lived in the desert city of Basrah on the Quraysh caravan route to Syria and who influenced Muhammad secretly and tremendously.

Bani Quraizah: A Jewish tribe who were living in Yathrib when the Prophet arrived. Several times they betrayed their covenant with the Prophet, forcing him to fight them.

Bedouin: Nomadic Arabs of the desert, usually shepherds.

Bismillah: The phrase meaning "In the Name of Allah."

Buraq: Animal ridden by the Prophet Muhammad on his supposed ascent to heaven (the Isra' and Mi'raj). It had two wings and an unveiled face of a beautiful woman who was well dressed, wearing cosmetics and ornaments.

Fatima: The daughter of Muhammad and his first wife, Khadija, and the wife of 'Ali, the fourth Khaliph.

Hadith: An account of what the Prophet said or did, or his silent approval of something said or done in his presence. It was handed down by oral tradition for generations after Muhammad's death until it was finally transcribed.

Hajj: A pilgrimage to Mecca. One of the five pillars of the Islamic faith.

Hijrah: Muhammad's flight from Mecca to Yathrib (present-day Medina) in A.D. 622.

Imam: A Muslim who is considered by Sunnis to be an authority in Islamic law and theology or the man who leads the prayers. Also refers to each of the founders of the four principal sects of Islam. The Shi'ites accept twelve great Imams.

Ishmael: The first son of Abraham by his wife's maid, Hagar of Egypt. Muslims believe he and his mother moved to the Valley of Mecca where Abraham joined him to rebuild the Ka'bah.

Islam: Religion revealed to the Prophet Muhammad; literally means "submission to the will of Allah."

Jihad: To struggle in the cause of Allah with pen, speech, or sword; Holy War.

Ka'bah: A small stone building located in the court of the great mosque at Mecca, containing the black stone (a meteorite) supposedly given to Adam by Gabriel and subsequently found by Abraham, who allegedly built the Ka'bah with Ishmael.

Khadija: The prophet Muhammad's first and only wife until her death. She was the first to believe in the Prophet and to accept as true the message he brought from Allah.

Khalid Ibn Al-walid: A great warrior. He planned the defeat of the Muslims at Uhud, but later converted to Islam and became one of the most famous Muslim generals.

Khaliph (Caliph): The title given to the office of the spiritual and political leader who took over after Muhammad's death, or the vice-regent of Muhammad.

Mahdi: "The guided one"; a leader who will cause righteousness to fill the earth. The Sunnis are still awaiting his initial appearance while the Shi'ites hold that the last Imam, who disappeared in A.D. 874 will someday reappear as the Mahdi—a type of Christ.

Mashaf: Another name for the Quran in handwritten form.

Mecca: The birthplace of Muhammad. This city, located in Saudi Arabia, is considered the most holy city by the Muslims. It must be visited by Muslims at least once in a lifetime.

Medina: A holy city of Islam named for Muhammad, it was previously named Yathrib. It is the city to which Muhammad fled in A.D. 622.

Minaret: Tower from which the call to prayer is made.

Mosque: Building in which Muslims pray.

Muhammad: The prophet and founder of Islam. Born around A.D. 570; died A.D. 632.

Muslim (Moslem): A follower of Muhammad; literally, "one who submits."

Omar: According to the Sunnis, the second Muslim Khaliph and principal advisor to the first Khaliph, Abu Bakr.

Paradise: Place to which the souls of good people go after death.

Pbuh: A salutation used by Muslims after the name of Muhammad is used.

Prophet: A man who comes with a message from God.

Quran (Koran): Said to be the final and complete inspired word of God, transmitted to the prophet Muhammad by the angel Gabriel over a period of twenty-three years.

Quraish: The descendants of Ishmael, son of Abraham, who became the most important tribe in Mecca; the tribe of the Prophet.

Ramadan: The ninth month of the Muslim year when the Quran was supposedly brought down to the first heaven; now devoted to fasting.

Sadaga: Alms to the poor and needy

Salah Eddin: The outstanding Muslim general who defeated the Crusaders at Hattin, near the Sea of Galilee.

Salat: The Muslim daily prayer ritual; one of the five pillars of Islamic faith.

Sheikh: Head of a tribe; old, respected, or learned man.

Shi'ites: A Muslim sect which rejects the first three Khaliphs, insisting that Muhammad's son-in-law, 'Ali, was Muhammad's rightful initial successor.

Suffis: Philosophical mystics who have largely adapted and reinterpreted Islam for themselves.

Sunnis: The largest Muslim sect, which acknowledges the first four Khaliphs as Muhammad's rightful successors.

Surat (Surah): Title of each chapter of the Quran.

'Umar Ibn Al-Khattab: One of the bravest and most important men of Quraish, who greatly influenced the course of Islam after his conversion to the faith.

Wadi: The channel of a water course, which is normally dry, except in the rainy season.

Zakat: A religious tax or offerings of a devout Muslim.

Zamzam: The famed well of Mecca from which every Muslim desires to drink.

NEW MATERIALS FROM THE ANIS SHORROSH EVANGELISTIC ASSOCIATION

ITEM	QUANTITY	PRICE	TOTAL
Islam Revealed: A Christian Arab's View of Islam Book	_____	$12.95	_____
Jesus, Prophecy & the Middle East Book	_____	$ 5.00	_____
6 cassette tapes narrated by Dr. Shorrosh	_____	$30.00	_____
4 cassette tapes narrated by Dr. Shorrosh	_____	$20.00	_____
The Liberated Palestinian (biography of Anish Shorrosh) 1 cassette tape only	_____	$ 4.00	_____
The Exciting Discovery of the Ark of the Covenant Book	_____	$ 3.00	_____
1 cassette tape narrated by Dr. Shorrosh	_____	$ 4.00	_____
"The Quran and the Bible, Which Is God's Word?" Christian-Muslim debate, National Exhibition Center, Birmingham, England 4-hour video	_____	$50.00	_____
3 cassettes	_____	$15.00	_____
"Is Jesus God," Christian-Muslim debate, Royal Albert Hall, London, England 2-hour video	_____	$25.00	_____
2 cassette tapes	_____	$10.00	_____
"Where Jesus Walked" 1-hour video of the Holy Land	_____	$25.00	_____

TOTAL AMOUNT ENCLOSED $_____

NAME _____

ADDRESS _____

CITY _____

STATE _____

ZIP CODE _____

COUNTRY _____

TELEPHONE _____

PLEASE RETURN THIS FORM WITH PAYMENT
TO

ANIS SHORROSH EVANGELISTIC ASSOCIATION
P.O. Box 7577
Spanish Fort, Al 36577

GRACE GOSPEL CHURCH

Falcon Avenue

Patchogue, New York

631-289-5495